MW00789876

Anatomy of a Purple State

Anatomy of a Purple State

A North Carolina Politics Primer

CHRISTOPHER A. COOPER

The University
of North Carolina
Press Chapel Hill

*This book was published with the assistance of
the Luther H. Hodges Jr. and Luther H. Hodges Sr. Fund
of the University of North Carolina Press.*

© 2024 Christopher A. Cooper
All rights reserved
Designed by Richard Hendel
Set in Miller and Neue Kabel
by Jamie McKee, MacKey Composition
Manufactured in the United States of America

Cover design by Amanda Weisse.

Library of Congress Cataloging-in-Publication Data
Names: Cooper, Christopher A. (Christopher Alan), 1975– author.
Title: Anatomy of a purple state : a North Carolina politics primer / Christopher A.
    Cooper.
Description: Chapel Hill : The University of North Carolina Press, [2024] | Includes
    bibliographical references and index.
Identifiers: LCCN 2024020846 | ISBN 9781469681702 (cloth) | ISBN 9781469681719
    (paperback) | ISBN 9781469681726 (epub) | ISBN 9781469681733 (pdf)
Subjects: LCSH: North Carolina—Politics and government—1951– | BISAC: POLITICAL
    SCIENCE / American Government / State | POLITICAL SCIENCE / History & Theory
Classification: LCC JK4116 .c66 2024 | DDC 320.9756—dc23/eng/20240603
LC record available at https://lccn.loc.gov/2024020846

Contents

Illustrations

Tables

Acknowledgments

This book is a product of a couple of decades of thinking, writing, and commenting about North Carolina politics (I know, you'd think the book would be longer). Not surprisingly, I have racked up a lot of debts and people I need to thank over that time. Typing their names in black font on a white page and sending it to a printer by way of an editor seems like an inadequate way to thank them, but it's the only tool I have at my disposal at the moment. Lavish gifts forthcoming for all (except where prohibited by law).

Somebody smart once reminded me that answers are easy to come by; the thought is in the question. I think of this adage a few times a week when the phone rings and there's a journalist on the other end of the line who asks questions that cause me to think about North Carolina politics in new ways. So, thanks to anyone who ever thought it was a good idea to give me a call and talk about the stuff that appears in this book, including, but not limited to, Brian Anderson, Mark Barrett, Danielle Battaglia, Charles Bethea, Russ Bowen, John Boyle, Tim Boyum, Jim Buchanan, Joel Burgess, Matt Bush, Colin Campbell, Mike Collins, Will Doran, Travis Fain, Tom Fielder, Steve Harrison, Michael Hyland, Kyle Ingram, Reuben Jones, Joe Killian, Lilly Knoepp, Laura Leslie, Michael Kruse, Paige Masten, Jim Morrill, Kyle Perotti, Gary Robertson, Kate Sheppard, Lucille Sherman, Peter Slevin, Jeff Tiberii, Dave Russell, Cory Vaillancourt, Dawn Vaughn, Kyle Villemain, and the crew at WLOS—past and present (yes Russ, that means you get the double shout-out).

My knowledge of North Carolina politics and government has also been strengthened by comments and conversations with a cast of characters—political scientists, lobbyists, candidates, consultants, and elected officials—many of whom have spoken in my classes, and some of whom talked to me for this book. That list includes Christy Agner, Matt Ballance, Michael Bitzer, Preston Blakely, Don Bryson, Gerry Cohen, Skye David, Blake Esselstyn, Rob Ferguson, Ferrel Guillory, Ben Guiney, Phil and Connie Haire, Asher Hildebrand, John Hood, Scott Huffmon, Andy Jackson, Andrew Judson, Justin King, Wayne King, Bryant Kinney, Martha Kropf, Brian Lewis, Alex Macauley, Joe Bill Mathews, Julie Mayfield, Mac McCorkle, Seth McKee, David McLennan, Justin Menickelli, Irwin Morris, Jim Perry,

Lindsey Prather, Libby and Steve McRae, Sean O'Connell, Bob Orr, Blair Reeves, Jennifer Roberts, Caleb Rudow, Rob Schofield, Zeb Smathers, Richard Starnes, Bill Studenc, Joe Stewart, Brian Turner, Kelly Turnow, Stephen Wiley, and the residents and staff of Christmas Village. The *Old North State Politics* blog has given me a great outlet to give some of the ideas in this book a test run—thanks to my friends Michael Bitzer, Whitney Ross Manzo, and Susan Roberts for allowing me to contribute. Special thanks to my friend and frequent collaborator Gibbs Knotts—many of the ideas in this book took root in my work with him. Many thanks also go to my colleagues and students in the Department of Political Science and Public Affairs at Western Carolina University.

Lucas Church and the team at the University of North Carolina Press have been incredibly supportive of this project since the first time I pitched the idea over a Shadowbox IPA at Craftboro. I appreciate Lucas's encouragement, ideas, and understanding throughout this process as well as the hard work of Thomas Bedenbaugh, Sonya Bonczek, Valerie Burton, and Madge Duffey. If you get a chance to work with Lucas or UNC Press, I encourage you to do so. You will not find a better partner.

My family deserves my thanks for putting up with too many conversations about state politics when we should have been talking about the new Eric Brace and Thomm Jutz album or a George Saunders short story. Thanks go to Wiley, Emily, Charlotte, and Baker Cooper, Al and Damon Smuzynski, Kathy Swigger, Keith Swigger, Robert Brazile, and a dozen or so other Coopers, Hughes, Stansells, Joneses, and Swiggers. My wife, Jessie Swigger, deserves the biggest thanks for reasons said and unsaid. Her love and support means the world to me. Our children, Jack and Maddie Cooper, did not read any of these pages, but to be fair to them, they are in elementary school and are more apt to share thoughts on Nintendo Switch games than on the nature of state politics today. But they sure do make my life better. Jack and Maddie, if you're reading this, put the book down; let's go for a bike ride.

We lost my mother, Pamela Hughes Cooper-Smuzynski, and my brother, Peter Cooper, while I was working on this book. Both were constant sources of encouragement in my life, but just as importantly, neither was afraid to challenge me on an idea, a phrase, or a conclusion. Mom would not have liked my penchant for beginning a sentence with the word "and." Peter would not have liked that I just used the word "penchant." But I hope they would have found a sentence or two in here that made them smile. I miss them both terribly.

Anatomy of a Purple State

INTRODUCTION The Path to Purple

The fubar meter affixed to the wall of the pressroom in the North Carolina State Legislative Building was moved to "10" at 11:57 p.m. on June 8, 2011, following the late-night passage of the "monster bill" that attempted to rewrite many of the state's voting laws.[1] While most people might have assumed that "10" represented maximum fubar, just eight days later, the North Carolina press corps added another tick past the theoretical top end of the scale to accommodate an unscheduled Friday and Saturday meeting of the general assembly.[2]

It is safe to assume that a fubar meter would not have been necessary in North Carolina before more recent times. Over the course of just a few years, however, the goings-on in the traditionally moderate North Carolina government have moved from something that was rarely discussed outside the 53,819 square miles that make up the Tar Heel State to something debated in the pages of America's prestige media.

For its part, the *New York Times* traced North Carolina's "decline" from "a beacon of farsightedness in the South" to a "demolition derby" and blamed the Republican general assembly for "tearing down years of progress in public education, tax policy, racial equality in the courtroom and access

Figure 0.1. The fubar meter. Photo by author.

to the ballot."[3] In response, an op-ed in the *Wall Street Journal* asked, rhetorically, "Why Are North Carolina Liberals So @&%*! Angry?" While acknowledging, "This isn't to say the Republicans have been saints," the *Wall Street Journal* piece highlighted the ability of Republican policies to "spur growth and job creation" and gave the impression that the protests coming from the left were nothing more than well-funded distractions from the real work of governing.[4]

More recently, this message of extreme partisanship and government dysfunction in the Tar Heel State was reinforced in a book ominously titled *How Democracies Die*. In a tour through failed democracies around the globe, Harvard University political scientists Steven Levitsky and Daniel Ziblatt single out North Carolina as an example of "politics without guardrails" and as a "microcosm of the country's hyperpartisan politics and growing mutual distrust."[5]

The debate over North Carolina's place in American politics has even bled past the relatively staid industries of academia and journalism. Comedy Central's *The Daily Show* and HBO's *Last Week Tonight* with John Oliver have increasingly peered into the Tar Heel State to mine for topical comedy gold.[6] Luckily for them, it was chock-full.

Putting aside the relative merits of any of these arguments, the fact that policies coming out of a once-moderate and relatively quiet state were now the topic of debate in national media, the subject of analysis by academics at Ivy League universities, and the butt of jokes from America's top comedians suggested that North Carolina politics had become relevant to a national audience in a way that would have seemed unlikely just a few years before.

Although the national story surrounding North Carolina politics is predicated on the idea that North Carolina experienced a rapid change from moderation and good governance to radical politics, the magnitude of the shift is more complicated and nuanced than many observers might have you believe. Things certainly changed in 2011, when the general assembly shifted from Democratic control to unified Republican control for the first time in more than 100 years, but North Carolina was never as progressive as the protestors who gathered for Moral Mondays maintained, nor was there a far-right silent majority just waiting to enact some of the most conservative policies in the country.

North Carolina is, and has always been, a divided state. From 1861 to 1865, those divisions were expressed through warfare, with pockets of constituents counting significant numbers of Union sympathizers among them, while the majority of the state's citizens supported the Confederate orthodoxy. Later, those divisions were characterized by the tension between "modernizers" and "traditionalists."[7] Today, the battle lines in the state are defined by political geography and partisan identification, two concepts that are increasingly intertwined.

It is also an ahistorical oversimplification to suggest that the Republican majority was unique in its attempts to use its power for its own gains. The Democratic majority engaged in many of the same tricks and shenanigans that the Republicans have used in more recent years. As we will see in later chapters, Democrats gerrymandered, kept power from the governor when it suited them, and generally manipulated the levers of power in pursuit of their own interests. In 2003, the Democratic Speaker of the North Carolina House of Representatives even arranged a bribe in an IHOP bathroom to avoid losing majority control of the lower chamber.[8]

It turns out that the competitiveness of North Carolina elections and the closely divided nature of the state are likely what led to the winner-take-all politics that defines North Carolina today. As political scientist Frances Lee demonstrates in her masterful book *Insecure Majorities*, in times when either party can realistically be expected to gain or lose power in the next election cycle, the party that is in power will engage in winner-take-all politics when it is in charge—precisely because it is aware that if it does not exercise power now, it might not get it back. The minority party, by contrast, is not apt to compromise because it realizes the precarious position of majority control and believes that it could take the reins after the next election.[9]

The states where insecure majorities lead to partisan discord and lack of compromise are not places such as Oklahoma, where the Republicans will likely hold power for the foreseeable future, or California, where the Democrats have held and (likely) will continue to hold power for decades. In these states, there is no reason to act with haste—the majority party has time to enact its policies. The minority parties in these states also know that they are likely to face long odds for decades. Compromise is their only chance to exert any power over public policy.

In states such as North Carolina that consistently rest on the razor's edge between Republican and Democratic rule, however, members of the majority party know that their power is fragile and can disappear in a single election. In such states, the majority party often acts quickly and without regard for the long-term consequences of its actions. The minority party likewise is unwilling to compromise, as its members know that they could be in the catbird seat just one election later. In Lee's words, "Looking toward the next elections, politicians under competitive conditions have stronger motivation to exploit legislative debate for purposes of electioneering and partisan mobilization."[10]

In a grand stroke of irony then, North Carolina's status as a swing state, a purple state, a competitive state, a two-party state, a moderate state, or whatever other middle-of-the-road moniker you want to throw at it, has led it to become the home of hyperpartisanship and a cautionary tale for those concerned about the state of democratic deliberation and representation in America.

Why North Carolina?

North Carolina is a perfect representation of the promise and peril of modern American democracy. Hyperpartisanship, paired with hypercompetitiveness, gerrymandering, dissatisfaction with the two-party system, the urban-rural divide, and the challenge of managing growth amid political change, is apparent across US politics but magnified in North Carolina. If national politics is Jack Daniel's whiskey, North Carolina politics is a twenty-year-old single malt scotch—perfectly distilled and with a bite that lingers long after the sip is over.

North Carolina is also an increasingly important state on the national stage. Former North Carolina governor Pat McCrory became the butt of comedian Trevor Noah's jokes for bragging too many times about the size of North Carolina's population, but McCrory was correct: North Carolina is a large and influential state, and one that is growing in both size and influence by the day.[11] Of the fourteen presidential "swing states," only Florida, Pennsylvania, Georgia, and Ohio have more electors up for grabs than North Carolina.[12] And, given recent Republican ascendency in Florida and Ohio, it can easily be argued that only Pennsylvania and Georgia remain as larger swing states. In a competitive national political environment, North Carolina can be the difference between winning and losing a presidential election or gaining majority control in the US Senate.

While North Carolina politics is important because of what it tells us about our political moment in general, it is also important to understand it as an end in itself. Politics as practiced in Washington, DC, may monopolize the attention of many in the Tar Heel State, but state politics has the most important and long-term effects for most North Carolinians. Raleigh, not Washington, is home to the people who manipulate the key levers of power that determine abortion rights, state tax rates, higher education funding, Medicaid expansion, marijuana laws, curriculum and instruction in high schools, economic development incentives, and a host of issues that sit at that critical point where the rubber meets the road in American politics. Although their number of Instagram followers might lead you to believe otherwise, when Madison Cawthorn served in the US House of Representatives and Tim Moore was in the North Carolina House of Representatives, it was Moore, not Cawthorn, whose actions mattered far more to the life of the average North Carolinian.

The Three Trends

Three trends run throughout modern North Carolina politics and government and are highlighted throughout this book—*nationalization*, *competition*, and *polarization*. As we will see, these trends reinforce one another, creating a state political environment that is becoming ever more divisive and less representative.

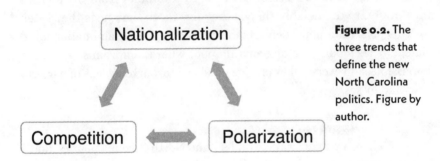

Figure 0.2. The three trends that define the new North Carolina politics. Figure by author.

Former Speaker of the House Tip O'Neill once quipped that "all politics is local."[13] Today the opposite is true. All politics are national. Voters' opinions on the president are increasingly tied to how they vote for state and local offices. National-level interest groups are active at the state and local levels, and bills are crafted not at the grass roots, by local activists aware of local issues, but at the grass tops, by national groups and consultants who might have never set foot in the state.[14] Whereas in the past some quirks of North Carolina politics were insulated from national forces, that is no longer the case.[15] Today, if you want to forecast how a county will vote for any partisan office—from US Senate to Soil and Water commissioner—the key metric, and arguably the only metric you need, is how that county voted in the last presidential election. North Carolina politics has become nationalized.

North Carolina politics is also increasingly competitive. Virtually every statewide election is competitive, and both parties have a legitimate shot at victory—no matter the candidate. Consider the 2020 presidential election, where Donald Trump's margin in North Carolina was the smallest of any state that he carried. Or the 2020 race for attorney general, where Democrat Josh Stein bested Republican Jim O'Neill by fewer than 14,000 votes. Or Republican Paul Newby's 401-vote victory over Cheri Beasley in the 2020 state supreme court chief justice election. Or Republican Ted Budd's 3.2 percentage-point victory for US Senate in 2022—the fourth closest US Senate election in the country (out of thirty-two). And the list goes on. The national parties are increasingly aware of this competitiveness, which is why they funnel tens of millions of dollars into North Carolina every election cycle. National interest groups are also at work to compete in this most-purple of states. The state's competitiveness fuels further nationalization, and vice versa.

North Carolina politics is polarized. Democrats and Republicans in the Old North State have increasingly little in common—from the policies they prefer, to the neighborhoods they live in, to the music they listen to. This polarization, particularly in such a competitive and nationalized state, creates a policymaking environment where compromise is next to impossible, and every policy change is viewed through the lens of partisan wins and losses.

The Approach

There are many ways to understand North Carolina politics. Some use insider accounts to uncover the dirt about North Carolina politicians and what happens in and around the state capitol. Others might take an anthropological tour through the state, focusing on the people who make it what it is. Another approach might turn the lens onto the key figures or events that have shaped the political history in the state. There are also a number of excellent books that take a traditional textbook-like approach—describing each of the institutions of state government in turn. And of course, many of the extant analyses of North Carolina politics are polemical—describing the state's politics through a particular partisan or ideological lens.

Anatomy of a Purple State takes a different approach. This book uses a multitude of methods to uncover various lessons about the politics of the Tar Heel State, but it relies heavily on the tools of social science—things such as voter files, surveys, and government data—to uncover important topical lessons about North Carolina politics. The North Carolina voter file and voter history file are available for download with the click of a button. Add in some minimal skills with data analysis and anyone can quickly get a good sense of who North Carolina's voters are and how they behave.

In a similar vein, we are fortunate to have a number of major polling organizations based in North Carolina. East Carolina University, Elon University, High Point University, Meredith College, and a host of other organizations all produce top-quality polling of the Tar Heel State multiple times a year. North Carolina is also fortunate to have active think tanks representing both sides of the aisle as well as municipal and county government organizations that provide constantly updated data for those interested in how local governments have evolved over time. Observers of politics in other states simply do not have the variety and quality of resources available to them that we have in North Carolina.

Political scientists have also supplemented these North Carolina–specific resources with measures of a variety of political phenomena across all fifty states, making it possible to compare, for example, the ideology of members of the North Carolina General Assembly to members of the Idaho State Legislature, or public sentiment on gun control in North Carolina to public sentiment in Oregon.

The availability of these tools does not mean that they speak for themselves, of course. A primer on North Carolina politics should blend this analysis with a focus on the key people, events, and historic moments that have driven politics in North Carolina. To achieve these goals, the chapters that follow are brief, and they are organized around central questions or takeaways rather than around broader subjects or institutions in general.[16] These chapters fall into four broad topics: "Part I. The Building Blocks of Purple Politics"; "Part II. The New Era of Voting, Parties, and the Information Industry in North Carolina Politics"; "Part III. First among Equals: The North Carolina General Assembly"; and "Part IV. Vying for Power: Other Institutional Actors in North Carolina Government." The conclusion, "Toward a Better North Carolina," looks forward and offers five policy solutions that can help improve politics and government in North Carolina.

Each chapter in this book could easily be expanded into a book on its own. And there are ideas, people, and institutions that receive only scant attention in the pages that follow but that could also easily warrant a chapter, or even a book, of their own. The mass media, runoff elections, boards and commissions, the politics of sexuality, the politics of the state budget, social movements, the state bureaucracy, and the council of state are just a few of the critical stories in North Carolina politics that deserve more mention than they receive in these pages.

The title of this book reflects what this book is and is not. Like a good anatomy lesson, this book gives you enough information to understand the mechanics, but it remains up to you to apply these lessons to future eventualities and events. Consequently, the appendix provides a guide to resources and attempts to improve information literacy about North Carolina politics. Finally, because much of this data changes so quickly, the website for this book, www.chriscooperwcu.com/anatomy, includes all graphs and tables from the book; these will be updated every six months. As new resources become available, I will also link to them.

In the end, this book attempts to marry two warring factions of political understanding—the social scientific use of data (some might argue *obsession* with data) and the more humanistic portrayals of people, places, and events. The goal is to describe, analyze, and contextualize the state of politics in North Carolina and maybe even entertain a bit in the process. Let's get to it.

Part I
The Building Blocks of Purple Politics

1   Third Time's a Charm
The North Carolina Constitution

Most Americans think of the US Constitution as sacrosanct. Even in today's acrimonious political times, Democrats and Republicans, liberals and conservatives, men and women, Duke fans and Tar Heel fans all hold a reverence for the US Constitution, a respect for its authors and a sense that it should not be altered, except in rare circumstances. The same cannot be said for state constitutions.[1] Since the founding of the country, the United States has held one federal constitutional convention, but during this same time, there have been 230 constitutional conventions held among the fifty states of the nation.[2] On average, there is a state constitutional convention about as often as there is a Super Bowl.

The states have also demonstrated remarkable willingness to alter their constitutions once they are passed. In contrast to the federal Constitution which has just twenty-seven amendments, state constitutions have been amended more than 7,500 times, to say nothing of those amendments that were proposed but that ultimately failed.[3] Americans are not afraid to tinker with their state constitutions.

State constitutions are best understood as blueprints for power. They delineate who has power, when, where, and over whom. It is in the state constitutions where we learn why certain states have virtually omnipotent governors, while in other states governors are relatively weak; why some lieutenant governors are separately elected and others are not; why some states' legislatures do the real work of government, while in other states they are relegated to the sidelines; and why local governments in some states are left alone, while in other states they have to ask permission from the state government before completing the most basic tasks.

This chapter tells the story of North Carolina's three constitutions, with a focus on the battles to pass and alter them. As will become clearer in the pages that follow, the North Carolina Constitution is fairly typical as far as state constitutions go. We've had a few constitutions, we're not afraid to amend them, but we don't approach the constitutional flexibility of other states that seem to alter their constitutions with the seasons.

The North Carolina Constitution of 1776

It took the federal government five years after the Declaration of Independence to ratify the first federal governing document, but the states were much quicker on the draw. Indeed, eleven of the thirteen original colonies (Connecticut and Rhode Island were the exceptions) adopted their first state constitutions in 1776.[4] North Carolina's first constitution made it in just under the wire, with its ratification on December 18, 1776.

This first North Carolina Constitution was passed not by the people but by a "provincial congress."[5] This small group of delegates first passed a twenty-five-item "declaration of rights" on December 17, 1776. The next day the delegates passed a more traditional constitution that, in just over 2,800 words, laid out the roles of the general assembly, the governor, the council of state, and the judicial system. Taken together, these two documents became known as the original Constitution of North Carolina.

This brief initial governing document purported to provide for separation of powers. In fact, it "reflected the great confidence that people of that time had in legislative bodies."[6] The original North Carolina Constitution placed an extraordinary amount of power in the hands of the bicameral general assembly, it gave some power to an ill-defined judiciary, and it left the governor with almost no formal power. "It was the bicameral legislature, the General Assembly that was supreme. The General Assembly, not the voters chose the governor and members of the Council of State, the treasurer, the secretary, the attorney general, and all the judges, as well as the officers of the state militia."[7]

This initial constitution was amended forty-six times on issues ranging from the requirement that a "Sheriff, Coroner or Coroners, and constables" be present in each county to a rule that practicing clergy could not be members of the legislature or council of state. All told, this initial state constitution lasted just shy of a century and came to an end after the South's failed attempt at secession. After Robert E. Lee and the Confederacy surrendered at Appomattox, one of the first acts of the reunited federal government was to direct the "rebel states" to rewrite their state constitutions "in conformity with the Constitution of the United States in all respects."[8]

On November 19 and 20, 1867, a special election of the people of North Carolina overwhelmingly supported the decision to call a constitutional convention (74 percent in favor and 26 percent against) and less than two months later, 120 delegates gathered in Raleigh to draft a new state constitution. Three months after that, North Carolina's second constitution passed by a vote of the people 56 percent to 44 percent.[9]

The North Carolina Constitution of 1868

In addition to expanding basic rights to include habeas corpus, extending the franchise to all men regardless of property-owning status (in word, if not in deed), and prohibiting slavery, North Carolina's second constitution provided a much more detailed description of the architecture of government than the state's initial foray into self-governance. The second constitution wrested some power away from the North Carolina General Assembly, shifted a few legislative appointments to direct election by the people, created a lieutenant governor, and increased the size and scope of the state supreme court.[10] Representation in both houses of the general assembly was also changed from a system based on counties to one based on population.[11]

The passage of the second constitution did not usher in a period of constitutional stasis in North Carolina. Quite the opposite. Just seven years after the ratification of the Constitution of 1868, the general assembly called another constitutional convention where it proposed and passed a whopping thirty changes that were then combined into a single amendment the following year. Continuing a theme that would define constitutional changes moving forward, the main goal of the 1876 amendment was "to restore to the General Assembly more of the power it had lost."[12]

After this flurry of activity, the constitutional churn in North Carolina quieted considerably; fewer changes were proposed, and those that were proposed were rarely passed. Starting in the 1930s, North Carolinians again became more eager to alter their governing document—passing more than forty additional amendments to a constitution that was already a bit unwieldy. Graph 1.1 shows both the amendments proposed and the amendments ratified for the duration of the second constitution.

During this period of rapid-fire amendments, calls for constitutional reform increased. In 1933, the general assembly created and passed a new constitution, which would have, in addition to other things, provided the governor with veto power. It never reached the people for a vote, however, and was relegated to the dustbin of good ideas that never became public policy.[13]

But some kept hope alive. A 1934 special issue of the UNC School of Government publication *Popular Government* noted that reform of the North Carolina Constitution was "not dead, but sleeping." Twenty years later, the nap had devolved into full-fledged hibernation, leading Duke University political scientist Robert Rankin to quip that "the length of this nap gives rise to real concern."[14]

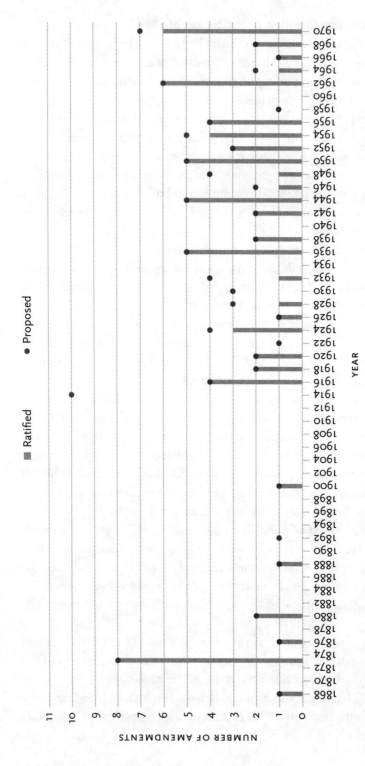

Graph 1.1. Amendments to the 1868 North Carolina Constitution, 1868–1970.

Source: Sanders, "Our Constitutions."

Table 1.1. Votes on November 3, 1970, constitutional amendments.

	"Yes" votes (%)	Number of votes cast
Adopt new Constitution of North Carolina	61.1	644,891
Reduce state administrative agencies	61.7	649,687
Allow legislature to call special sessions	53.8	618,568
Revise limits on state and local taxing and borrowing	53.5	604,218
Fix personal income tax exemptions	54.4	619,357
Allow escheats to be used for higher education	59.3	610,548
Abolish literacy test	44.0	634,479

Source: North Carolina Department of the Secretary of State, *North Carolina Manual of 1973.*

In late October 1967, Democratic governor Dan Moore rekindled the push for a new constitution by calling for a "study of North Carolina's state Constitution with the view of amending or rewriting it."[15] Other prominent politicians such as Terry Sanford lined up alongside him to call for a new constitution.

The lone holdout to constitutional change among the North Carolina political elite of the time was secretary of state and "oldest rat in the barn" Thad Eure.[16] Eure maintained that the Constitution of 1868 just needed "tidying up"; but speculation at the time held that his opposition was rooted in fears that the new constitution might shift the council of state from elected to appointed positions—effectively putting him out of a job.[17]

Sensing that public and elite opinion was on the side of constitutional change, Governor Moore secured $25,000 ($221,500 in 2024 dollars) in support from the Z. Smith Reynolds Foundation, and on December 9, 1967, Moore formally appointed a twenty-nine-member steering committee of lawyers to examine the North Carolina Constitution of 1868, by then amended more than sixty-five times.[18]

Ultimately, the general assembly approved seven changes to the North Carolina Constitution and put those changes to the people for a vote on November 3, 1970. The first ballot item asked citizens whether they approved a "revision and amendment of the Constitution of North Carolina." The other six authorized a number of specific changes that are listed in table 1.1.

It is notable, and more than a bit concerning, that the amendment to repeal the racist literacy requirement for voting was the sole amendment that was not enacted into law. While the measure passed handily in North Carolina's most populous counties—including Mecklenburg (61 percent), Guilford (64 percent), Buncombe (64 percent), Forsyth (57 percent), Orange (68 percent), and Durham (61 percent)—it failed to achieve support in thirty-six counties and garnered only 44 percent of the vote statewide. As a result, the literacy test, a vestige of the racist Jim Crow South, remains enshrined in our state constitution today. See the conclusion of this book for more about the literacy test and the prospects for its repeal.

The North Carolina Constitution of 1971

With a few decades of hindsight, constitutional scholar John Orth described the North Carolina Constitution of 1971 in positive, but less than revolutionary, terms. According to Orth, it was not "a product of haste and social turmoil. It was instead a good-government measure, long matured and carefully crafted by the state's lawyers and politicians, designed to consolidate and conserve the best features of the past, not to break with it."[19] The fourteen-article structure of the previous constitution remained, including basic features such as due process, a declaration of rights, a rhetorical commitment to separation of powers, and the primacy of the general assembly among supposedly equal branches of government.

Like the Constitution of 1868, the newly passed Constitution of 1971 did not sit idle for long. The first change occurred just as the ink was drying, thanks to the passage of the Twenty-Sixth Amendment to the US Constitution, which dropped the voting age nationwide from twenty-one to eighteen. Other changes took effect in rapid succession—in 1972 alone, five amendments were brought to the people and approved. Unlike lowering the voting age to eighteen, most were not proposed at the behest of the federal government but rather born out of homegrown concerns. For example, two 1972 amendments increased the requirements to be a judge and implemented a way for the general assembly to remove judges. Both passed easily (with 73 and 75 percent of the vote, respectively).

As graph 1.2 demonstrates, amendments have continued to accumulate at the rate of about one per year. The passage rate is fairly high, with only eight failing since the 1970 vote on ending the literacy test. Four of the failed amendments would have authorized bonds or made it easier for

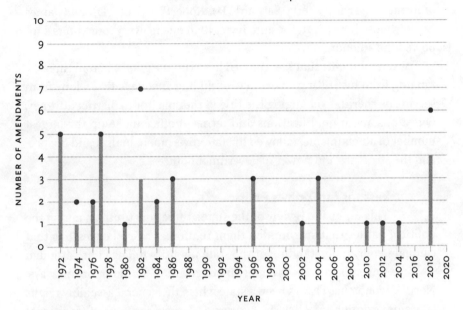

Graph 1.2. Amendments to the 1971 North Carolina Constitution, 1972–2020. *Source:* Sanders, "Our Constitutions."

local government to authorize bonds (one in 1974, two in 1982, and one in 1993). Another one would have allowed public bodies to "acquire, construct, finance, refinance, sell, or lease lands and facilities and to Finance for Private interests Seaport, Airport, and other related commercial facilities." The sixth would have increased the length of terms of state senators and representatives from two to four years. In 2018, two amendments failed that would have adjusted midterm judicial selection and changed the makeup of the North Carolina State Board of Elections. When amendments fail in North Carolina, they fail spectacularly; the average failing amendment garners less than one-third (31.7 percent) of the vote.

These failures are usually easily foretold. For example, an editorial in the *News and Observer* described the amendment to move from two- to four-year legislative terms in fairly unequivocal terms: "Rarely has such a self-serving piece of legislation ever been introduced in Raleigh. It came in response to no great public hue and cry for reform. Indeed, it seemed to come only in response to the perceived needs of some incumbent legislators."[20] The "vote no" campaign was spurred on by the "Keep the Two-Year

Term Committee," a coalition of political actors led by the bipartisan team of former governors, Terry Sanford (D), Robert W. Scott (D), and James E. Holshouser Jr. (R). In the end, fewer than one in every four voters supported the amendment.

The amendments that have passed have run the gamut in topic areas— ranging from instituting voter ID to excluding anyone with a felony from serving as sheriff, to changing the title of the solicitor to district attorney. Questions about qualifications and terms of office make up the largest number of amendments, followed by state government budget and finance, and the structure and power of government offices.

Lessons for Today's Politics

This rapid-fire review of the state's three constitutions and of the political battles that surrounded them reinforces a few key lessons that can guide our understanding of the state's politics today. First, although we have tinkered with the architecture of government in important ways, North Carolina has always been a state where the general assembly reigns supreme over public policy. The governor, largely shut out of traditional formal power channels, has been forced to "go public" and use his bully pulpit to appeal to voters rather than to work through the legislative process (see chapter 13 for more). Local governments must go to the state government to ask permission for basic tasks of governing (see chapter 15); and the state supreme court's role in enforcing guardrails on the legislature is frequently called into question (see chapter 14).[21]

The story of North Carolina's three constitutions also demonstrates that despite considerable continuity, change is possible in North Carolina politics. The amendment process has been used frequently in the state's history, and often to good ends. We should not be afraid of constitutional change but rather accept it for what it is—a necessary but not a sufficient condition for good government.

But will change continue at this rate, in this current era of polarized, nationalized, and competitive politics that defines North Carolina today? For constitutional change to occur, the general assembly must be faced with either a policy that requires alteration of the state constitution or a policy it prefers that cannot make it past the governor's desk but that will likely be supported by the majority of North Carolina voters. Otherwise, why would a rational general assembly go through the amendment process if it didn't have to? If the governor likes the policy, or if the general assembly can override the governor's veto, that is clearly the preferred path. Likewise, if the policy is not the clear preference of a majority of North Carolinians, then the majority in the general assembly will not bring it to the people. At least in the near future, the period of rapid constitutional change may be on pause.

2   North Carolina Is a Purple State

The national political environment in 1976 looked almost nothing like it does today. In contrast to today's near constant onslaught of political information, there were just three network television stations, and there was no social media. The daily fix of political news came in the morning and in the evening, leaving the middle of the day mercifully free of politics and government, save for the occasional emergency cut-in. Regional patterns in partisanship also looked a lot different. California was solidly red, while many of today's red-state stalwarts such as Mississippi, Alabama, and Texas were bright blue. From the vantage point of 2024, the 1976 electoral map is unrecognizable.

One thing that has remained constant across the decades, however, is that a victory in North Carolina was not and is not a foregone conclusion for either political party.

About a month out from the 1976 general election, a poll revealed that Republican incumbent Gerald Ford trailed Democrat Jimmy Carter in North Carolina by just 2 percentage points, with almost a quarter of voters (24 percent) undecided.[1] Soon after this neck and neck poll was released, a national publication concluded that North Carolina, unlike its neighbors south of the Mason-Dixon Line, was "not strongly committed" to Carter.[2] Both presidential candidates responded by spending on North Carolina the scarcest resource in American politics: time. In June, Jimmy Carter hosted a $1,000-a-plate fundraising dinner at the home of George Vanderbilt's grandson.[3] Carter made a second stop in Winston-Salem in October, and Gerald Ford followed suit with an appearance at the North Carolina State Fair.[4] After they had both completed their North Carolina visits, a poll showed that the gap in North Carolina was down to just 1 percentage point.[5]

After Carter's victory in the 1976 election, the idea that North Carolina was up for grabs by either party was ingrained in the national conversation. Four years later, Republican Cass Ballenger declared, "North Carolina is a swing state in that no one is taking it for granted."[6] In 1984, Republican Ronald Reagan was expected to beat his Democratic opponent, Walter

Mondale, in North Carolina handily. To be fair, though, Reagan won every state except for Mondale's home state of Minnesota and Washington, DC, so there wasn't much swinging to be done anywhere. In 1988, the George H. W. Bush versus Michael Dukakis election saw North Carolina return to swing state status—a narrative that was reinforced in 1992 and 1996.[7]

The first two decades of the twenty-first century saw no relief for North Carolina residents who might have wanted to trade political coverage for more basketball instead. In 2000, the rise of US Senator John Edwards from North Carolina to national prominence was due, in no small part, to his ability to "prompt some oohs and ahhs in swing states such as North Carolina."[8] When John Kerry selected Edwards as his running mate four years later, the same logic applied, with journalists and political observers noting that his home state's status as a swing state contributed to his appeal as a running mate.[9]

The 2008 election brought North Carolina's swing state status into even sharper relief. Robert Gibbs, a North Carolina State alumnus and Barack Obama aide, called the Old North State a "major battleground" and a "swing state in recent years."[10] Gibbs's words turned out to be prescient as Obama won North Carolina in 2008, cementing North Carolina's status as a swing state.

In each presidential election that followed, North Carolina has contin-ued to be labeled a swing state—a fact reinforced by how candidates have allocated their resources and attention. It is not a coincidence that Donald Trump also made fourteen trips to North Carolina in 2020; only Florida and Virginia saw more visits.[11] Joe Biden was also no stranger to North Carolina, traveling to Charlotte in September and Durham in October.[12]

Despite the fact that the state has not given the plurality of its votes to a Democratic presidential candidate since 2008, the 2024 election will provide no relief from the swing state narrative. Whether you want to call it a "purple state," a "swing state," a "center-center state," a "smack in the middle state," a "competitive state," or a "battleground state," the idea that North Carolina does not lean consistently toward one party or the other but rather sits somewhere in the blurry middle is ingrained in the country's collective political mind. It has been that way for a long time and shows no signs of letting up anytime soon.

Political observers generally agree on the character and charac-teristics of most American states. Mississippians are conservative; Califor-nians are liberal. Vermonters support Democratic socialist Bernie Sanders, while Oklahomans would prefer just about anyone to the Vermont liberal. Identifying the political leanings of North Carolina, by contrast, is a bit of a Rorschach test.

From some angles, North Carolina politics looks overwhelmingly conservative. The general assembly has been in Republican control for over a decade and is known for passing some of the most conservative policies in the country. The Republicans also control both of the state's US Senate seats, and the Republican candidate for president has won the last three presidential elections in North Carolina. A quick reading of the state's political history might yield a similar conclusion. After all, the most prominent politician in the state's history is "Senator No" himself, Jesse Helms.[13]

From another vantage point, North Carolina politics appears positively progressive. Southern liberals look at Asheville as a Shangri-la of sorts; and the City of Charlotte is increasingly known for taking left-leaning political stances, such as in its nationally prominent fight over transgender bathrooms. The two-term governor of North Carolina is Democrat Roy Cooper, and the state's voters have never elected a Republican attorney general. Historically, political scientists, historians, and political commentators have considered North Carolina progressive, particularly when compared to its southern neighbors. V. O. Key Jr., the North Star of southern politics scholars, called North Carolina a "progressive plutocracy" in 1949; and dean emeritus of the North Carolina press corps Rob Christensen remarked in 2008 that "what sets North Carolina apart is its progressive streak."[14]

The fact that both sides of the political spectrum can find resonance in North Carolina's political leanings reinforces the central point of this chapter: taken as a whole, North Carolina is neither liberal nor conservative. It is brightly and undeniably purple. This chapter relies on two measures to buttress the claim of a purple North Carolina: political ideology and partisan preferences as expressed through presidential vote choice.

Let's get the definitions out of the way. According to political scientist Hans Noel, "Ideologies and parties tell you who is on your side and who is not." The key difference is that "ideology is built around a set of abstract principles," whereas "parties are constructed around coalitions of people who seek to win an election."[15] While political parties and ideologies have become synonymous in American politics (liberals are Democrats and conservatives are Republicans), this does not have to be the case. Indeed, the almost complete convergence of party and ideology is a relatively recent phenomenon in American politics. There is no better example of this fact than the experience of North Carolina. North Carolina's congressional delegation used to be populated with conservative Democrats, a species that moved from the endangered to extinct list when blue dog Democrat Heath Shuler left the Old North State for the hills of East Tennessee.[16] And believe it or not, there used to be some examples of liberal Republicans throughout the Tar Heel State, too.

Today, most political scientists believe that political attitudes, opinions, and behaviors can be arrayed on a left (liberal, Democratic) to right (conservative, Republican) spectrum. And since 2000, these ideological and party orientations are often summarized as red (Republican, conservative) or blue (Democratic, liberal).[17] States and voters that are more difficult to characterize became known as a mix of red and blue. As anyone who has ever left a red crayon and a blue crayon next to each other in the Carolina sun too long knows, that color is purple.

There is no clear, concise, or agreed-upon definition for a purple state, so I will offer mine: a purple state is a state that holds roughly equal elements of liberal, Democratic sentiment and conservative, Republican sentiment. If a state is "near the middle," let's say in the middle 10 percent of states, it might be thought to be "purple." It is not necessary for purple states to "swing" from one party or the other. If a state is consistently just to the left or the right side of center, it is purple, even if the election winner does not change.

Public Opinion in North Carolina

Since at least the 1940s, we have relied on public opinion polls to estimate what the public thinks about a host of issues ranging from opinions on abortion to the relative likability of Congress and cockroaches.[18] For about half a century, these opinion polls tended to be focused at the national level, and reliable estimates of state-level opinion were difficult to come by.

When we could find state opinion polls, they tended to be inconsistent—a poll of California here, a poll of Wyoming there—making it difficult, if not impossible, to compare and contrast political preferences across states. In the 1990s, however, a group of political scientists decided that a solution to the problem of estimating opinion at smaller geographic levels was not to field more subnational polls but rather to pool all the responses from existing state polls together into one measure for each state.[19]

The details are complicated and sometimes use phrases like "Bayesian item response," "joint posterior density," or "multilevel regression and post-stratification," but the idea is fairly simple: aggregate a bunch of polls from a particular geographic area together using the best statistical practices, array the results on a left-to-right continuum, and voilà—you have an accurate portrayal of the "ideological preferences of the mass public" in a given place.[20]

Over the years, political scientists have developed a host of these metrics, all relying on the same basic idea but each employing slightly different methods to arrive at their answer. One of these metrics is from political scientist William Berry and colleagues.[21] The states on the most conservative end of their scale include Oklahoma and Idaho; and the residents of Connecticut and Vermont emerge as the most liberal in the country. Makes sense, right? According to Berry and colleagues, North Carolina falls smack in the middle of the country (the twenty-seventh most conservative and twenty-fourth most liberal state in the country). Using the arithmetic average of the same measure produces a similar result—North Carolina has a score of 52.38, whereas the average state has a score of 52.33. It's hard to get much more purple than that.

A similar measure, produced by political scientists Chris Tausanovitch and Christopher Warshaw, comes to largely the same conclusion. With their measure, North Carolina is the twenty-seventh most liberal state in the country. There are other available measures, but the bottom line is that, regardless of the specifics of the measure, public opinion in North Carolina falls somewhere in the middle of the country—neither bright red nor bright blue, but undeniably purple.

Slouching toward Moderation

While the analysis described above gives us a clear picture of a moderate North Carolina electorate today, it does not address change over time; thus, we are left unsure whether the state taken as a whole has become more liberal over time, or whether moderation is a relatively constant feature of the Old North State. Two competing predictions come to mind. On the one hand, given the rapid in-migration to North Carolina, particularly to the state's urban areas, and given the empirical reality that people who move are more liberal than people who live in their hometowns, it is possible that, over time, the state has become more liberal relative to other states.[22] On the other hand, the well-publicized change from Democratic to Republican rule in the general assembly and the recent dominance of Republican officeholders at the county commission levels might be reflective of steady movement toward the conservative direction.

Graph 2.1 attempts to answer this question by presenting the now familiar Berry and colleagues estimates of public opinion from 1960 to 2016. The solid line represents the North Carolina estimate, while the dashed

— North Carolina   - - Nationwide average

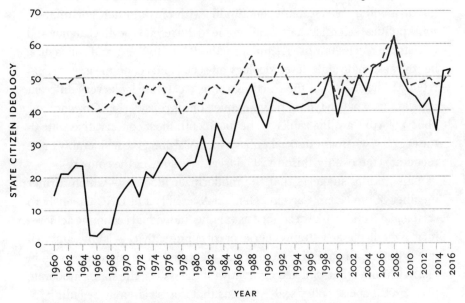

Graph 2.1. Comparing North Carolina public opinion to the nationwide average, 1960–2016.
Source: Data from Berry et al., "Measuring Citizen and Government Ideology"; and Fording, "Updated Measures of Citizen and Government Ideology." Analysis and graph by author.
Note: "State citizen ideology" is a measure of a state's aggregate political ideology on a scale from 1 to 100. Higher numbers indicate more liberal public opinion.

line represents the fifty-state average for the year in question. Three major stories emerge from this graph. First, aggregate public opinion across all fifty states has stayed remarkably stable, whereas the North Carolina electorate has become steadily more liberal over time. Indeed, North Carolina was the fourth most conservative state in the country in 1960. From 1960 to 1999, North Carolinians steadily became more liberal until 1999, when they became the definition of moderation. Immediately following this creeping ideological movement toward becoming a less conservative state, the North Carolina General Assembly moved the opposite direction and flipped to unified Republican control for the first time in more than a century.

Separating Social from Economic

Of course, placing citizens on a one-dimensional liberal-conservative scale presents a limited view of ideology. This unidimensional view may present particular problems in the American South, where social and economic ideology have often been at odds with one another. Fortunately, some political scientists have again come to the rescue. Devin Caughey and Christopher Warshaw use a similar methodology to Berry and colleagues, but they estimate state-level ideology on social and economic issues separately.[23] They find that the North Carolina electorate looks very different depending on which type of policy opinion one is considering. On economic policy, North Carolina ranks as the fourteenth most conservative state in the country, whereas on social policy, North Carolina is considerably more moderate (the twenty-third most conservative state in the country).

This finding suggests that the modernizer ideology—which former member of the North Carolina General Assembly and UNC Greensboro sociologist Paul Luebke described as valuing "individual economic achievement, whether as an entrepreneurial or corporate activity"—is alive and well in North Carolina politics. Luebke also identified a traditionalist strain in North Carolina that valued conservative social issues; the state's moderate place on the social policy scale suggests that that strain may be fading.[24]

Presidential Vote Choice

So, the people on average are moderate. But this is a book about politics, so you can be forgiven if you're thinking, "That's all well and good, but what about election results?"[25]

We might expect that a purple state would fall in the middle of the country in terms of presidential elections results. If a state typically gives the Republican candidate the largest vote share of any state in the country, that is a pretty good sign that the state is a conservative state. Similarly, if a state is consistently the most Democratic in the country, you can assume that its residents are likely quite liberal.[26] By that reasoning, a purple state should hover somewhere around the middle of the country.

To learn where North Carolina fits in this admittedly simple, but I would argue telling, indicator, graph 2.2 plots where North Carolina fell in terms of presidential vote share in every presidential election from 1960 to 2020. As you can see, North Carolina increasingly rests near the middle of the country. In 2008, North Carolina gave all its electoral votes to Barack Obama for president, leading many commentators to proclaim that North Carolina had "turned blue." In 2012, the national media narrative indicated that North Carolina had "returned to red." The reality is more complicated.

In 2008, Democrat Barack Obama did win North Carolina, but his margin of victory was the smallest of any state he won. In 2012, Republican

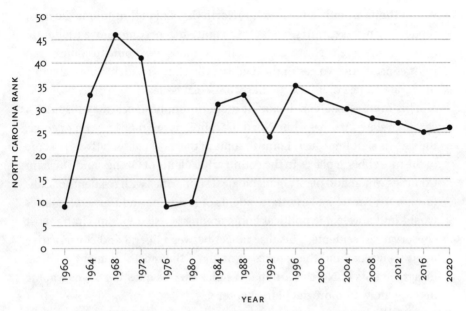

Graph 2.2. North Carolina rank in Republican vote share for president, 1960–2020. *Source:* Data from David Leip's Atlas of US Presidential Elections. Analysis and graph by author.

Note: Dots indicate North Carolina's rank relative to other states. For example, in 1960 North Carolina's support for the Democratic candidate for president (Jimmy Carter) was the ninth highest in the country. In 2020, North Carolina's support for the Democratic candidate for president (Joe Biden) was twenty-sixth highest among the fifty states. Higher numbers indicate more Republican votes.

Mitt Romney's victory in North Carolina was the smallest of any state he won. Moving forward to 2020, there was a narrative that Georgia "flipped" blue while North Carolina remained stubbornly red.[27] The reality is that North Carolina was the bluest red state in the country and that Georgia was the reddest blue state in the country. They were both on different sides of a razor's edge; an edge that, thanks to the winner-take-all Electoral College, results in the flip of all a state's electoral votes.

Conclusion

The evidence explored in this chapter helps us solve some of the puzzle that is North Carolina politics. North Carolina is often misunderstood and mischaracterized not because the people of North Carolina are particularly liberal or particularly conservative but because, taken as a whole, they are neither. On average, North Carolinians are among the most moderate in the country. In fact, the state has become more moderate over time. Whereas North Carolina in the 1960s was home to some of the most conservative voices in the country, the state's residents have steadily moderated since then—particularly on social issues.

This overarching conclusion of moderation, however, may disguise a second, related truth—while North Carolinians are moderate *on average*, the state is simultaneously home to some of the most conservative and some of the most liberal places in the country. Residents of Orange and Durham Counties would find plenty of ideological similarities with residents of California's Bay Area. Similarly, the residents of Randolph and Harnett Counties would find a welcome political home among Mississippi's or Utah's most conservative residents. This disconnect between liberal and conservative helps us understand the sources of many of the most vehement political disagreements in North Carolina. We pick up this question of geographic heterogeneity in more detail in chapter 3.

Partially because of this geographic ideological heterogeneity, various elected officials may be pulled away from the ideological center and toward one pole or another. And over the last decade, it seems that our elected officials have tended toward much more conservative policies—while at the same time, the public is moderating. In fact, the gap between public opinion and government ideology in North Carolina is among the largest in the country. This growing gap may explain why many North Carolinians rate the state government's performance relatively poorly at the same time that the state's economy—often thought of as the linchpin of government success—is doing exceedingly well.

Understanding the reality of a purple North Carolina helps explain a tremendous amount about North Carolina politics as the 2024 election approaches. Neither party is guaranteed a victory in North Carolina for any statewide office.[28] The sense, therefore, is that small changes in the electorate have the potential to shift the election in one direction or another. Changes to voting laws that may affect only 10,000 voters could make the difference between victory and defeat. The investment of a few million dollars in the right television market could result in a different winner. And even a candidate's travel schedule and attention to the state could swing an election.

All of it matters in a purple North Carolina.

3   The Where Matters

The Changing Political Geography
of North Carolina

Senator Corbin, we don't have shark fishing in the mountains.
—Senator Carl Ford (R-Rowan) to Senator Kevin Corbin
(R-Macon), when debating House Bill 544 during the 2023
legislative session, which limited on-beach shark-fishing
tournaments during the tourist season.

The first mention of the phrase "Murphy to Manteo" came just after the 1876 gubernatorial election when Democrat Zebulon Vance's supporters celebrated his victory from "Murphy to Manteo."[1] The phrase is not meant to be literal, of course (if people really were celebrating from Murphy to Manteo, it would have been a party to rival the first Mardi Gras after prohibition) but rather to conjure thoughts of the long distance from the western to the eastern end of the state. Murphy is situated close to the western border, a stone's throw from Tennessee and Georgia, whereas Manteo is located on Roanoke Island, between the Roanoke and Croatan Sounds. About 500 miles separate the two. Truthiness and familiar alliteration have kept the phrase alive for almost 150 years.[2]

"Murphy to Manteo" resonates politically because it reveals two long-standing fault lines in North Carolina politics—region and distance. In 1949, after examining the politics of the American South, V. O. Key concluded, "North Carolina has more-tender sectional sensibilities than any other state in the South, including even tripartite Tennessee."[3] Writing in 1955, political scientist Robert Rankin agreed, noting that perhaps the key division in one-party North Carolina was that the mountains of Western North Carolina contained pockets of Republican strength, whereas the rest of the state was dominated by the Democratic Party. Subsequent updates on North Carolina's politics almost always included a tip of the hat to the regional distinctions within the state.[4]

Political observers over the last half century have homed in on three generally agreed upon regions that define the state's politics and culture. These dividing lines affect the likelihood of Republican victory and even the type of barbecue you can find at the roadside restaurants that line North Carolina's highways.

Eastern North Carolina, also known as the Coastal Plains, runs from the coast to a diagonal line stretching from Northampton County at its northwest corner to Scotland County at its southeastern point. This fifty-three-county region includes Fayetteville, Greenville, and Wilmington and has the largest percentage of African Americans in the state. The region includes coastal towns, estuaries, and the sandy site of the Wright brothers' first flight. The barbecue is vinegar based.

Sparsely populated Western North Carolina spans from the western border of the state to the eastern borders of Rutherford, Burke, Cald-well, Wilkes, and Alleghany Counties. This twenty-three-county region has always stood apart from the rest of the state. Given that the rocky terrain is not conducive to large-scale farming, the enslaved population in Western North Carolina was much smaller than it was in the rest of the state. As a result, during the Civil War, the mountain region contained pockets of Union sympathizers and later was the state's lone Republican stronghold. Today it is the most racially homogenous region and includes just one medium-sized city, Asheville. The barbecue style in Western North Carolina is tomato based.

Although Asheville provides the heartbeat of the region, the city does not represent its western edge. There is a lot of North Carolina past Asheville—hours of it, in fact. The region comprises a midsized university, the gateway to the most visited national park in the country, a portion of the Blue Ridge Parkway, eight counties, a separate nation, a bear sighting every few hours, some talented flat-pickers, terrific whitewater, three North Carolina House districts, two North Carolina Senate districts, and the better part of a congressional district. It is a big region.

The lion's share of population, economic growth, and political power in North Carolina is contained in the populous Piedmont region. This largely urbanized region rests in the middle of the state and includes the urban centers of Charlotte, Winston-Salem, Greensboro, Durham, and Raleigh. Belying its actual geographic location, "Western North Carolina barbecue" has its origins in the Piedmont, although you're likely to find vinegar-based barbecue on smokers in the eastern reaches of the region. The Piedmont is home to the only professional sports franchises in the state, the state's largest universities, and, of course, the state capital and all its attendant infrastructure. As a result, when many people outside the state think of North Carolina politics, they are thinking of the Piedmont.

Distinctions between the three regions have shaped the politics of the state for centuries. In the mid-twentieth century, there was even an informal understanding that the president pro tem of the senate should shift from one region to the next, so no one region would have too much influence.[5] When boards and commissions want to signal an awareness of region, they are careful to have meetings in the east and in the west. Most importantly for our purposes, regional distinctions continue to shape partisanship and voting patterns.

Graph 3.1 shows the average county-level Republican vote share for every presidential election from 1980 to 2020, with lines representing the Coastal Plains (dashed line), Piedmont (solid gray line), and mountain region (solid black line). Despite scores of changes to politics in the state of North Carolina, the partisan distinctiveness of each region continues to hold some weight. Counties in the west have long been the most Republican in the state and continued to be so in 2020. If anything, Republicanism in the west, at least when measured at the county level, continues to grow. Similarly, the Coastal Plains, largely because of racial diversity, continue to be the home to the most Democratic counties in the state. Piedmont counties continue to reside between the two extremes.[6]

Region and Distance

Regionalism also defines the state because of the realities of travel, social networks, and information flow. Citizens at the far ends of the state have a much more difficult time accessing information about their state government or gaining access to the levers of power.

Consider Western North Carolina. Even in today's hyper-connected age, information about state politics is difficult to find in the far-western counties. The region's largest daily newspaper, the *Asheville Citizen Times* does not offer home delivery in most of the far-western counties. Some counties receive local television signals from Tennessee, Georgia, or South Carolina. Just as importantly, the informal networks, where people receive cues about politics (diners, bars, hardware stores, beauty shops, and the like), are less connected to state politics the farther you get from Raleigh. As a result, on average, people in the far western regions of the state know less about state politics.[7]

The choice of candidates for state legislative office also shifts in consequential ways as you get farther from the state capital. The reason is simple: it's easier (and cheaper) to maintain a life at home when your legislative work and home life are close to one another. The "cost" of service in the legislature (whether measured by actual or social costs) is higher for a person living in Bryson City than for someone living in

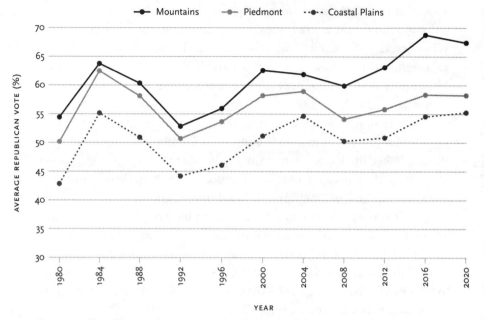

Graph 3.1. Republican average county-level presidential vote share by North Carolina region, 1980–2020.
Source: Data from David Leip's Atlas of US Presidential Elections. Analysis and graph by author.
Note: All figures exclude third-party candidates.

Bethesda. Perhaps for this reason, legislative districts farther from the state capital are less likely to have contested elections than districts closer to the state capital.

It is not just that people farther from the state capital have fewer choices when voting; distance also shapes the types of people who choose to run. Political scientist Rachel Silbermann finds that distance has a particularly profound effect on women who might be considering a legislative run—each hour farther away from the state capital equates to about a 7-percentage-point reduction in the likelihood that a woman will run for office.[8] In North Carolina terms, the odds that a woman will run for office in Robbinsville is about 35 percentage points less likely than in Raleigh.

Regions, therefore, are important not only because of how the land shapes attitudes and behaviors but also because of how they are overlaid on the realities of location and distance.

Toward a New Divide: Urban vs. Rural

In the 2020s, it is taken for granted that urban areas are more likely to vote Democratic and rural areas are more likely to vote Republican. But once you adjust the aperture, you can see that it is a relatively new phenomenon in American and North Carolina politics.

The 2000 election was among the closest elections in American history. Democrat Al Gore garnered around half a million more popular votes than his Republican challenger George W. Bush, but after a recount and a Supreme Court decision, Bush secured more electoral votes and, therefore, the presidency. In some ways, 2000 foretold a new era of polarized, competitive American politics. In another way, however, it was the last gasp of the old orthodoxy. Many of North Carolina's urban counties—counties that we think of as Democratic strongholds today—supported Bush. The majority of voters in Buncombe County (which includes Asheville), Mecklenburg County (Charlotte), Wake County (Raleigh), and New Hanover County (Wilmington) supported the Republican Bush over the Democrat Gore.

Many rural counties—counties that we associate with Republican strength today—supported Gore. These included not just the traditional rural Democratic strongholds in the northeastern part of the state but also places such as Richmond, Scotland, Hoke, Cumberland, and Columbus Counties that are located just to the east of Charlotte.

Graph 3.2 shows the long sweep of that story by displaying the percentage of voters who supported the Republican presidential candidate separated into urban, suburban, and rural counties.

The graph demonstrates that the urban-rural divide—what Zeb Smathers, the mayor of Canton, North Carolina, calls the "country mouse/city mouse divide"—is somewhat new in North Carolina politics, but the degree of the divide today is massive. As political scientists Trey Hood and Seth McKee remind us, the realignment of southern rural white people to the Republican Party is "America's longest and deepest realignment."[9] It is the longest because whereas many examples of the partisan realignment occurred quickly, often centered around a single "critical" election, the rural realignment has been a slow movement over decades. It is the deepest in their estimation because it is not just that average rural white southerners hail from a different party today than they did around the midpoint of the twentieth century, but that they went from the *most reliable Democratic voters* to the *most reliable Republican voters*.

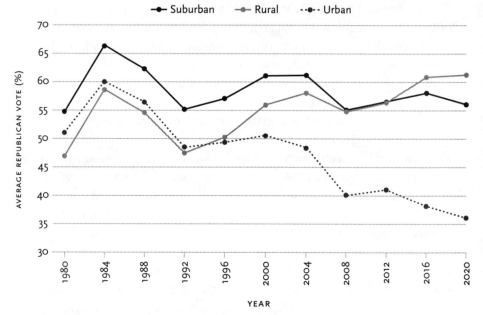

Graph 3.2. Republican average county-level presidential vote share by urban, suburban, and rural North Carolina counties, 1980–2020.
Source: Data from David Leip's Atlas of US Presidential Elections. Analysis and graph by author.
Note: All figures exclude third-party candidates.

This increasing urban-rural divide is not merely an interesting footnote on modern North Carolina politics but rather a central fault line that can help explain election outcomes and governance choices. North Carolina is second only to Texas in the number of rural voters.[10] Despite increasing urbanization, rural voters have an outsized influence in North Carolina politics, as compared to rural voters in other states.

The urban-rural partisan divide combined with the large number of rural voters in North Carolina helps explain partisan outcomes in the state. North Carolina is often compared to Georgia; as discussed in chapter 2, North Carolina and Georgia have almost the same voting patterns, yet in the 2020 election, Georgia, not North Carolina, "flipped" from red to blue. Part of the reason for North Carolina's status as the purple state that is too stubborn to flip is the reliably Republican rural vote. There are over 80,000 more rural residents in the Old North State than in the Peach State, despite the fact that Georgia's overall population is larger than North Carolina's. A Democrat can win Georgia simply by running up the score in Atlanta and other urban centers. A similar strategy in North Carolina centered around Charlotte (the largest city in the state) will not get a Democrat a victory. Candidates for elected office in North Carolina need the rural vote.

Geographic Predictability and
Polarization Is Growing, Not Shrinking

Whether looked at through the lens of region or distance from the capital, there is no doubt that the political geography of North Carolina tells a story of heterogeneity. North Carolinians are divided by region, distance, and rurality. The effect of this is that every unit of geography votes in increasingly predictable ways.

For example, from the 1980 presidential election to the 1984 presidential election, the average county in North Carolina "swung" from one political party to the other by an average of almost 12 percentage points. From 2016 to 2020, the average county swung by less than 2 percentage points. Looking at county-level data in a slightly different way, between 1972 and 1976, eighty-three counties switched partisan allegiances in their presidential vote choice (see graph 3.3.). The number of "swing counties" dropped to thirty-four from 1976 to 1980 and has continued to drop since. As graph 3.3 shows, between 2016 and 2020, just three counties (New Hanover, Nash, and Scotland) changed partisan allegiances from one presidential election to the next. If you are looking for which counties to watch in 2024, you could do worse than to keep an eye on these three.

Political scientist Michael Bitzer has shown that the increasing tendency of geographic areas to strongly favor one party or the other extends down to the precinct level. In the 2020 election, more than seven in every ten precincts in North Carolina gave more than 60 percent of their vote to one party's candidate for president. Only 14 percent of the state's precincts are truly competitive.[11]

Geographic polarization is also evident when you compare the political attitudes and behaviors of people who settle in municipalities versus those who settle in unincorporated areas in the same county. Whereas Democrats make up the largest number of registered voters within municipal boundaries, they trail both unaffiliated and Republican registered voters in the unincorporated parts of the state. Simply put: people who live in municipalities are more left-leaning than those who live outside city limits. This trend exists in big cities (Charlotte) and small towns (Sylva), in urban counties (Forsyth) and in rural counties (Swain).

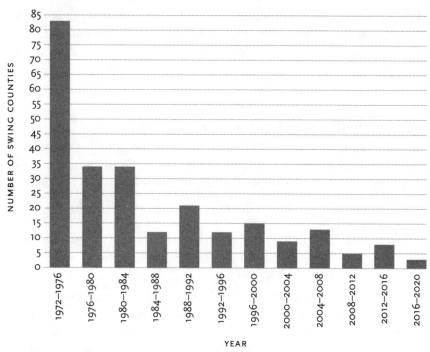

Graph 3.3. Swing counties in North Carolina, 1972–2020.
Source: Data from David Leip's Atlas of US Presidential Elections. Analysis and graph by author.
Note: Bars indicate the number of North Carolina counties that switched partisan support from one presidential election to the next.

The Reality of a Purple, Polarized State

Chapter 2 established that North Carolina has been, is, and is likely to remain a purple state—at least for the foreseeable future. The palpable evidence for purple, however, should not disguise another related truth: North Carolina is increasingly divided. Long-standing regional divides (west/Piedmont/east) in voting patterns, although perhaps relaxing a bit, are still evident in North Carolina politics. The urban-rural divide, which did not exist two decades ago, is today a primary driver of voting patterns and representation in North Carolina. Counties and even smaller geographic units like precincts are also increasingly reliable supporters of one party or the other. North Carolina is a divided state.

In a state whose politics is as competitive and nationalized as North Carolina's, this means that for political parties, candidates, and elected officials there is very little incentive to moderate, at least for those not running for statewide office. Politicians listen to their constituents. Thanks to a growing urban-rural divide, constituents self-sorting into like-minded communities, and strategic gerrymandering that takes advantage of these facts, "listening" to constituents may increasingly mean echoing partisan extremists.

4   The Past Is Not Dead, It's Not Even Past
Race and North Carolina Politics

Thirty years after the conclusion of the Civil War, the City of Wilmington, North Carolina, was governed by a biracial coalition of white and Black leaders. African Americans held significant power in what was then the largest city in the state, and white supremacists, including former Confederate soldier Alfred Moore Waddell, were not happy about it. In a speech that would provide the rhetorical spark to ignite rising racial tensions, Waddell called for overthrowing the government. His goals were clear, as were his methods.

Following Waddell's directives, on November 10, 1898, an armed mob of more than 2,000 white rioters descended upon Wilmington with the intent to overthrow the local government by any means necessary. If anyone got in their way, Waddell proclaimed that the mob should "choke the Cape Fear with carcasses."[1] What transpired was the only successful coup in American history—a coup whose racist roots were not hidden but rather on full display.[2]

Four days earlier and 388 miles to the west in Franklin, North Carolina, a Black man named Mitchell Mozeley was murdered by lynching at the hands of the Red Shirts, a group of white supremacists who planted the seeds for what would become the Ku Klux Klan. Mozeley was one of three African Americans killed that week in Franklin; all three murders were racially motivated.[3]

These are not isolated incidents. The political history of North Carolina is littered with acts of racial oppression, violence, and discrimination, often carried out with the goal of gaining and maintaining political power for white people. While it would be convenient to dismiss these incidents as horrible examples from a bygone era, human behavior does not work that way. Patterns of behavior do not just disappear as one generation passes the baton to the next; rather, some behaviors are passed down and remain in some form or another. The patterns may fade, but many can still be seen in sepia tones.

Political scientists Avidit Acharya, Matthew Blackwell, and Maya Sen argue that these patterns are passed down from one generation to the next through a process called behavioral path dependence.[4] The phenomenon of behavioral path dependence explains, for example, why white residents in counties that had higher slave populations in 1850 have more racist attitudes today, or why white residents in counties with more Klan chapters have different voting patterns today.[5]

Not convinced by social scientists? How about some Faulkner? "The past is never dead. It's not even past."[6]

From Jim Crow Laws to a Racially Polarized Electorate

Following the Civil War, North Carolina, like all Southern states, adopted a new state constitution with the goal of moving closer to something resembling a multiracial democracy—at least on paper. Some positive change did come as a result. African Americans began to gain a small foothold in elected office. From the end of the Civil War to 1876, thirty African Americans were elected to the North Carolina General Assembly, and former state senator John Hyman was elected to the US Congress from the Second Congressional District (known at the time as the "Black Second").[7]

As often happens, however, progress was met with resistance. White North Carolina lawmakers, like white lawmakers throughout the South, passed a series of laws that attempted to restrict this newfound Black influence on politics. One of these Jim Crow laws, as they came to be known, required North Carolinians to "be able to read and write any section of the Constitution in the English language" before they were eligible to vote. The catch? Men who were eligible to vote or were directly related to people eligible to vote prior to 1867 did not have to comply with this rule. That grandfather clause made it clear that white men could continue to vote, regardless of literacy.

Jim Crow laws, along with various other legal manifestations of racism, restricted African American voting power, and therefore African American political influence for most of the twentieth century. During the middle of the twentieth century, these formal tools of racism were aided by campaigns of racial terror headed by Ku Klux Klan leaders such as Bob Jones and James "Catfish" Cole. For a time, North Carolina, not Mississippi, Alabama, or any of the Deep South states was home to the largest number of Klan chapters in the country.[8]

One of the first major pieces of federal legislation that threatened to break, or at least bend, the orthodoxy of white supremacy in political representation was the Voting Rights Act (VRA) of 1965. With the stroke of a pen, President Lyndon B. Johnson rendered the literacy test unenforceable and outlawed a host of other Jim Crow laws. Counties that were "covered" by the VRA were required to ask the federal government for permission before they could make any changes to voting or elections—a process known as "preclearance." In all, 41 of North Carolina's 100 counties were covered by the VRA at some point.[9]

To say that the VRA was successful in reaching its goals would be like calling Michael Jordan a pretty good basketball player. Black voter registration skyrocketed throughout the South, including a rise of 59 percentage points in Mississippi between 1964 and 1970. In North Carolina, Black voter registration rose almost 5 percentage points over the same period—an impressive gain, particularly given that the majority of North Carolina counties were not covered by the VRA.[10] Today, African Americans make up more than one in every five registered voters in North Carolina, just slightly below the 22 percent figure for the population as a whole.

The overall numbers, while important, mask large variations across the state. African Americans currently make up more than half of the registered voters in five North Carolina counties—Hertford, Bertie, Edgecombe, Northampton, and Halifax—all of which are located in the northeastern quadrant of the state. On the other end of the spectrum, African Americans make up less than 10 percent of registered voters in ten counties, all mostly located in the western part of the state. In the most extreme example, there are just nine registered Black voters in Swain County. Not 9 percent. Nine registered voters.

Of course, the key to the partisan change caused by the VRA was not just that African Americans registered to vote but that African Americans overwhelmingly registered with the Democratic Party. By contrast, white voters, who had formerly been in control of the Democratic Party, lost power and influence in the party across the South. As a result, they left the Democratic Party in droves, registering with the only other viable political party in the region, the GOP.[11]

The post-VRA partisan landscape soon inspired a strategic and successful southern strategy, wherein Republicans courted the white southern vote through the trinity of conservative racial politics, appeals to sexism, and conservative Christianity.[12] Race remained central to the state's politics throughout the 1970s as support of de facto segregation was thinly disguised as debates over busing.[13] In the 1980s, racial divisions were coded but still ever-present. Republican political strategist and native southerner Lee Atwater admitted as much in an interview with political scientist Alexander Lamis. Atwater said that in 1954, racist rhetoric was explicit. By 1968, however, it became coded because explicit appeals to race began to backfire. As he explained, "So you say stuff like, uh, forced busing, states' rights and all that stuff, and you're getting so abstract. Now you're talking about cutting taxes, and all these things that you're talking about are totally economic things and a byproduct of them is, blacks get hurt worse than whites."[14]

The use of race as a wedge issue in North Carolina was perhaps most clearly seen in the 1990 North Carolina Senate election between Republican senator Jesse Helms and his Democratic challenger, the African American mayor of Charlotte, Harvey Gantt. The election was littered with examples of thinly disguised, racially coded language, but none was more obvious than Helms's infamous "white hands" ad, where a white hand crumpled up a piece of paper with a voiceover that said, "You needed that job. And you were the best qualified. But they had to give it to a minority because of a racial quota. Is that really fair?" Helms won the election, and many credit the power of that advertisement as giving him the final boost he needed.[15]

The racial politics at play in "white hands" are not up for debate. Republican strategist Carter Wrenn, who was part of the team that produced and approved the ad affirms, "That was absolutely a racial ad. That was the race card. . . . We played the race card and I'm not proud of it. . . . There's no point in trying to say it wasn't because it was that."[16]

In 2013, the US Supreme Court released a decision (*Shelby County v. Holder*) that once again fundamentally altered racial politics in North Carolina and in the South more generally.[17] In a five-to-four ruling, the conservative majority decreed that the formula that determined which counties were covered by the VRA no longer applied. As a result, covered North Carolina counties were no longer required to go to the federal government for preclearance before making changes to election laws. Immediately following the Shelby County decision, a member of the North Carolina General Assembly legislative staff asked the state board of elections, "Is there any way to get a breakdown of the 2008 voter turnout by race (black and white) and type of vote (early and Election Day)?"[18] Not partisanship. Race. Clearly the political distinctions between Black and white were important.

The evidence of a racially polarized North Carolina electorate today is unequivocal. Fewer than 2 percent of the North Carolinians registered with the Republican Party identify as Black, whereas 45 percent of Democratic Party registrants are Black. In another way of looking at the same data: 77 percent of Black registered voters in North Carolina are registered with the Democratic Party; just 2.5 percent of Black registered voters are registered

Republicans. Even African Americans who register as unaffiliated overwhelmingly choose the Democratic primary.

Clearly race continues to define voting patterns, political representation, and the exercise of power in the Old North State. As I discuss below, just as voting rights for African Americans have lagged in North Carolina, so too has representation of African Americans in elected office.

Black Representation in North Carolina Politics

At the time of the 1966 presidential election, just fourteen African Americans (all men, of course) served on city councils throughout the state of North Carolina, and there was not a single Black representative in the general assembly. In fact, no African Americans had served in the general assembly in the entirety of the twentieth century up to that point. Because of the near-uniformity of white officeholding, a Black candidate losing an election did not make for a newsworthy or surprising event. Henry Frye's loss in his 1966 bid for general assembly was no exception. "He was just another casualty."[19] Never one to be easily discouraged, however, Frye ran again in 1968 and this time emerged victorious thanks to heavy turnout in his hometown of Greensboro. After Frye's victory, Black representation in the general assembly also increased, albeit slowly. Dr. Joy Johnson was elected from Robeson County two years later, and Mickey Michaux won election in 1972. In 1974, John Winters Sr. and Fred Alexander were elected as the first Black state senators from North Carolina in the modern era.

The next major increase in Black representation occurred in the 1982 election, when thirteen Black legislators gained office—an increase of ten from the previous legislative session. Although some of this gain was likely due to changing attitudes, most can be chalked up to the effects of institutional change. North Carolina, like many Southern states, had used multimember districts. As the name suggests, a multimember district is an electoral structure where multiple legislators represent the same district. While there are some advantages to having multimember districts, research finds that they consistently depress minority representation. Just before the 1982 election, North Carolina, like many states, reduced its use of multimember districts and, as a result, Black representation increased in the state as it did throughout the South and across the country.[20]

After the 1982 election, there were enough African American legislators to formalize a North Carolina Legislative Black Caucus (NCLBC). The NCLBC holds biweekly meetings, when possible, and helps coordinate

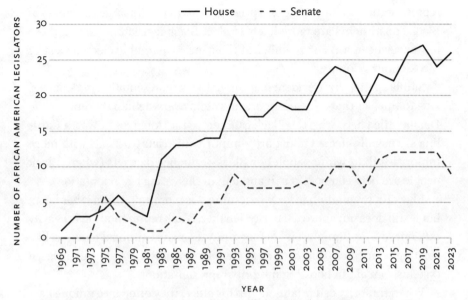

Graph 4.1. African American North Carolina state legislators, 1969–2023.
Source: Data from North Carolina Legislative Library, "North Carolina African-American Legislators 1969–2023," accessed March 25, 2024, chrome-extension://
efaidnbmnnnibpcajpcglclefindmkaj/https://sites.ncleg.gov/library/wp-content
/uploads/sites/5/2023/03/African-Americans.pdf. Analysis and graph by author.

legislative action to further its agenda. Membership is open to members
of any race, although at least once in its history, the NCLBC has denied
membership to a white legislator believed to have been insincere about his
desire to work for the caucus's agenda.[21]

Analysis of the demographic and occupational patterns of these early
Black legislators in North Carolina indicates that, apart from their race,
they were quite similar to their white counterparts. Lawyers predominated
in both groups, the vast majority had at least a college education, their ages
were similar, and both groups were overwhelmingly male.[22]

There is a plaque on the top floor of the legislative building in Raleigh
that lists every Black North Carolina legislator from Reconstruction through
2000. For those who want to understand the trends but who do not want
to make the trek to Raleigh, or for those who would like data updated with
the last two decades, graph 4.1 shows the number of African Americans who
have served in the North Carolina General Assembly from 1969 to 2023.
As you can see, the situation is improving, but few would describe current

representation as robust. Not surprisingly, districts with larger numbers of Black constituents are more likely to elect Black legislators. To wit, there has never been a Black member of the general assembly elected west of Mecklenburg County.

Similar patterns are evident in terms of Black representation in Congress. Due to the fact that African American voters overwhelmingly support the Democratic party, whereas Black candidates for Congress in North Carolina are usually elected to majority-minority districts (districts with more minorities than white people) or Black-influence districts (where Black people are between one-fourth and half of the voting age population).

Black representation in local government is more equal than it has been, but it still does not approach parity. Further, Black representation is heavily influenced by geography and demography. Even institutional features, like electing councillors and commissioners in districts instead of in at-large systems, can aid in boosting minority representation.

When minority candidates do run for office, they often face unique barriers not experienced by white candidates. When Preston Blakely, a Black candidate for mayor of Fletcher, North Carolina, was running for office, someone placed anonymous flyers around Fletcher claiming that Blakely favored "the urbanization of Fletcher, low-income housing and a racially based allocation of government resources."[23] Reflecting on the incident, Blakely affirmed, "Race in politics matters in North Carolina. I found myself dealing with microaggression and dog whistles often."[24] Blakely did win the election, but unfortunately, the racism he experienced in his run is not unique.

This lack of representation is not just symbolically important; it matters in terms of who gets what, when, where, and how. Even when they hail from similarly constituted districts, Black legislators and white legislators represent their constituents differently. Black members of Congress are more likely than their white counterparts to provide earmarks for Black residents, Black communities, and Black colleges. The color line even influences where and how members of Congress place their district offices; Black legislators are more likely to place their offices proximate to a Black community and to employ Black staffers.[25]

Using examples closer to home, Black legislators "saved the law school at predominately Black North Carolina Central University in Durham from closure when other legislators were grumbling about the school." In 1987, Black legislators "fought and won the legislative battle to have Dr. Martin Luther King's birthday become a paid state holiday for state employees."

Black state legislators in North Carolina have also led legislative changes around voting rights and elections on multiple occasions over the past half century.[26]

Electing African Americans to office matters.

The Changing Racial Demography of North Carolina

Racial politics in North Carolina have long been defined in the scholarly literature by a single color line—one separating Black and white people. The most prominent works on North Carolina politics bear this out. V. O. Key makes no mention of any races other than Black and white people in *Southern Politics in State and Nation*, nor do later treatments of the state's politics.[27] Paul Luebke does tip his hat to the importance of "beyond black-white relations" in his 1998 book but concludes, "For the foreseeable future the additional coloring and diversity of North Carolina's population will have little effect on politics."[28]

The times, however, are a-changin'.

LATINOS AND LATINAS IN NORTH CAROLINA POLITICS

In 1994, Danny McComas, a Republican from New Hanover County, became the first Latino elected to the North Carolina General Assembly. Although he understood the significance of his electoral victory, McComas told me that he identified much more as a Republican than as a Latino candidate.[29] Eight years later Republican Tom Apodaca became the first Latino elected to the North Carolina Senate. In 2020, Alamance County's Ricky Hurtado became the first Latino Democrat elected to either the house or the general assembly. Three legislators do not exactly constitute a tsunami of influence, but clearly Latino power is growing.

Census numbers show that the potential political power of the Hispanic and Latino vote is increasing as well. Although the size of the Hispanic population in North Carolina pales in comparison to states like Texas and Florida, it is growing; and given the tight margins that govern North Carolina elections, it is meaningful. One study indicates that North Carolina was one of three states where the Latinx vote may have tilted the election toward Barack Obama in the 2008 presidential election.[30]

Like in most Southern states, the lion's share of Latino in-migrants trace their heritage to Mexico, followed by Puerto Rico, El Salvador, Honduras, and Colombia. In contrast to many other racial groups, Latinos in North Carolina are often concentrated in rural areas. After the 2010 Census, there were "more than twenty-five small cities and towns throughout the state with Latino Populations exceeding 20 percent. . . . Latino areas are often the backbone of these towns."[31]

Overall, Hispanic and Latino voters make up just shy of 3.5 percent of the registered voters in the state. The specifics, of course, vary by county. At the high end, almost 8 in every 100 registered voters (7.67 percent) in Lee County identify as Hispanic, compared to a low of less than half of 1 percent (0.45 percent) in Northampton County. The Hispanic-identifying electorate is more likely to register with the Democratic Party (39 percent of Hispanic voters) than the Republican Party (15 percent), but it is the unaffiliated registration group that takes most of Hispanic registered voters (45 percent). In the 2022 election, the majority of Latino unaffiliated voters who cast votes in the primary election chose the Democratic primary.

The Latinx vote, therefore, leans toward the Democratic Party, but Democratic allegiance is much stronger among African Americans in North Carolina than among Latinos. As a result, both the Republican and the Democratic Parties have made and will continue to make a play for this group. With that said, there is considerable evidence from other states that the Latinx vote should be thought of in plural rather than in singular terms. Given the wildly different backgrounds and heritage of the various groups who identify as Latino, their political attitudes, opinions, and behaviors should not be thought of as monolithic.

ASIAN AMERICANS IN NORTH CAROLINA POLITICS

As with many other racial and ethnic minorities, the number of Asian Americans in the general assembly has also been increasing. In 2017, Jay Chaudhuri became the first Indian American elected to the North Carolina General Assembly.[32] There were more firsts in the 2022 election when Maria Cervania and Ya Liu became the first two Asian American women elected to the North Carolina House of Representatives. The 2023 legislative session even saw the creation of an Asian American and Pacific Islander (AAPI) caucus in the general assembly—a group that aims to "tackle issues that are important to Asian Americans," and "engage Asian American voters outside the General Assembly."[33]

Although the size of the Asian American population in North Carolina is smaller than that of the Latino or Black populations, Asian American identifiers are the fastest growing racial category in the state—a rate of growth that places North Carolina third in the country.[34] Much of this growth has taken place in the counties that make up the Research Triangle.[35]

In terms of voting power, Asian Americans make up about 1.5 percent of registered voters in North Carolina. Once again, there is considerable variation across the state. The largest concentration of AAPI registered voters lives in Orange, Wake, Durham, Mecklenburg, Guilford, and Union Counties (more than 2 percent of registered voters in all those counties identify as AAPI). Almost half (45 percent) of the registered AAPI voters in the state are in Wake and Mecklenburg Counties. On the other end of the spectrum, there is a single Asian American identifying registered voter in Hyde County, and there are just five in Alleghany County.

NATIVE AMERICANS IN NORTH CAROLINA POLITICS
Just four years after North Carolina elected its first Black state legislator of the twentieth century, the voters of Robeson County, North Carolina, elected the first Native American to the general assembly. Henry Ward Oxendine (Lumbee) took office in 1973. Charles Graham (Lumbee) from Robeson County became the first Native American elected to the North Carolina General Assembly in the twenty-first century when he won election in 2011. North Carolina has never had a Native American member of Congress. Whereas Black, Latino, and Asian American representation seems to be on an upward trajectory, the same cannot be said of Native American representation.

The North Carolina voter registration database indicates that a little less than 1 percent (0.73 percent) of registered voters in North Carolina identify as Native American. Almost half (47 percent) of those Native American registered voters live in Robeson County. The majority of the remainder live in Swain, Scotland, Hoke, and Jackson Counties—in and around the boundaries that mark the Eastern Band of the Cherokee Indians in Western North Carolina and the Lumbee Indian homeland in Eastern North Carolina.

In terms of partisanship, 44 percent of Native American affiliated voters in North Carolina are registered with the Democratic Party, 21 percent are registered with the Republican Party, and 34 percent are unaffiliated. These data are comparable to nationwide studies that find that Native Americans are more likely to identify with the Democratic than with the Republican Party. This connection to the Democratic Party is magnified among Native Americans who have a strong sense of collective identity with their race.[36]

Conclusion

There is perhaps no part of North Carolina politics where the past plays a bigger role than in the interplay of race and politics. Patterns of political participation and political preferences do not just flip on a dime—they take decades, and sometimes generations, to change. As in the case of the literacy test, sometimes the vestiges of the past still exist in today's governing documents. North Carolina politics is still defined by political differences in race—a reality that will be evident throughout the remainder of this book.

These differences are magnified in the competitive, polarized, and nationalized political environment that dominates current North Carolina politics. Minority voter turnout continues to lag behind white voter turnout, and partially as a result of this, minority representation in elected offices lags behind as well.[37] But, of course, minority voices are not homogenous. As discussed in this chapter, the political realities of Black, Asian, Latino, and Native American voters and representatives vary dramatically, making generalities about the role of minority groups writ large more misleading than illuminating.

Every day the state of North Carolina grows in population. And that population growth does not mirror the state's previous demographics, but rather represents a movement toward a more diverse politics and society. Astute analysts of North Carolina politics will be attuned to these shifts and will not simply assume that past trends will continue. A new North Carolina will require a new understanding.

5   Women Are Underrepresented at Every Level of North Carolina Politics

It is a pretty safe assumption that when the curtains close around the ballot box, the people running for elected office cast a vote for themselves. Not so for Lillian Exum Clement. When Clement was elected as the first female legislator in the Southern United States in 1920, she did not have the right to enter the polling place, much less to cast a vote. Clement would not get the right to vote until after the passage of the Nineteenth Amendment later that year.[1]

Breaking the glass ceiling in an era during which women had no voting rights made Clement's selection as the Democratic Party nominee for state senator from Buncombe County critically important, but that should not imply that she was treated with anything approaching equity. Press coverage of Clement's candidacy dripped with sexism. The *Charlotte News*, for example, thought it appropriate to focus not on the importance of a woman being elected, or on what Clement planned to accomplish in office, but rather on how men might change their behaviors in response to her election. "We can already see a reduction in the amount of chewing tobacco consumed by North Carolina saloons during their deliberations. . . . These be curious times, my masters and my mistresses."[2] Clement served one term in the general assembly before returning to her law practice in Asheville.

Over the course of the next century, women have been elected to office in North Carolina with increasing frequency, but they remain a long way off from parity. And while press coverage may not include as much explicit sexism as it did in Clement's day, the experience of women and men in elected office is still distinct, and in many ways not equitable.

Lindsey Prather, a Democratic representative to the North Carolina General Assembly told me that the gendered expectations and treatment differ all the way from the campaign trail to the legislative building. She explained, "One of the first people I contacted after I decided to run was an image consultant. I had been recommended to contact the consultant on two separate occasions by female elected officials. I know many women in politics who have hired one but no men." Prather added that when she was running, she "was often assumed to be the campaign manager (instead of candidate)"; and when she was serving, she was frequently "assumed to be the Legislative Assistant instead of the member."[3]

Political theorist Hanna Pitkin offers us a useful framework to help us think about how representation (or lack thereof) matters. Descriptive representation, according to Pitkin, summarizes the degree to which representatives resemble their constituents. For the purposes of this chapter, we will assess the degree to which the number of female representatives matches the number of women in the electorate. Symbolic representation in Pitkin's formulation embodies the ways that a representative "stands for the represented." Substantive representation assesses the degree to which elected representatives take action on behalf of those they represent. As we will see, the lack of descriptive representation of women in North Carolina politics influences both substantive and symbolic representation.[4]

Descriptive Representation

Gains in female descriptive representation in North Carolina government came in fits and starts and, in many cases, did not come at all until fairly recently. Clement was elected in 1920, but the first female member of US Congress from North Carolina was not elected until more than a quarter-century later (1946); and the Old North State did not elect its first female US senator, Republican Elizabeth Dole, until 2002. It was not until 1974, six years after Neil Armstrong took a stroll on the moon, that a woman was elected as North Carolina's chief justice (Susie Sharp); until 1977, that a woman was elected as mayor of a major city in North Carolina (Isabella Cannon, Raleigh); until 1996, that a woman served on the North Carolina Council of State (Elaine Marshall, secretary of state); and until 2008, that a woman was elected governor of North Carolina (Beverly Perdue). Although the recency of many of these firsts is startling, the story is similar in almost every state in the country.

WOMEN IN FEDERAL GOVERNMENT

When Eliza Jane Pratt was elected to the US Congress from North Carolina's Eighth Congressional District in 1946, her term of office began twenty-nine years after the first women had been elected to Congress. A total of thirty-five women from twenty-one states had served in Congress up to that point. In addition to the timing, the circumstances of Pratt's election were also noteworthy. She did not rise through the ranks of elective office like most of her male colleagues; rather, she had served as a secretary for four different members of Congress. When the fourth, William O. Burgin,

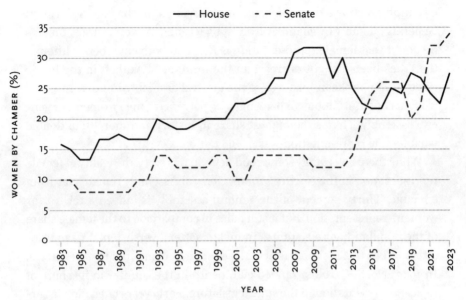

Graph 5.1. Female representation in North Carolina General Assembly by chamber, 1983–2023.
Source: Data from Center for American Women and Politics at Rutgers University, "Find Women Elected Officials," accessed March 25, 2024, https://cawpdata.rutgers.edu/. Analysis and graph by author.

passed away in office, Pratt was elected in a special election. After three months in office, an article in the Durham *Herald-Sun* complimented her for her attendance, "poise and dignity," and her ability to play "hostess to her friends from the Eighth District, who stop in her office to see her."[5] Pratt did not run for reelection and served a mere 223 days. The Old North State did not elect another woman to Congress for another 44 years. Pratt remains the only women ever to serve in Congress from the Eighth Congressional District.

WOMEN IN THE GENERAL ASSEMBLY

The fifty years following Lillian Clement's election to the general assembly saw slight improvement in the representation of women in the North Carolina state legislature. Two more women were elected in the 1920s, two in the 1930s, four in the 1940s, three in the 1950s, and ten in the 1960s. A steady increase did not begin until the 1970s, and numbers large enough to enable any sort of voting bloc did not emerge until the early 1980s.

Graph 5.1 shows the representation of women in the North Carolina General Assembly by chamber from 1983 to 2023. As you can see, there is no doubt that female representation is rising in both chambers, although there has been a slight decrease in the number of women in the house since the Republican takeover of the general assembly in 2011. In 2023, women constitute about 30 percent (29.5 percent) of the 170-member general assembly. That is the highest share in history and more than double what female representation was in 1983.

While there is certainly some good news in this story, the reality of female representation in the North Carolina General Assembly remains far from enviable. Thirty percent of the general assembly is indeed a record for women's representation, but it still pales in comparison to the female share of the population or electorate. To make matters worse, female representation in North Carolina has actually decreased compared to other states. In 1983, North Carolina ranked eighteenth in the country in its share of female representation in the state legislature. Forty years later, North Carolina ranks thirty-fourth out of the fifty states. North Carolina has not kept pace with other states.

While graph 5.1 is helpful in understanding the overall patterns of female representation by chamber, it does not tell us anything about female representation within each political party. Graph 5.2 charts the percent of women in the North Carolina General Assembly (both chambers combined) by political party. From 1983 to 2001, between 10 and 20 percent of both major political parties were women. There was almost no difference between the parties in terms of gender representation. If anything, Republicans were slightly *more* likely to elect women than Democrats. Beginning in 2001, however, a partisan gap in gender representation began to develop, and it has grown ever since. By 2023 there was a 43 percent gap between the representation of women in both parties. Almost 56 percent of Democrats in the North Carolina General Assembly are women, compared to about 12 percent of the GOP. This discrepancy between the parties has occurred as Republicans have expanded their share of seats in the general assembly. These two factors (widening gender gap and increasing Republican representation overall) can help us understand why North Carolina lags behind other states when it comes to gender representation in the general assembly.

WOMEN IN LOCAL GOVERNMENT

In November 2020, voters in Asheville elected three new city councillors. These newly elected officials, Sandra Kilgore, Sage Turner, and Kim Roney,

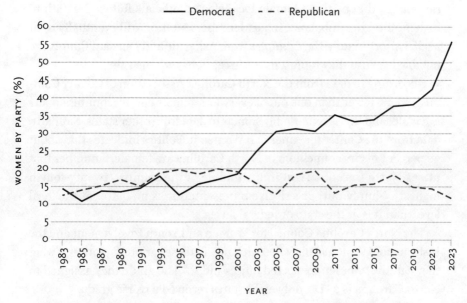

Graph 5.2. Female representation in North Carolina General Assembly by party affiliation, 1983–2023.
Source: Data from Center for American Women and Politics at Rutgers University, "Find Women Elected Officials," accessed March 25, 2024, https://cawpdata.rutgers.edu/. Analysis and graph by author.

joined Mayor Esther Manheimer, Vice Mayor Gwen Wisler, and Councillors Antanette Mosley and Sheneika Smith to make up the first all-female city council in North Carolina history. "It matters that there's an all-female Council because it represents a glass ceiling that's being shattered," said Leisha DeHart-Davis, scholar of public administration at the UNC School of Government. "It's important for little girls to be able to see themselves in their leaders," added Councillor Mosley.[6]

On the same day about 225 miles to the east, a similar vote took place for the Durham County Commission. Nimasheena Burns and Nida Allam joined incumbent commissioners Brenda Howerton, Wendy Jacobs, and Heidi Carter to make up the first female commission in Durham's history. "We are making history in Durham County," remarked Commissioner Jacobs.[7]

From these two snapshots, you might think that the rise in female representation in local government is more robust than female representation in higher office. Perhaps, if this were the case, the best hope for advocates of female descriptive representation might be simply to wait. You might rationalize that as these female local elected officials follow the path to higher office, the imbalance in gender representation will eventually right itself. Unfortunately, the examples from Asheville and Durham County are notable because they represent the exceptions, not the rule.

According to data from the North Carolina Association of County Commissioners, fewer than one out of every four female county commissioners is female; and this is remarkably similar to data from other states. Similarly, data from the Center for American Women in Politics indicates that about 30 percent of city councillors in North Carolina are female, a number that places North Carolina right in the middle of the country (twenty-fourth highest). Simply put: descriptive representation is no better at the local level than it is at the state or federal levels.

The North Carolina Council for Women and Youth Involvement and the Institute for Women's Policy Research put all these various factors into what they call the "women in elected offices index." The grade they assigned to North Carolina is a "D"; only eight states received a worse grade.[8]

The Importance of Descriptive Representation

Skeptics might be wondering why descriptive representation is so important. After all, if a city councillor, state legislator, or member of Congress represents the interests of his or her constituents and acts responsibly and ethically, why should their gender matter?

As Karen Kedrowski, director of the Carrie Chapman Catt Center for Women and Politics at Iowa State University, told me, legislators' backgrounds and life experiences are critically important for how they represent their constituents. "People with diverse backgrounds bring different issues to the public agenda." Issues like "breast cancer research funding, child care subsidies, and health disparities" are much more likely to be issues for female than for male state legislators.[9]

Kedrowski also pointed out that female elected officials tend to propose, support, and pass different types of policies than men do, resulting in more funding for social service programs and a variety of women-friendly policies.[10] Studies at the federal, state, and local levels reinforce that, on average, women focus on different types of issues than men do, even after controlling for factors like partisanship, district preferences, and the like.[11] Recent evidence even suggests that female state legislators tend to sponsor more innovative public policy.[12]

It is not just about policy, however. Women relate to their constituencies differently than men, and they promote different work styles. For example,

women tend to promote more citizen participation through greater empha-
sis on constituent contact and attention to citizen participation in meetings
and decision-making.[13] They are also more likely to emphasize cooperation
and coalition-building in their work.[14]

According to Kedrowski, "Having a government that 'looks like America' enhances the legitimacy of that government, especially among underrepresented groups." When states have higher proportions of female representatives, female citizens notice and respond with greater feelings of
efficacy toward politics and toward the elected officials in their states.[15]
Women constituents are even more likely to closely follow the voting records
of their US senators when their senators are women.[16]

Summing up a large literature on women elected officials, journalist
Sarah Kliff cuts to the chase: "Women legislators sponsor more bills, pass
more laws, and send their districts more money."[17] It doesn't get much
clearer than that.

What's the Problem?

So, if electing women to office is generally considered a good thing,
then why don't we have more gender parity in elected office? The answer, as
you might imagine, is complicated. And the root of the problem starts early
in life. In one study, a group of political scientists interviewed over 1,600
children from first to sixth grade. They asked them questions, documented
conversations, and even told these children, "Close your eyes and imagine a
political leader at work. A political leader is a person who wins an election
and then has the job of helping people and solving problems in the community and country. Some examples of political leaders are people like the
mayor, the governor, people who work in Congress."[18] The children were
then asked to draw a picture of what they imagined. After that prompt, just
13 percent of the students drew figures who were clearly women, whereas
two-thirds drew figures that were clearly identified as men. They also found
that girls were less likely to aspire to be politicians than boys, a reality that
became more pronounced as the children aged. At age six, girls were more
interested in politics than boys; but as they "internalize[d] gender roles
and gendered traits with age, girls [were] pulled toward feminine roles and
move[d] away from politics."[19]

This "gendered political socialization" has long-term effects. Female
adults tend to express less political ambition and are less likely to run for
office than their male counterparts.[20] A 2011 survey, for example, found that
women were 16 percentage points less likely to say they have "considered

running for office" than men. This is a clear indication of a "gender ambition gap."[21]

The difficulty of electing women to office, therefore, is not that they don't win when they run. In fact, female candidates are slightly more likely to win than male candidates. The problem is in the pipeline. To elect more women to office, more women need to run for office. Solving the pipeline problem is the work of groups like Lillian's List, a nonprofit organization named for Lillian Exum Clement that is "committed to increasing the diversity of women in elected offices in our state."[22]

While problems stemming from gendered political ambition explain the low level of gender representation overall, it does not explain the variation across the country. Why, for example, does Nevada have a majority female state legislature when North Carolina can't crack the one-third mark? Part of the answer has to do with the attitudes of citizens in the states. States where public opinion is more supportive of feminist policies are, not surprisingly, more likely to elect female state legislators.[23] Women are also more likely to be elected in less professional states and from districts that are urban and closer to the capital.[24] Multimember districts are also more likely to elect women.[25]

Put together, the research on what limits female representation suggests that a combination of cultural factors related to gendered political socialization, a political ambition gap, and institutional factors have all combined to create the lamentable situation of female representation in North Carolina politics today.

The Experience of Women in Office

But the story does not end once the election is over. Once women are elected, they may have very different experiences in office than men do. Representative Prather shared the following:

I have been spoken down to on a number of occasions, always by older, white, male, Republican members. Specifically, a few weeks ago a colleague fitting that description followed me to my office after session and gave me a "friendly warning" that I needed to "tone it down." He went on to explain that I was making too many floor speeches on too many issues outside of Buncombe. That the way *he* preferred to work was behind the scenes, quietly. He told me he was giving me this advice because he wanted me to be successful. I'll note that the preceding session involved floor speeches from all three freshmen Buncombe house members about a Buncombe County Schools issue. I confirmed later that the member did not speak with either of the other two (male) delegation members about their tone or political approach.[26]

Representative Prather's experience is borne out in study after study that finds that the experience of women in office is very different from that experienced by men. This finding holds in state legislatures as well as in other institutions. Not surprisingly, reported levels of discrimination tend to be reduced in legislatures with a greater number of women in office.

Conclusion

It is clear that women are underrepresented in North Carolina politics. That underrepresentation exists regardless of the level of government or the part of the state, and it exists despite the fact that women in North Carolina are more likely to be registered to vote than men and are more likely to cast votes than men.[27] Further, the underrepresentation of women in North Carolina politics is a problem, regardless of your political ideology or partisan allegiances. If you want to achieve a better-functioning government that includes more voices, you must elect more women to office.

Although the problem is easy to identify, the solution is much more difficult to achieve. Particularly in the hyperpolarized, nationalized, hyper-competitive environment that rules North Carolina politics today, appeals to gender representation might be successful in a primary election but rarely, if ever, will such appeals drive a voter's decision at the ballot box in a general election. No matter how much voters may want more women in office, they will want to have a member of their party in office more. This problem is compounded in a world where women make up a larger and larger proportion of Democratic representatives and a smaller and smaller proportion of Republican representatives. Advocates for change, therefore, should focus on the pipeline problem. Getting more women to serve in elected office requires getting more women to run for elected office.

Part II

The New Era of Voting, Parties, and the Information Industry in North Carolina Politics

6   Even the Way We Vote Is Polarized

Voter Turnout and Election Administration in North Carolina

In September 2020, Republicans Ken Raymond and David Black resigned their positions on the North Carolina State Board of Elections, claiming they had been misled by their Democratic colleagues. Amid a global pandemic, the majority Democratic state board had agreed to settle a lawsuit and make it easier to "cure" ballots, a process by which voters could fix errors in their ballots without having their ballots rejected. Despite voting for the measure, Raymond and Black wrote in a letter that they believed the Democrats were using the pandemic as an excuse to make changes to election administration without proper oversight or input from the general assembly. Republican senator Ralph Hise, never one to mince words, called it "a slow-motion mugging of North Carolina's election integrity."[1]

These high-profile resignations might be used as examples of an increasingly partisan atmosphere surrounding election administration. And to some degree, that is a fair conclusion to draw. But there are no halcyon days of bipartisan agreement when it comes to election administration in North Carolina. Just over a century ago, on the same legislative docket that included setting the weight for a bushel of onions, a bill to allow for absentee voting in North Carolina saw almost no partisan agreement. Only one Republican supported the bill, and the Republicans in opposition argued the bill had "dangerous tendencies" and might result in "double-voting," whereby North Carolinians who lived near the South Carolina border would cast a vote in both states.[2]

While there has always been partisan disagreement over the process and details of casting a ballot, there is no doubt that the forces of nationalization, competition, and polarization have combined to shine a brighter light on the administration of elections. Recently, that light has been blinding. In the 2022 elections in North Carolina, there were two incidents of poll-worker intimidation on Election Day and over a dozen during the early voting period.[3] Entering the 2024 election, election officials across the country are bracing for even more incidents of threats and intimidation.[4]

The Structure of Election Administration in North Carolina: The Basics

In contrast to many other developed nations, election administration in America is incredibly decentralized. The federal government plays a role, but its power is dwarfed by the power of state and local governments. This decentralization means that as long as states stay within federally prescribed guardrails, each state gets to choose its own adventure when it comes to administering elections. It also means that the details can be confusing.

The head election official in North Carolina is not the secretary of state but rather the executive director of the North Carolina State Board of Elections. That executive director (currently Karen Brinson Bell) was appointed by a five-member board that consisted of three members of the political party of the governor and two members of the political party with the second most registered voters in the state. Thanks to the passage of a recent bill, however, that arrangement is in question. Senate Bill 749 mandated, among other things, that boards should be made up of an even number of Democrats and Republicans. A March 2024 court ruling declared this bill unconstitutional, so its future remains uncertain.

North Carolina is one of just seven states where the chief election official is appointed by a board or commission. In the majority of states (thirty-three), the chief election official is elected by a vote of the people. The remainder of states select the chief official by appointment—either by the governor (in six states) or by the legislature (in the remaining four). If you think the election process in North Carolina is political, imagine if the Old North State put the chief election officer up to a vote of the people!

Each of North Carolina's 100 counties has its own board of elections with a parallel structure. County board chairs are hired and fired by the state board of elections, but the majority of each county's election budget is controlled by a partisan board of county commissioners. County directors, therefore, are influenced vertically by the state board and horizontally by the county commissioners. They have a lot of bosses.

It is safe to assume that the next few legislative sessions will continue to see legislation that may alter the details of election administration in North Carolina—legislation that will almost undoubtedly be followed by litigation.

Voter Turnout

The structure of election administration described above has overseen increasing voter turnout in recent years. Graph 6.1 shows presidential

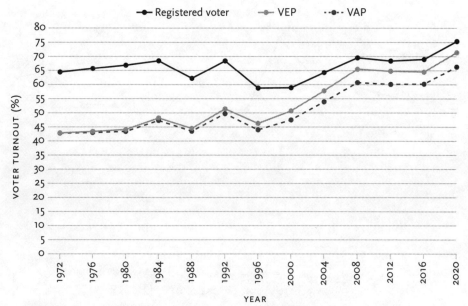

Graph 6.1. Voter turnout in North Carolina presidential elections, 1972–2020.
Source: Voting eligible population data from electproject.org. Registered voter data from North Carolina State Board of Elections. Voting age population data from David Leip's Atlas of US Presidential Elections. Graph by author.
Note: VAP: voting age population; VEP: voting eligible population.

voter turnout in North Carolina from 1972 to 2020 measured three different ways. The dashed line indicates voting age population (VAP) turnout.
This is simply the number of people who voted divided by the number of
people in the state of North Carolina who are above the age of eighteen.
That measure tells us a lot of the story, but it includes too much noise. After
all, not every person who is living in a state and above the age of eighteen
is eligible to vote.[5] The solid black line is the registered voter turnout—the
number of people who voted in a given election divided by the number of
registered voters in the state. The final indicator, the solid light gray line, is
the gold standard in the measurement of voter turnout—the voting eligible
population (VEP) measure. University of Florida political scientist Michael
McDonald developed this measure, which removes ineligible voters from
the equation, leaving just eligible voters in the denominator.

As graph 6.1 indicates, regardless of the measure, 2020 was a high-water
mark in presidential election voter turnout in North Carolina. Turning
to midterm elections presented in graph 6.2 reveals a similarly positive

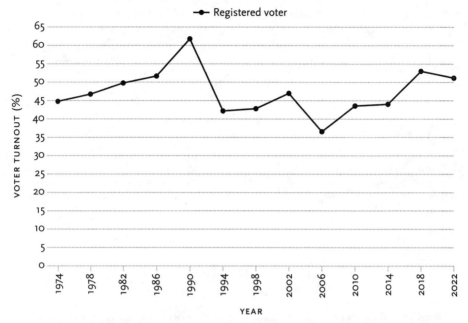

Registered voter

Graph 6.2. Registered voter turnout in North Carolina midterm elections, 1974–2022.

Source: Data from North Carolina State Board of Elections, "Voter Turnout," accessed March 25, 2024, www.ncsbe.gov/results-data/voter-turnout. Analysis and graph by author.

storyline. Midterm turnout in 2022 exceeded turnout in the 2014, 2010, 2006, 2002, 1998, and 1994 midterms. The only year with significantly higher midterm turnout was 1990, a year that featured perhaps the most famous election in North Carolina history: Republican senate incumbent Jesse Helms versus Democratic challenger and former mayor of Charlotte Harvey Gantt. It's hard to look at the turnout glass as anything other than half-full.

While some may think this high turnout is a positive sign for the Democratic Party, nothing could be further from the truth. As political scientists have demonstrated time and time again, the idea that Democrats benefit and Republicans suffer in elections with higher voter turnout is a myth; voter turnout and partisan electoral outcomes are unrelated.[6] As a result, the notion that higher voter turnout is a good thing should be something we can all agree on. And to some degree, we do. In 2022, I conducted a poll of Western North Carolina voters and found that 98 percent of the registered voters surveyed think that all else being equal, an election where more people turn out is a better election.

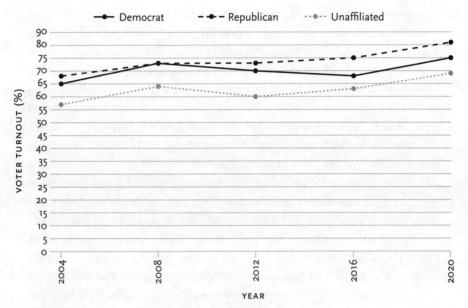

Graph 6.3. Registered voter turnout in North Carolina presidential elections by political party, 2004–2020.
Source: Data from North Carolina State Board of Elections. Analysis and graph by author.

While overall turnout does not signify anything about which party is favored, comparing the voter turnout of each party reveals a different story. Graph 6.3 shows the voter turnout (measured as a percentage of registered voters) for the three largest party registration groups (Democrat, Republican, and unaffiliated) in each presidential election from 2004 to 2020. As you can see, the Republican Party consistently does a better job than the Democratic Party at turning out its voters. Notably, the only year where Democratic voter turnout equaled Republican voter turnout was 2008; that was the last year in which Democrats won North Carolina's presidential electoral votes. Unaffiliated turnout lags behind, although that gap is closing.

Election Day Has Been a Misnomer for a Long Time

While all votes are eventually counted and aggregated into one election result, not all votes are cast the same way. In fact, "Election Day" has been a misnomer in North Carolina for more than a century. In 1917 the general assembly created "absentee voting," which allowed eligible voters who expected to be absent on Election Day to request and complete an absentee ballot for most elections before Election Day. Even prior to 1917, wartime election provisions made it possible for soldiers fighting in the Civil War and the Spanish-American War to vote before Election Day.

From 1918 to 1938, most elections in North Carolina offered the possibility of voting by absentee ballot for some elections. In 1939, North Carolina eliminated the absentee option for political primaries, but it restored that right in 1972 with House Bill 1606, An Act of Limited Duration to Permit Absentee Voting by Students and Others in the 1972 Primaries. The ability to vote absentee was then made permanent the following year, and the possibility of absentee balloting for municipal elections was granted in 1975. Around that same time, the state began using the phrase "one-stop" to describe the process by which people could vote early. In contrast to the old system—which required the voter to make a written request for an application, then submit the application, then get the ballot, and finally drop it off—the new system allowed the voter to request the ballot, fill it out, and return it in "one stop." No one seems certain exactly where the name originated, although former general assembly legal counsel Gerry Cohen is the likely culprit. He quipped, "Ha, ha, ha, I may have coined the phrase in the absentee ballot amendments."[7]

The next major expansion of the ability for voters to cast ballots not on Election Day occurred not just in North Carolina, but nationwide. The Uniformed and Overseas Citizens Absentee Voting Act of 1986 required all states to allow certain people to vote by absentee ballot in federal elections. The 1986 voting act remains the law of the land and supersedes any state law that may pass.

The Election Day voting standard in North Carolina shifted again in 1999 with the passage of Senate Bill 568, which created one-stop voting as we know it now. From 1999 on, a voter could cast an in-person early vote not just at the county board of elections office but at any early voting location throughout the county. Critically, Senate Bill 568 also removed the need for voters to supply an excuse for casting an early vote. In 2001, the general assembly expanded the possibility for one-stop voting to all elections (not just elections in even-numbered years), and it removed the need for excuses for mail-in voting.[8] And while there have been changes in receipt deadlines and the one-stop moniker was dropped in 2024, the basics of in-person early voting and absentee mailing in North Carolina have remained fairly constant throughout the twenty-first century. In the third decade of the twenty-first century, North Carolina voters have three ways to vote: mail, in-person early voting (formerly called one-stop voting), and Election Day voting. And as we will see, the patterns in usage are increasingly lining up along partisan lines.

Changes to Patterns in the Way We Vote

The 2014 election was the end of an era in North Carolina politics not because of the particulars of the candidates who won and lost but because 2014 was the last election in North Carolina where Election Day voting was the most popular way to cast a vote. The 2016 election saw a dramatic reduction in the share of North Carolina voters who cast their votes on Election Day and a dramatic, and likely permanent, increase in the share who cast their votes early. About 62 percent of North Carolina ballots were cast using one-stop voting in 2016, 51 percent in 2018, 65 percent in 2020, and 51 percent in 2022.

The election of 2020 was also critical to our understanding of the way we vote as the global COVID-19 pandemic caused voting by mail to temporarily surpass Election Day voting to become the second most popular way to vote (19 percent of all voters). In-person early voting increased to 65 percent of all votes cast in 2020. Only about 16 percent of all votes in 2020 were cast on Election Day.

The 2022 election saw a bounce back to what seems to be the new normal in North Carolina elections. Over half of all ballots were cast at one-stop voting locations, 42 percent were cast on Election Day, and the remainder were cast via mail-in ballots. Barring another pandemic or similar society-changing event, the 2024 election should see well over half of votes cast in person before Election Day, about 4 or 5 percent cast using mail-in ballots, and the remainder cast on Election Day.

As important as these patterns are, they are accompanied by equally important changes in who uses each of the three methods of voting. Prior to Donald Trump's entrance onto the national political stage, the plurality of mail-in votes were cast by Republicans. After falsely beating the drum of rampant mail voter fraud, however, those patterns changed—and changed dramatically. In 2020, mail-in voting became the purview of Democratic, not Republican, voters—a pattern that continued, although in reduced intensity, in 2022. One-stop voting had always been used predominately by Democratic voters, and that pattern seems to be intensifying as well. Republicans, by contrast, make up an increasing number of Election Day voters. It will be interesting to watch these trends in the future. There is some evidence that Republicans may not want to cede the early vote entirely as there is a movement by Republicans in the lead-up to the 2024 election, reminding their voters to "bank your vote" by voting early.[9]

Conclusion

The increasing partisan divide in the way we vote and in public opinion on election administration has important political implications for North Carolina politics—implications that are magnified in a competitive, nationalized, and polarized environment. Partisan battles over recent legislation changing the partisan distribution of election board members and the deadline for mail-in ballots certainly reinforce this conclusion. And we haven't even mentioned voter ID. The North Carolina electoral system finds itself squarely in the middle of what one scholar calls the "voting wars."[10]

These voting wars are taking place in an environment where any small edge can matter in electoral outcomes; and similar wars are taking place across the country. In addition to the usual suspects in North Carolina politics, there are new groups, such as the North Carolina Elections Integrity Team (NCEIT), sprouting up across the state with the goal of changing the way we conduct elections.[11] Cleta Mitchell, a former attorney for then president Trump, even visited North Carolina and took aim at college student voting locations, stating, "They basically put the polling place next to the student dorm so they just have to roll out of bed, vote, and go back to bed."[12]

With stakes this high and partisan patterns extending not just to who we vote for but to how we vote, the voting wars in North Carolina will not be going away anytime soon.

7   The Largest Political Party in North Carolina Is None of the Above

September 12, 2017, was a historic day in North Carolina politics that reflected an unprecedented shift in voter behavior, changed campaign strategy, and signaled a new era in political parties. Despite the importance of that day, the Democratic and Republican Parties did not send out a press release marking the occasion, the governor did not make a public proclamation, and the state's major newspapers were mostly silent on the issue, save for a brief mention in the aptly named *NC Insider* quoting a tweet from political scientist Michael Bitzer. Looking back, pundits, political consultants, and party officials should have been ringing alarm bells, because that was the day when the number of North Carolinians registered to vote as unaffiliated surpassed the number of North Carolinians who were registered as Republicans. Democrats who marked this occasion with anything other than trepidation missed the fundamental message: they were next. In March 2022, unaffiliated voters surpassed those registered as Democrats to become the largest group of registered voters in North Carolina.

The North Carolina Party System: Where Independents Are Unaffiliated

States have remarkable flexibility in how they structure their party system and party nominating contests.[1] In nine "closed primary" states, independent voters cannot vote in either party's primary. In fifteen states (including our Carolina neighbor to the south), voters do not register by party at all. By contrast, voters in North Carolina register by party, and that party registration has consequences for which primaries voters can participate in. Unaffiliated voters can vote in any primary they choose, whereas members of a political party are limited to voting in their own party's primary.

This feature of North Carolina elections means that voters have a choice to make. They can choose to register as a partisan, receive the (mostly social) benefits of party membership, but be limited in which primary they may participate in, or they can choose to register as an unaffiliated voter, "cover" their political beliefs, and maximize their choices in the primary elections. Given the incentives at play and the broader suspicions of the political parties, it is probably not surprising that an increasing number of North Carolinians have chosen the latter option.

Changes in the North Carolina Political Party System

In 1977, the North Carolina General Assembly passed a bill that collapsed the previous voter registration categories of "independent" and "no party" registrants to a new category called "unaffiliated."[2] This was a necessary but not a sufficient condition for opening up the party system in North Carolina. Initially, choosing the unaffiliated option rendered voters *unable* to vote in either primary—essentially disenfranchising them from the nomination process and ensuring that few would take advantage of this new option.

In 1986, after a US Supreme Court decision affirmed the right of state parties to open their primaries to unaffiliated voters, the North Carolina Republican Party began to consider the possibility of changing its party rules. According to Republican political operative Carter Wrenn, opening the primary system would "strengthen the Republican Party because a lot of conservative Democrats would support a conservative candidate in the Republican primary." The idea, while popular among Republicans, was unpopular among the state's Democratic leadership, including state Democratic Party chair James Van Hecke, who argued, "That's why we have political parties. If folks want to participate in primaries, they ought to register and be part of a party."[3]

The general assembly gave final clearance to the idea of opening up primaries in June 1987, when it passed House Bill 559, giving any voter the right to vote in a party primary if the state party agreed.[4] About one year after the idea surfaced, the state GOP Executive Committee voted to allow North Carolinians registered as unaffiliated to vote in the Republican primary. Although the state Republican Party chair remarked that he didn't think the decision would make "any appreciable difference," he did tip his hat to the politics of the decision, adding, "We think it will help us register people." The Democrats, for their part, held steadfast to the decision that their party primaries would include Democratic voters only. In the words of Democratic executive director Ken Eudy, "Democrats should continue to nominate Democrats."[5]

The Democratic Party's commitment to excluding unaffiliated voters from its primaries continued for the next eight years. Finally, as the 1996 elections approached, the North Carolina Democratic Party Executive Committee relented and voted 187 to 64 to open the Democratic primary to unaffiliated voters. Although the vote reflected clear support, that should not imply that there was no resistance. Democratic Party Executive Committee member Lavonia Allison cited fears that unaffiliated voters, who were mostly white, might "dilute the influence of blacks." Others were fearful that voters from outside the party might commit "electioneering mischief" that would hurt the party. The ultimate Democratic Party position was perhaps best summarized by Democrat Herbert Hyde who admitted, "We have been outmaneuvered by the other party. . . . They have made it look like they are inviting people into their party." And with that, the current primary rules in North Carolina were set.[6]

The Rise in Unaffiliated Voters

To provide a better sense of how these changes influenced party registration, graph 7.1 shows the percentage of the North Carolina electorate who were registered as either Democrat, Republican, or unaffiliated voters from 1977 to 2023.[7] The dashed vertical lines mark the boundaries of the three eras of party registration in North Carolina. The first era is the *closed primary era*, from 1977 to 1987, when unaffiliated voters could not vote in either party's primary. The second era, *asymmetric semi-closed primary era*, spans from 1988 to 1995. During this period, unaffiliated voters could vote in the Republican, but not in the Democratic primary. The current era, from 1996 to the present, is the *semi-closed primary era*, when unaffiliated voters can vote in either party's primary.

Graph 7.1 also makes clear the effects of policy choices on party registration. In the closed primary era, the rise of unaffiliated registrants was almost imperceptible—averaging an increase of only 0.02 of a percentage point per year. The second era, however, when unaffiliated voters were permitted to vote in the Republican primary, saw a rate of increase about thirty-two times the increase in the first era—from an average of 0.02 percentage points per year to an increase of 0.64 percentage points per year. During the current semi-closed primary era, unaffiliated registration has increased by almost 1 percentage point per year—by far the highest of the three eras.

These changes are not only evident when looking in the rearview mirror but were apparent to the political observers of the time. As early as 1996, the *News and Observer* featured an article proclaiming, "Independents' Day Is Here."[8] The same article quoted the chair of the Wake County Democratic Party as saying, "We've gone from a traditionally one-party state to a two-party state with a bunch of people who don't want to be in either one."

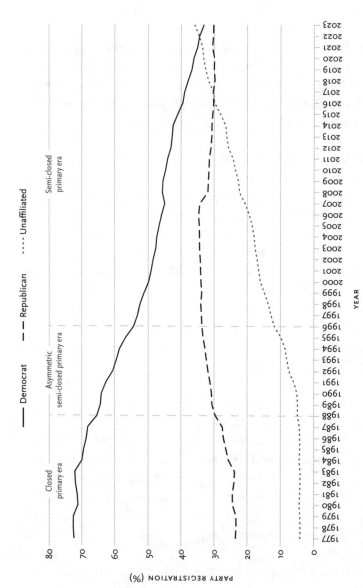

Graph 7.1. Party registration in North Carolina, 1977–2023.

Source: Data for 1977 to 2010 come from North Carolina Department of the Secretary of State, *North Carolina Manual.* Data for 2011 to 2023 come from North Carolina State Board of Elections, "Voter Registration Statistics," accessed March 25, 2024, https://vt.ncsbe.gov/RegStat/. Analysis and graph by author.

Note: Vertical lines indicate when Republicans and then Democrats opened their primaries to unaffiliated voters.

Unlike most trends in North Carolina politics, the rise in the unaffiliated vote is staggering in its geographic consistency. The average county in North Carolina experienced a 15-percentage-point increase in unaffiliated voters from 2004 to 2022, and *every county* in North Carolina experienced at least a 9-percentage-point increase in unaffiliated voters during the same time period.

By 2022, unaffiliated voters were the largest group of registered voters in twenty-two North Carolina counties and the second largest group in seventy-four additional counties. The counties where unaffiliated registrants outnumber registered Democrats or Republicans run the gamut in terms of region and urbanity. They include urban counties like Wake and New Hanover, suburban counties like Buncombe and Henderson, and rural counties like Transylvania and Camden. They also include counties from the east like Dare and Currituck, from the Piedmont like Camden and Chatham, and from the mountain region like Haywood and Henderson. Unaffiliated registrants trail the two major parties in just four counties: Nash, Jones, Sampson, and Wayne.

Who Are These People?

Clearly the number of unaffiliated voters is rapidly increasing in the Tar Heel State, and those voters are spread far and wide across the state. But the question remains whether they are demographically distinct from members of the two major parties and, if so, in what ways. After all, if unaffiliated voters do not differ from their partisan-identifying counterparts, perhaps this rise is much ado about nothing.

As table 7.1 illustrates, unaffiliated voters are indeed distinct from their Democratic and Republican counterparts on every available demographic metric. For example, in terms of the racial composition of the electorate, unaffiliated voters in North Carolina fall somewhere between the two major parties. Unaffiliated registrants are less likely to be white than those registered as Republicans; but they are much more likely to be white than are registered Democrats. In total, unaffiliated voters more closely resemble the overall racial composition of North Carolina residents than the overwhelmingly white Republican Party and the racially bifurcated Democratic Party.

Unaffiliated voters are also distinct in the length of their connection to the state. Unaffiliated registrants in North Carolina are less likely to be born in North Carolina or in the South than either registered Democrats or registered Republicans. Perhaps most telling is the distribution of age across the various party groupings. Whereas the average Democrat and

Table 7.1. Demographics of registered Democrat, Republican, and unaffiliated voters in North Carolina, November 18, 2023.

	Registered Democrats	Registered Republican	Registered Unaffiliated
Average age	53	54	46
Race	(%)	(%)	(%)
Asian	1	1	2
Black	45	2	12
American Indian / Alaska Native	<1	<1	<1
Multiracial	<1	<1	<1
Other	4	2	4
Native Hawaiian / Pacific Islander	<1	<1	<1
Undesignated	6	6	13
White	42	89	67
Ethnicity	(%)	(%)	(%)
Hispanic / Latino	4	2	5
Not Hispanic / Latino	71	75	65
Unknown	25	23	31
Gender	(%)	(%)	(%)
Female	57	47	45
Male	38	48	44
Unknown	5	5	11
Birthplace	(%)	(%)	(%)
North Carolina	52	50	41
Elsewhere	48	50	59

Source: North Carolina State Board of Elections, "Voter Registration Data."

Republican registered voters are fifty-three and fifty-four years old, respectively, unaffiliated voters are a full seven years younger, on average. Graph 7.2 plots the distribution of partisan identification by age in 2023. As is evident, unaffiliated is the party registration category most represented among people between the ages of seventeen and fifty-one. From the age of fifty-four onward, however, unaffiliated voters are the smallest category. As these younger people age into the electorate, and those at the upper end of the age range leave the electorate, we can expect unaffiliated voters to increase in number and influence.[9]

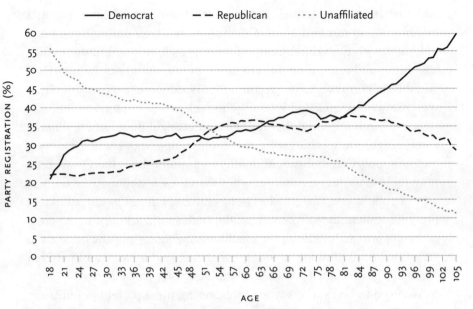

Graph 7.2. Party registration by age in North Carolina, 2023.
Source: Data from North Carolina State Board of Elections, "NC Voter Registration Database," accessed March 25, 2024, https://dl.ncsbe.gov/?prefix=data/. Analysis and graph by author.

Revealed Preferences

While there is no way to know how a person votes, examining who votes in party primaries can offer some clues about which party unaffiliated voters may prefer—or at least which contests they participate in.

More than three in every four unaffiliated voters chose the Democratic primary in 2008. Viewed slightly differently, unaffiliated voters made up more than one in every five participants in the Democratic primary. While that is not ironclad evidence that unaffiliated voters in 2008 preferred the Democratic candidate, political scientists Trey Hood and Seth McKee combined these data with available survey data and concluded that unaffiliated voters in 2008 did in fact prefer Democrat Barack Obama to Republican Mitt Romney. It was likely these unaffiliated voters who ultimately "turned North Carolina blue" in 2008.[10]

From 2010 to 2016, the tables were turned—more unaffiliated voters chose the Republican than the Democratic primary in 2010, 2012, 2014, and 2016. The gap in primary election only grew between these years, experiencing the largest Republican advantage in 2014 (for a midterm election) and 2016 (for a presidential election year). There is good circumstantial evidence to suggest that North Carolina Republicans during these years did a better job than North Carolina Democrats in reaching these unaffiliated voters and convincing them to support their candidates. In 2017, then Republican Party executive director Dallas Woodhouse noted that the GOP was "winning" unaffiliated voters.[11] The evidence is on his side.

Just when it appeared that the Democrats might have lost unaffiliated voters for the foreseeable future, the 2018 election began to turn this pattern of support on its head, as unaffiliated voters chose the Democratic primary with slightly greater frequency than the Republican primary. The year 2020 added to the growing Democratic advantage as almost two in every three unaffiliated voters chose the Democratic primary. In the 2022 and 2024 primary elections, the unaffiliated pendulum swung back to the Republicans, reinforcing the notion that there is no consistent partisan winner or loser when it comes to unaffiliated voter participation.

We need to be cautious when interpreting these patterns in primary voting. Race-specific dynamics, such as who is running and the competitiveness of the primary, certainly play a role in determining which primary voters choose. And the often-rumored "sabotage" vote, where unaffiliated voters choose the least desirable and least electable candidate from the party they deplore, may be at play from time to time, as it was in the 2022 Eleventh Congressional District Republican primary election, when unaffiliated voters bolted to the Republican primary to vote out embattled Republican incumbent Madison Cawthorn.[12] Nonetheless, this analysis suggests that the unaffiliated vote may be more up for grabs than is generally acknowledged.

The Tsunami That's Still Cresting

Unaffiliated voters are the future of North Carolina politics. They are the largest group of registered voters in North Carolina, and every day more people register as unaffiliated than as Democrat or Republican. This trend is not just confined to a particular type of place. Urban, rural, predominately Black, or overwhelmingly white—all parts of North Carolina are experiencing this trend. No matter what one thinks about a person's motivations to register as unaffiliated, it is a reality that any observer, analyst, or practitioner of North Carolina politics must accept.

Of course, unaffiliated does not equate to independent. In related work with my colleagues Michael Bitzer, Whitney Ross Manzo, and Susan Roberts, we argue that unaffiliated voters in North Carolina are instead best understood as "unmoored voters." Democrats and Republicans are tethered to their partisan docks and cannot drift away, but unaffiliated voters are akin to unmoored boats floating near a dock. As long as the weather is calm, they will likely stay, but a strong political wind may cause them to be pushed to an entirely different partisan dock.[13]

The rise in unaffiliated voters also has important impacts on the political parties themselves. Elected officials are, almost without exception, from one of the two major parties (see chapter 8). With young people choosing unaffiliated in such great numbers, it is hard to imagine who will be left to run for office when the next generation comes of age. Similarly, political parties need officers and others to do the work of the party. As former Buncombe County Democratic Party chair Jeff Rose stated, "We have to tell that story better, because otherwise people will just continue to drift into the unaffiliated category, and it'll be harder and harder to fill some of the party offices. Because you do have to be a registered Democrat to be a local organizer in the party. And we need more people to do that."[14]

With apologies to American Express, the two major political parties need to better articulate why "membership has its privileges."

While I have no expectation that the traditional two-party system is on the decline in North Carolina (see chapter 8 for more on this point), the decoupling of an increasing number of North Carolinians from party registration does reflect a large-scale dissatisfaction with parties and politics as we know it—dissatisfaction that is occurring while the two major parties are pursuing nationalized agendas in a purple state. In addition, this movement toward unaffiliated registration reflects an increasing political sophistication among North Carolina voters and creates a series of problems for the two major political parties, particularly in relation to candidate recruitment and party organizing.

8   The Dog That Wouldn't Hunt
Unaffiliated Candidates in North Carolina Politics

By most accounts, Jennifer Moxley was a good candidate. A young, engaged, and engaging communications professional, Moxley was embarking on a run for Charlotte City Council in District 1. She seemed to fit the district she was hoping to represent. She was a center-left candidate in a district that included the left-leaning, but by no means radical, areas of Dillworth, and NoDa (think seven-dollar IPAs, not anarchist bookstores). She was also registered with the most popular political party in the district, "none of the above."

Unfortunately for Moxley, qualifications and ideological fit were not the key factors in her election. For those factors to matter, she would have had to get on the ballot.

In North Carolina, unaffiliated candidates for city council must collect signatures from 1.5 percent of the registered voters in their district. In Moxley's case, that amounted to 1,323 verified signatures. When the election took place in May 2022, voters were presented with a ballot with three candidate, all Democrats. Moxley's name was nowhere to be found. After thirty-three days of chasing signatures, she realized "it was near impossible for an unaffiliated candidate to make it on the ballot."[1]

Moxley is not alone. Despite the massive rise in unaffiliated voters cataloged in chapter 7, people who want to run for office as unaffiliated face a host of barriers that are not faced by members of recognized political parties. As a result, they rarely appear on the ballot, and when they do, they have about the same odds of being elected as they would hitting a bullseye while blindfolded in a hurricane.

A Brief History of Unaffiliated Candidates
The history of unaffiliated candidates in North Carolina is surprisingly murky. There is no authoritative list of candidates and winners, and newspaper accounts, particularly in the early days of the unaffiliated designation, often refer to unaffiliated candidates as "independent" candidates, making the details difficult to track.

With that caveat in mind, the first unaffiliated candidate in North Carolina was likely two-term state Democrat senator Jim McDuffie, who attempted to use the new unaffiliated categorization in 1978 to resurrect a failed campaign for reelection. McDuffie had been defeated in the primary after campaigning for, but ultimately voting against, the Equal Rights Amendment.[2] His plan was to rinse and repeat and run again, only this time as an unaffiliated candidate. His plan failed, and failed spectacularly. He finished sixth in a six-person field.[3]

The effects of McDuffie's defeat were not limited to a rather embarrassing loss. His failed end run around the system inspired "McDuffie's law," which prohibits a person who loses a primary from running as unaffiliated in the general election.[4]

It was not until 1990 that an unaffiliated candidate was finally elected to the general assembly, and even that came with an asterisk. Carolyn Russell was the first unaffiliated candidate to win election to the North Carolina General Assembly, although it turns out her unaffiliated label was a bit of a temporary disguise. Russell affiliated with the Republicans just after the legislature convened in 1991.[5]

A smattering of other candidates ran as unaffiliated in the 1990s, but most lost. Things began to look up a bit for unaffiliated candidates in 2010 when Bert Jones became the second unaffiliated candidate to win election to the North Carolina General Assembly and the first to maintain the unaffiliated label throughout an entire term.[6] The same year, Jackson County's Jack Debnam became possibly the first unaffiliated county commission chair in North Carolina.[7] The election of Jones and Debnam was important, but it by no means ushered in a new era of unaffiliated candidates and officeholders. From 2010 to 2022, just 261 unaffiliated candidates ran for partisan offices in North Carolina; that is less than 3 percent of the total number of candidates over a dozen years.

Graph 8.1 shows the percentage of candidates running for partisan offices in North Carolina in even-year elections who were members of the Democratic Party, the Republican Party, unaffiliated, or members of a third party. From 2010 to 2022, the share of unaffiliated registered voters rose from 23 percent of the electorate to 35 percent. Over the same time period, the share of unaffiliated candidates running for partisan office rose from 3.58 percent to 3.64 percent—a small blip on the electoral radar and one that would not even be apparent if I didn't round to the hundredth place.

Graph 8.2 illustrates which office those unaffiliated candidates ran for. As you can see, the majority of unaffiliated candidates run for county commissioner (52 percent), followed by board of education member (18 percent), and sheriff (17 percent). A smattering of unaffiliated candidates over the last

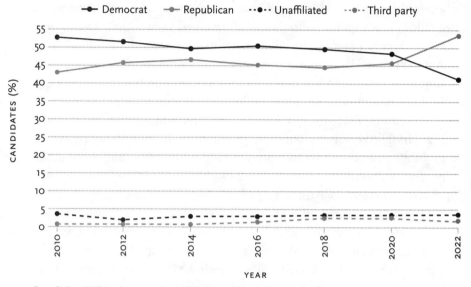

Graph 8.1. Political party of candidates in North Carolina even-year elections, 2010–2022.

Source: Data from North Carolina State Board of Elections, "Candidate Lists," accessed March 25, 2024, www.ncsbe.gov/results-data/candidate-lists. Analysis and graph by author.

dozen years has run for partisan elections for clerk of court, judge, member of the general assembly, register of deeds, and other local offices. No one has run as an unaffiliated candidate for statewide office.

Clearly, unaffiliated candidates rarely appear on the ballot, and when they do, they tend to run for local offices. But what about the electoral fortunes of the few who are able to navigate the ballot access process? From 2010 to 2022, unaffiliated candidates have chalked up forty-two victories. That is a 16 percent winning percentage. If unaffiliated candidates joined together to form a Major League Baseball team, they would have the worst record since 1899.

It gets worse: in eleven of those forty-two electoral victories, there were no Democrats or Republicans on the ballot, meaning that an unaffiliated candidate was guaranteed victory before a single vote was cast. And just when you thought it could not get any worse for unaffiliated candidates, here is one more unfortunate fact: when unaffiliated candidates lose, they tend to lose badly. In three out of every four elections where unaffiliated candidates ran for office over the last dozen years, they finished in last place.

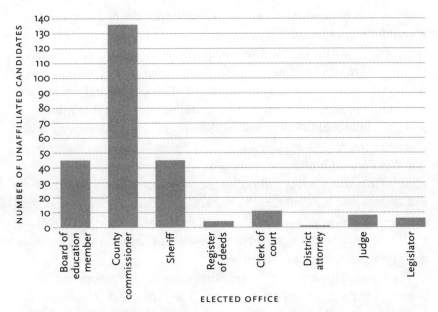

Graph 8.2. Unaffiliated candidates in North Carolina politics by office, 2010–2022. *Source:* Data from North Carolina State Board of Elections, "Candidate Lists," accessed March 25, 2024, www.ncsbe.gov/results-data/candidate-lists. Analysis and graph by author.

There are a lot of quixotic efforts in American politics. Running as a Democrat in bright red Graham County, or running as a Republican in bright blue Durham might come to mind. But both stand a greater chance at victory than an unaffiliated candidate staging a campaign in North Carolina.

But Why?

The reasons for the lack of unaffiliated representation are both structural and cultural.

The key structural barrier is ballot access. If you are a member of a recognized political party, you pay a filing fee and register with the appropriate board of elections. If you want to run as an unaffiliated candidate, however, the process of getting your name on the ballot is much more complicated.

First, you have to petition to get on the ballot. Sounds easy, right? Well, the user-friendly fact sheet from the North Carolina State Board of Elections comes in at six pages and over 2,000 words.[8] That's 2,000 words to tell you how to fill out a form. If that is too complicated and you just want the bare-bones facts, you can always go to the twenty-four-cell table that tells you how many signatures you need and when the petitions are due.[9] It's not an easy or intuitive process.

Once you have the instructions, it's time to get the signatures themselves. If you want to run for statewide office, you will need signatures from 1.5 percent of the people who voted in the most recent general election for governor.[10] In 2022, that was 83,188 signatures. But even that will not be enough, as the board of elections needs to confirm that the signatures are from registered, eligible voters. If Robert Zimmerman signs his name as Bob Zimmerman, it might not count. And if a well-meaning college student signs your petition but is still registered to vote in Atlanta, the signature definitely would not count. So, to be safe, candidates for statewide office must secure well in excess of 100,000 signatures to get on the ballot. Meanwhile, their partisan counterparts are spending their time securing votes and donations rather than signatures.

The required total number of signatures necessary to run for lower offices is fewer, but the act of collecting them is still quite a task. Macon County Commission candidate Jerry Moore explained to Blue Ridge Public Radio's Lilly Knoepp, "Well, when I first started thinking of getting 1,100 signatures, it didn't seem that bad. But then when I started with my first sheet and tried to get 20, I said to myself, 'wow this is going to be a process.'"[11] Michael Zytkow, who successfully petitioned to be listed on the ballot for Charlotte City Council in 2013, described the effort it takes to get on the ballot as virtually all-consuming. "I mean, the last nine weeks of my life have been dedicated to getting on the ballot."[12]

After the signatures are secured, the candidate can turn in the signature pages, pay a filing fee, and hopefully the board of elections will verify the application. Only at that point will the unaffiliated candidate and the candidates affiliated with a partisan label appear on the same ballot.[13]

Once an unaffiliated candidate has secured access to the ballot, the next stage of the longshot election effort begins. Members of the two major parties have a large apparatus behind them. For example, Republicans running for the North Carolina House of Representatives can rely on the intellectual firepower and data wizardry of Stephen Wiley, the caucus director of the North Carolina House GOP. Wiley's job is to elect Republicans to the North Carolina House. There is no Stephen Wiley for unaffiliated candidates. You can try to call the head of the unaffiliated caucus, but there will not be anyone at the other end to answer.

So the few intrepid unaffiliated candidates who get onto the ballot must set out on their own. They must create their own lists, develop their own strategies, and communicate their own message. And the people they are running against have the political equivalent of the 1927 Yankees backing them up.

Unaffiliated candidates are also less likely to receive media coverage, and they are less likely to be asked to participate in debates than their partisan counterparts. This isn't a conspiracy but rather a practical reality. Journalists have decisions to make and if they think a candidate is assured defeat, they will be less likely to cover them. Likewise, time in a debate is finite; every minute given to an unaffiliated candidate is a minute that will not be devoted to the candidates who will likely serve in elective office.

And then there are the voters themselves. Voting is a habitual act. People tend to vote in the same place, using the same methods, and for candidates from the same party. Even unaffiliated voters have had very few opportunities to vote for anyone who is not accompanied by an R or a D. For example, I am an unaffiliated voter who has lived in Jackson County, North Carolina, for twenty-one years. In that time, I have had the opportunity to vote for unaffiliated candidates only twice. When it comes to voting for unaffiliated candidates, I'm simply out of practice. And so are most North Carolinians.

Given all that is working against unaffiliated candidates, perhaps it should be no surprise that fewer than fifty candidates have won election under the unaffiliated label. Perhaps the surprise is that the number is that high.

What about Third Parties?

Some might wonder whether the hope for people to be elected outside the two major parties rests not with unaffiliated candidates but rather with the prospects of a new party—one that will appeal to the disaffected unaffiliated voters as well as to some members of one of the two major parties. At least thus far, third-party candidacies have not proven to be a magic bullet, either.

Third parties just are not that successful. Nationwide, less than 4 percent of the votes for the US House of Representatives are for third-party candidates. Even at the peak of third-party popularity during the early twentieth century, they accounted for only about one in every five votes for Congress.[14]

Returning to graph 8.1, you can see that as a percentage of candidates, third parties trail even their unaffiliated counterparts in North Carolina. The path to representation beyond the two parties likely isn't to be found in the Green, Libertarian, or No Labels Parties, or whatever is to come next.

What Can Be Done?

The two major parties hold a nearly hegemonic grip over electoral politics in North Carolina. And this conclusion holds despite the fact that every day more and more people are choosing to register with neither the Republican nor the Democratic Parties. This may seem counterintuitive (isn't politics supposed to represent the will of the people?), but political scientists reading this are nodding their heads while smugly repeating, "I told you so," under their breaths.

The reason is that most political scientists have read the work of a French sociologist named Maurice Duverger.[15] In a series of papers and books beginning in 1964, Duverger observed that electoral systems where people compete for one seat per district (single-member districts) and where the person with the most votes wins (first-past-the-post systems) inevitably produce two and only two major political parties. Electoral systems that feature proportional representation and multiple seats per district, by contrast, tend to spawn many political parties. Duverger's insight has become so ingrained in political science that it is now referred to not as an observation, theory, or a hypothesis but rather as Duverger's law.[16]

The application of Duverger's law means that no matter how hard the candidates try, unaffiliated and third-party candidates are unlikely to break the two-party stronghold. Then, add the other institutional roadblocks that are set up by the state in terms of ballot access, the layers of the culture of a two-party politics, and the work of the two major political parties themselves to protect the system, and it becomes clear that the problem is close to intractable.

It's not that candidates outside the two major parties aren't good enough, aren't smart enough, or that people don't like them.[17] The problem is much more fundamental. To change their electoral fortunes would take fundamental changes to the system. And in a nationalized, competitive, and polarized environment, any such changes are almost certainly dead on arrival.

9 The Information Industry in North Carolina Politics

Lobbyists, Think Tanks, and Extra-Party Organizations, Oh My!

When Skye David was a kid, she collected quarters from her parents' chain of car washes in southern Illinois. Today she works with legislators to craft public policy that benefits the organizations that contract with her firm, New Frame Lobbying. David's clients range from the North Carolina Coalition Against Sexual Assault to the Elevator Industry Work Preservation Fund.

Donald Bryson grew up in Henderson County, Tennessee, and has always had an interest in politics. Today he heads up the John Locke Foundation, the preeminent conservative think tank in North Carolina. The Locke Foundation does a bit of lobbying but most of its attempts to influence government do not occur through face-to-face conversations with legislators but rather through research and writing meant to change the broader conversation in North Carolina politics.

Politics is Blair Reeves's side job. A full-time software product manager and part-time powerlifter, Reeves joined with some like-minded friends in 2021 to start a group called Carolina Forward, whose aim is to combat what he describes as a "lack of compelling leadership on North Carolina's center-left."[1]

These three individuals have wildly different backgrounds and perspectives, but all are part of the information industry in North Carolina politics. They need money to accomplish their goals, but their primary tool to influence policy and politics is not cash on the barrelhead but rather information and attention—two resources that are critical in any state, but particularly in North Carolina, where an under-resourced state legislature reigns supreme.

Just like the other areas of North Carolina politics and government, the information industry has changed dramatically over the last two decades. The forces of nationalization, competition, and polarization have created a fundamentally different environment than what existed just a few years ago.

Lobbyists

Lobbyists are in the information business.

Sometimes they collect information to monitor their clients' interests, while at other times they dispense information to legislators and staffers. Often this information is used to help pass policy, but at other times lobbyists may want to make sure a certain policy *doesn't* pass. As registered lobbyist Joe Stewart explains, "What a lobbyist brings to the public policy business is akin to what an architect does in the construction of a building: mapping how what's imagined can be real, accounting for how the parts must fit together, and ensuring the finished product is more or less what was envisioned."[2]

The specifics fluctuate a bit from month to month, but as of April 3, 2023, there were 736 registered lobbyists in the state of North Carolina—that is more than 4 lobbyists per legislator. That total does not include the 96 liaisons who lobby the legislature on behalf of other state government organizations. If you graduated from a University of North Carolina System institution, there is a liaison working on behalf of your alma mater as well as another two registered liaisons who have the interests of the university system in mind. Even the office of the governor employs two liaisons whose job it is to lobby the general assembly on behalf of the governor's office.

Lobbyists and liaisons come from a host of different backgrounds and have different work styles. Some live and work in Raleigh, while others visit the general assembly for a few days or a few weeks each session. Still others live out of state and may be registered to lobby in multiple states. Some, like Steven Webb, represent a single client (the North Carolina Home Builders Association, in Webb's case). Others, like Nelson Freeman, represent dozens of clients (fifty-five in Freeman's case).

Those 736 lobbyists represent 1,183 principals, which is government-speak for clients. The list of principals includes many of the groups you might imagine, including the National Rifle Association (NRA), the National Association for the Advancement of Colored Persons (NAACP), the Audubon Society, and the American Civil Liberties Union (ACLU). But, depending on how deeply you dive into the world of state politics, some of the principals might come as a surprise. Plasma Games, Buc-ee's, and the Charlotte Hornets NBA team all employ people who lobby the general assembly.[3]

Even local governments employ lobbyists to represent them in the general assembly. As of April 2023, 26 of North Carolina's 100 counties had at least one lobbyist registered with the general assembly. There are also dozens of municipalities who employ lobbyists—ranging from smaller cities like Lexington all the way up to large cities like Charlotte.

Political scientist Julia Payson spent years studying local government lobbying efforts across the country. She concluded that the economic benefits of municipal lobbying are far from a sure thing. In some cases, municipalities that lobby receive large economic benefits from the state; in other cases, their lobbying efforts are essentially for naught. Local government lobbying, therefore, is more a gamble than a safe economic investment.[4]

Despite the lack of a guaranteed win, many local governments have chosen to ante up and gamble. Because local governments are subject to open records laws, it is relatively easy to peer inside and to see how the process of hiring a lobbyist works. In 2022, Buncombe County, North Carolina, put out a request for proposals (RFP) to hire a lobbying firm to represent its interests.[5] According to the RFP, its objectives were to:

- Lobby the general assembly based on county priorities, including, but not limited to: early childhood education, economic development, environmental quality, equity and inclusion, planning and land use, public safety, public transportation, renewable energy, tax policies, telecommunication, and other board priorities
- Liaise with the leadership of the general assembly and the county's state delegation
- Alert the county to potential new opportunities that could further or limit the county's interests
- Review state proposals, legislation, administrative rules/regulations, and other developments for their impacts on the county
- Confer with elected and staff members on the development of a legislative agenda

Nine lobbying firms bid on the contract, and after a scoring process, the county selected Ward and Smith, a North Carolina–based firm at the cost of $72,000 per year. That sum is about $2,000 more per year than the combined annual salaries of the five state legislators who are elected to represent Buncombe County in the general assembly.

Why do these local governments hire lobbyists instead of relying on their elected legislators who are supposed to represent them in Raleigh? In the case of Buncombe County, the answer may be obvious: the Republicans have majority control in the North Carolina General Assembly, and Buncombe

County's entire house delegation is made up of Democrats. Other local governments might believe that their local legislators are spread too thin to advocate effectively on their behalf. According to Payson, "City officials don't sit back passively and hope for favorable treatment. Instead, cities jostle for influence over the state policies that affect them through lobbying. Local leaders often describe their lobbyists as being essential to the process of navigating increasingly complex state policy environments."[6]

Regardless of the clients they represent, lobbyists gather and dispense information to help craft public policy that is of interest to their clients. That work is not free (over $62 million was spent on lobbying in North Carolina's general assembly in 2022). That money primarily funds time, information and expertise—all of which are intended to further the principal's policy goals.

To achieve the policy ends they are seeking, North Carolina lobbyists spend a good bit of time doing what their name suggests—they hang out in the lobby of the legislative building, talking to legislators and keeping tabs on the goings-on in the general assembly. When they become aware of a bill (or the potential of a bill) that would affect one of their clients, they inform the client and work with legislators to block, alter, or pass the bill in question, depending on what is in the best interests of their clients. As longtime North Carolina lobbyist Joe Stewart revealed, "The magic pixie dust of it is that a lobbyist spends a lot of unseen time getting familiar with how the public policymaking process works, who the players within the process are and going about the business of maintaining a good working relationship with them, and having a good sense of the current conditions within the political landscape—all of which must be applied to succeed."[7]

Like a surfer waiting for the perfect wave, when the time is right, a lobbyist must act quickly and proactively—meeting with legislators to raise the need for a bill, engaging in public relations campaigns, or even crafting draft model legislation for legislators.[8] Joe Stewart offered me one such example.

"That Is Lobbying": A Case Study

In 2005, Stewart was lobbying for an association representing property and insurance companies. According to Stewart, his client was "concerned that the very political rate-making process had resulted in coastal insurance rates that were not sufficient to cover the actual cost of the peril to the state of getting hit by a major hurricane." But Stewart had a problem: legislators knew that he was a lobbyist for the insurance industry and might discount his opinion as a result.

To combat this credibility problem, Stewart engaged a professor from Appalachian State University to conduct an independent analysis of the insurance marketplace. If the professor's study was consistent with the conclusion of the insurance companies, perhaps Stewart and his clients could get legislators to listen. After a few months of study, the professor concluded that "North Carolina was just one major storm away from plunging into a price and availability crisis."[9]

But favorable information is not enough by itself. It still needs to be communicated effectively to the right audiences. So, Stewart and his colleagues encouraged the legislature to form an official legislative study commission on the topic that, according to Stewart, meant "the legislation proposed would be perceived as coming from the legislature, not [from] the insurance industry."

At that point, Stewart and his colleagues shifted to what political scientists refer to as "outside lobbying."[10] They held public symposia and invited the press to cover the issue. They also held forums throughout the state, where they asked candidates for the elected office of insurance commissioner about the issue. At one of those forums, they received a gift—a candidate referred to the coastal insurance marketplace as a "ticking time bomb." Knowing a catchy phrase when he saw one, that became the language Stewart and his colleagues would use to communicate the nature of the problem they sought to solve.

In 2009, after getting the facts down and engaging in a public campaign to make the issue more salient (or at least as salient as coastal insurance rates can be) attention turned back to lobbying the general assembly directly. Stewart and his clients developed a strategy to focus in on particular legislators who did not represent the coast. After all, why should North Carolinians in the mountains be subsidizing people on the coast who aren't paying sufficient rates? There was also some simple math that reinforced this strategy. "There are more non-coastal legislators than coastal legislators, and getting legislation passed is about numbers," Stewart reminded me.

A lobbying strategy executed over five years paid off in 2009 with the passage of House Bill 1305. As Stewart told me when reflecting on the entire story, "That is lobbying."

Think Tanks

Think tanks are in the information business.

The North Carolina Center for Public Policy Research (NCCPPR) was founded in 1977 with the goal to improve information in North Carolina politics. According to its first director, John Eslinger, the NCCPPR would "do what any good newspaper would do if it had the time and resources."[11] Eslinger insisted that the organization was "not an advocacy group" but rather would be "absolutely nonpartisan and work just for good government." Its initial activities were to publish research reports as well as a bimonthly magazine and short pieces on various aspects of public policy in North Carolina. For over a dozen years, NCCPPR was the only game in town as far as North Carolina think tanks were concerned.

In 1990 things began to change when then state senator Art Pope announced an alternative think tank for North Carolina, the John Locke Foundation. Although Pope argued that his foundation's goal was "to be non-partisan and not be captive of any one political persuasion," he also cited the need for a more "free-market, limited government perspective" to be represented in the state's information ecosystem. Speaking of his competition in the marketplace of ideas and information, Pope noted, "The N.C. Center for Public Policy Research does good, quality research, but it leans toward the progressive, liberal side." The newly formed John Locke Foundation would provide a different perspective.[12]

It did not take long for the idea to move into action. Two months after the January announcement of the new institute, the Locke Foundation named its permanent director (Marc Rotterman), and by April the publications director (John Hood) was penning op-eds in the state's newspapers on the political issues of the day. Rotterman and Hood would go on to be two of the most prominent free-market voices in the state.

Over the course of the next few decades, the Locke Foundation would eclipse the NCCPPR in terms of prominence and influence. Today, Locke employees write op-eds, testify before the general assembly, conduct polls, appear on statewide and local media, and do some direct lobbying. They also have a nonprofit journalism arm known as the *Carolina Journal*.

The Locke Foundation owes its prominence and success in no small part to its ties to the State Policy Network, a group of sixty-five state-focused think tanks spread across all fifty states that pursue conservative, free-market policies. SPN member organizations do not exist in silos; they come together annually for a conference and have a variety of means to talk with one another and share ideas.

Another national group that attempts to shift state policy in a conservative direction is the American Legislative Exchange Council. Founded in 1973, ALEC describes itself as "America's largest nonpartisan, voluntary membership organization of state legislators dedicated to the principles of limited government, free markets, and federalism."[13]

In addition to the usual slate of activities—conferences, op-eds, research reports, and the like—ALEC hosts a model policy library. This library is exactly what it sounds like—a place for legislators to go to find language that supports conservative perspectives. The effectiveness of the model legislation idea explains why a bill introduced in one state looks like it has been copied and pasted from a bill in another state. It probably has been.

Research finds that ALEC legislation is most likely to be implemented in states with fewer resources (less professional states) and states where legislators share a conservative ideological perspective. Given what we know about North Carolina, it is probably not surprising that North Carolina has led the way in ALEC-proposed legislation and that a prominent North Carolina legislator (Representative Jason Saine) recently served as ALEC's national chair.[14]

A series of studies by political scientists Theda Skocpol and Alexander Hertel-Fernandez finds that this nationalization of state politics through the SPN has been incredibly effective. Liberal groups have attempted to follow this model (see the rise of left-leaning journalism outlets associated with States Newsroom), but they simply have not been as effective as the well-funded, nationalized movement from the right.[15]

But some individuals and groups are attempting to challenge that narrative.

Blair Reeves cofounded the nonprofit Carolina Forward "to inform and engage voters about what goes on in Raleigh, because when people have full information, they'll usually choose to embrace the future. Our state is changing, and we choose to lean into it."[16] Carolina Forward pursues an explicitly progressive agenda. Although its budget is smaller, its tools are similar to those you might see from the Locke Foundation. It conducts public opinion polls and publicizes research on politics and policy issues. In 2022 and 2024, Carolina Forward published a slate of legislative candidates whom it supported and believed other progressives should support as well.

Not all groups that peddle in the information business are organized around ideas or legislation, however. In 2021, the American Muckrakers LLC (aka Fire Madison) was founded with the explicit goal of firing freshman member of Congress Madison Cawthorn. The tools at its disposal in this effort were not research and polls but rather amplifying negative information about the incumbent member of Congress (including, but not limited to, publicizing salacious videos) and attempting to bypass the Democratic Party structure to facilitate Cawthorn's loss by advocating that Democrats leave the party to vote Cawthorn out in the Republican primary.[17] Fire Madison's goal was met, although some disagree about the group's impact on Cawthorn's loss.

Underrated

Economist Tyler Cowen has a segment on his podcast, *Conversations with Tyler*, where he asks guests whether various ideas in economics, politics, and society are "overrated" or "underrated" and why. One guest might argue that markets are overrated and that Vladamir Putin's power is underrated. The next guest might conclude that the Allman Brothers are overrated while the Marshall Tucker Band is underrated. There is no doubt, however, that the power of information in North Carolina politics is underrated. State government in North Carolina encompasses hundreds of policy areas, and the number of technical details needed to understand how our state works is mind-boggling. From insurance premiums to ranked choice voting to certificate-of-need laws for hospitals, there's just no way that any one person can know what one needs to know to make informed decisions about politics in North Carolina. Legislators, bureaucrats, and voters need people and institutions to help filter, translate, and interpret this information.

As a result, a host of institutions and organizations that work in the information industry have sprung up across the state and nation in an attempt to fill this critical need. And in a North Carolina politics that is defined by polarization, competition, and nationalization, the importance, power, and influence of these groups is growing.

Part III

First among Equals

The North Carolina General Assembly

10 The General Assembly Does Not
Have Much Capacity to Govern

The office is small and does not have much to recommend it, save for the windows that remind the occupant that there is life beyond the legislative building. The walls are cinder block, and the legislative assistant sits just outside the inner office door.[1] Depending on which office legislators are assigned to, they might have to squeeze past the legislative assistant to get to the bathroom.

The building, which was the first building in the country dedicated to the state legislative branch, is a maze of cinder block, red carpet, brass handles, 1,700-pound doors, and garish indoor fountains. It was designed by Edward Durell Stone, a man who was once described by the *Los Angeles Review of Books* as "the most hated of architects" and whose "fall from favor" was described with glib derision in the pages of Tom Wolfe's *From Bauhaus to Our House*.[2] If feng shui has an antonym, it might be the North Carolina legislative building.

The legislator labors in this labyrinthian structure for an unpredictable number of days each year. There is a long session and a short session that should provide some guidance, but from time to time, the long session is shorter than the short session.

Then there's the pay. Legislators who might have raised a million dollars to gain their seat earn an annual salary of $13,951 for toiling away in an accidental anathema of architecture and commuting back and forth to their district. By comparison, the average malpractice attorney in North Carolina earns that before the calendar turns to March.

Such is the life of a member of the North Carolina General Assembly.

This lack of institutional support, which political scientists call state legislative professionalism, is critically important in shaping and influencing who runs for office and how they behave once they have been elected. And in a state that gives the legislature the lion's share of power, the effects of this low level of professionalism are magnified.

A Brief History of State Legislative Professionalism
The mismatch between responsibilities and resources in American state legislatures is not new, although for some time it was considered a

feature of the system and not a bug. At the turn of the twentieth century, state legislators in North Carolina and elsewhere were encouraged to see their positions in the legislature as a sideline, not as their primary careers. Instead, they were meant to work full time on their real careers and head to the capitol for short spurts to perform their legislative duties. This division of labor, it was thought, would keep legislators rooted in the real lives of the citizens of the state and less concerned with the elite issues and interests of full-time politicians.

While this citizen legislature model, as it was called, had its benefits, it did not take long for legislators to realize that their responsibilities exceeded their limited resources. And so, they began to ask for more.

Initially, "more" focused on salary. And it worked, at least to a point. From 1910 to 1935, the average state legislative salary increased two-fold, and the majority of the states replaced daily allowances with salaries. Despite those changes, however, the average annual state legislative salary in 1935 still represented just 6 percent of what a member of Congress earned.[3]

North Carolina was a late adopter of the notion of legislative salary. Instead, North Carolina slowly increased legislative per diem through various constitutional amendments. In 1928, the per diem moved from $4 dollars a day to $10 dollars a day for a maximum of 60 days. Constitutional amendments to increase the per diem in 1946 and 1948 failed by small margins—just 897 votes stopped the bill from passing in 1946, and about 13,000 votes separated the "yes" and "no" votes in 1948 (a difference of fewer than 3 percent of the total votes cast).[4] In 1950, the advocates for salary increases finally won; a constitutional amendment that passed 70 percent to 30 percent increased the maximum compensation to $1,350 a year plus an additional $375 for special sessions, for a grand total of $1,725 (about $22,800 in 2024 dollars).[5] Finally, in 1968, the people voted 55 percent to 45 percent to give the general assembly power to set an annual compensation, as long as the increase did not take effect until the next legislative session.[6]

Session length and staff support also began to increase in the 1940s and 1950s. But it took the efforts of a political entrepreneur in California named Jesse Unruh to give the movement a stable foothold. Unruh successfully championed Proposition 1A in California in 1966 that gave the legislature power to set salaries and session length. The movement that Unruh started was later amplified through the publication of a small paperback book published by the Citizens Conference on State Legislatures and John Burns titled *The Sometime Governments: A Critical Study of the 50 American Legislatures*.[7] The book ranked the fifty American state legislatures on five criteria to determine to what degree they were: functional, accountable, informed, independent, and representative (FAIIR). North Carolina ranked forty-seventh.

Although *The Sometime Governments* was a major step forward in the pursuit of a better resourced legislature, its authors did not use the term professionalism to describe the object of their study. That term was first used in a book chapter by political scientist John Grumm who argued:

> Some legislatures may be characterized as highly professional. By this I mean that their members and their committees are well staffed [and] good information services are available to them; a variety of services and aids, such as bill drafting and statutory revision, are maintained and well-supported; the legislators themselves are well paid, tend to think of their legislative jobs as full time or close to it, and regard their legislative role as a professional one. Other legislatures are poorly staffed, with little or nothing in the way of legislative services, and the members are poorly paid and regard their legislative work as encompassing a very insignificant part of their lives. It happens that most of these factors go together in patterns of professionalism or amateurism.[8]

Measuring State Legislative Professionalism

By the early 1970s, political scientists and political reformers were beginning to coalesce around the idea that a more professional legislature would produce better outcomes, but how best to measure professionalism remained an open question. In 1992, a bespectacled midwestern political scientist named Peverill Squire came up with what would become the most commonly used and accepted measure of professionalism. His measure rests on two central insights.

First, Squire concluded that professionalism could be captured by measuring three things: salary, staff, and session length. More of any of those three would constitute a more professional legislature. Sure, you could include other factors, but in the parlance of the day, the juice isn't worth the squeeze.

Second, Squire held that for all its faults, the US Congress represents the epitome of legislative professionalism. As such, he could create a measure that placed all other states in comparison to Congress. A state equally professional as Congress would receive a 1 on his measure; a state that was half as professional would receive a 0.5, and so on.

So, how does North Carolina stack up?

State Legislative Professionalism Today

The short answer is: not well. North Carolina has the ninth largest population of any state in the country and the tenth highest gross domestic product. The legislature is the most powerful branch of government in this growing and prosperous state, but its resources do not follow.

Members of the North Carolina General Assembly earn $13,951 per year and have not had a raise since 1994, when they received a 7 percent raise from their previous base salary of $13,026.[9] Always scared of political blowback, even that $925 raise was hidden in a larger package of raises given to a variety of state employees.

Although they do receive mileage reimbursement, the salary is the same whether legislators are commuting from Millbrook or Murphy. That salary places North Carolina thirty-sixth in the country, sandwiched between Maine and Utah—two states that, when combined, have less than half of the population of North Carolina.

As of 2021, the North Carolina General Assembly employed 493 full-time staff, an average of just fewer than 3 staffers per member. North Carolina ranks sixteenth in the country for its number of permanent staff members—just under the nationwide average of 528 staff. Hidden within these numbers are radical disparities. Rank-and-file members generally employ one legislative assistant, while the remainder of the staff are spread across leadership, committees, bill drafting departments, and the like.

In North Carolina, years that end in an odd number are considered "long sessions," because that is when the general assembly is required to adopt the biennial budget. "Short sessions" occur in the even-numbered years, when the general assembly is meant to make some tweaks to the budget but not to adopt a new budget wholesale. However, there is no statute that says that the long session needs to be longer than the short session, nor is there one that says anything about session length. A study examining 2009 and 2010 session length data found North Carolina's session length to be the sixteenth longest in the country. And it has only gotten longer in the years since.

North Carolina senator Jim Perry recently explained that the lack of session length rules has created real problems for the general assembly. "Session length has gotten out of hand. We need to provide lawmakers, their family members and the people of North Carolina with more certainty." Perry continued, "We are kidding ourselves when we say we are a part-time, citizen legislature without proper bumpers."[10] One of Perry's colleagues across the aisle relayed similar sentiments regarding the calendar. Describing uncertainty around the 2023 calendar, Democratic house member Lindsey Prather said, "Are we going to work straight through from the budget to redistricting because Republicans want to go home? Or are we going to push redistricting back as close to the filing deadline as possible because Republicans want to make it harder for us to find candidates? It sucks."[11]

The solution, according to Perry, is a constitutional amendment. "In order to establish session lengths, we would need to amend our constitution to allow the general assembly to call themselves back into session with simple majorities, versus only with supermajorities. We need deadlines in place, and we must hold our leaders accountable for hitting those deadlines in order to avoid excessive gamesmanship with regards to internal negotiations."

None of the three indicators of professionalism places North Carolina's legislature commensurate with other states of its size or complexity, with the salary figures being the most out of line. In terms of overall state legislative professionalism, the Old North State ranks twenty-first in the country, sandwiched between Oklahoma and Indiana.

Effects of State Legislative Professionalism

The fact that North Carolina has a relatively unprofessional legislature is not just an interesting footnote but also critical to understanding the nature of representation in the Old North State.

Scores of studies find that professional legislatures are more representative, more responsive, and function better than their less professional counterparts. When legislators have professional resources, they spend more time communicating with constituents and responding to constituency requests. Armed with time and staff, they are also less apt to rely on interest groups and lobbyists for information, generating information from within their offices instead. They are also more likely to create and pass policies that follow the wishes of their constituents; and perhaps just as importantly, the policies they do pass are more likely to be effective. One study even found that professional legislatures are associated with more environmental regulations that improve the quality of drinking water.[12] Professionalism makes a difference.

Professionalism also has an impact on the types of people who decide to run for office. According to Squire, "It's clear that with higher salaries, you get a broader range of people serving in the legislature that more accurately reflects the population as a whole."[13] The lived experiences of legislators I have talked to reinforce this notion. Representative Lindsey Prather told me: "I'm hyper aware of all the little things that aligned to make it possible for me to run and serve. An understanding spouse. No children. A flexible employer. Most of all: a family (that I get along with) that lives in Cary with a spare guest room. It should not require all of those things in order to serve." Prather continued, "My biggest concern is that the pay and long-uncertain session lengths are what prevent more regular people from running for office."[14]

These effects can be magnified for districts farther from the state capital. Consider the experience of Kevin Corbin, a North Carolina senator from Macon County. Every time the general assembly gavels into session, Corbin must make the five-hour trek to Raleigh from his home near Franklin. He must secure a place to sleep and find a way to squeeze in some meals.[15] To maintain financial viability, he keeps an insurance practice in Macon County while all this is going on. Meanwhile, his colleagues who live in Wake County can see their families at night and even make it home for a tuna-fish sandwich at lunchtime, should they wish.

Tuna-fish sandwich notwithstanding, the effects of North Carolina's lack of legislative professionalism vary based on where you live.

Potential for Reform

It is clear that the North Carolina General Assembly is relatively unprofessional, particularly compared with the legislatures of states of similar size and complexity. Further, there is little doubt that the more professional legislatures produce better outcomes. So, why haven't we managed to build a better mousetrap when the blueprints are right in front of us?

The answer lies with the public.

If you ask a random sample of people whether state legislators deserve a pay raise, the answer comes back with a resounding no. In fall 2021, I surveyed hundreds of North Carolinians and asked this very question. Fewer than one in five (18 percent) North Carolinians surveyed said that state legislators should receive a salary increase.[16]

These patterns are borne out not just in survey data but in the legislative arena as well. In 2016, the North Carolina General Assembly considered a bill to increase legislative pay. It never made it to committee. A recent bill in Maine (2019) suffered a similar fate, as did popular referenda in Arizona (2014) and Nebraska (2012).

The blowback on legislators who support pay increases can be swift and harsh. As Prather told me, "A tweet of mine about legislator pay was referenced with the taglines 'Lindsey Prather already wants to give herself a raise!' and 'Prather wants to give politicians like herself a raise,' along with an image of my face drowning in money. It was honestly pretty funny." This much is clear: giving legislators a pay raise is an unpopular idea.

It turns out that part of the reason for the relatively unpopularity of legislative pay raises is that most people have absolutely no idea what their state legislator makes. In the same survey referenced above, I asked people to estimate how much legislators in their states earn in salary. The average estimate in North Carolina was $124,705—almost nine times the actual salary! Survey respondents in California, New Hampshire, and Wisconsin provided similarly unrealistic estimates.

But the same survey also provides a possible path forward to reform. I split the sample referenced above in half. Half of the respondents were told the actual legislative salary, and the other half were not corrected. Respondents who received the correct information were much more likely to support a legislative pay increase than the ones who were able to keep their preconceived notions. This finding was true in North Carolina as well as in New Hampshire and Wisconsin.[17]

But don't take my word for it. Political scientists David Fortunato, Josh McCrain, and Kaylyn Jackson Schiff conducted a similar study to see whether they could increase support for legislative salary and staffing.[18] Instead of correcting misinformation, they simply explained the benefits of legislative professionalism to portions of their sample. They found that exposure to what they call a "good governance frame" can improve support for legislative salary and staffing increases. Their frame wasn't lengthy and simply said, "Research shows that, when legislators have more resources like salary and staff, they are better equipped to deal with real problems. For example, states that provide their legislators with more resources had better responses to the opioid crisis and therefore fewer overdose deaths."

Small nudges can result in large opinion change.

Conclusion

Although we may wish to return to the days of citizen legislators who are deeply rooted in their community and have a day job that takes precedence over their work in the legislature, the reality is that those days are long gone, if they ever existed in the first place.

State governments are asked to do more and more of the heavy lifting in American politics. From abortion policy to transportation policy to health care to voting rights, the power has devolved from the federal government to the states. The job of state government is complicated and critical. We need institutions that provide the best chance for success.

This increased pressure on state government is particularly pronounced in a place like North Carolina that has experienced dramatic population growth and sits on the line between red and blue. And, perhaps most importantly, the pressure on state government in North Carolina is not evenly distributed but instead rests most heavily on the legislative branch.

If we are comfortable with the legislature having the lion's share of power, maybe it's time to give them the resources to roar.

11 It's Not All Cookies and Ice Cream
Polarization in the North Carolina
General Assembly

The Moravian cookie presents more like a cracker than a cookie. It is wafer thin, and there is not a chocolate chip to be found. In addition to the traditional cookie ingredients of flour, butter, sugar, and eggs, the Moravian cookie recipe calls for molasses, ginger, cinnamon, and cloves, and then—and here is the key—rolling to "infinite" thinness.[1] It's a North Carolina original.[2] Who doesn't like the Moravian cookie?

Fourth-graders at Brooks Global Elementary School in Greensboro asked themselves that very question and suspected the answer was "no one." So they worked with Republican lawmaker Jon Hardister to draft a bill to make the Moravian cookie the state cookie of North Carolina. After minimal debate House Bill 394 passed the North Carolina House 115 to 0.[3]

There are more Moravian cookie bills than you might think. A number of bills in the 2023 legislative session passed unanimously, including a moratorium on shark-fishing tournaments from shore during tourist season, an act to increase the punishment for certain types of property crimes, and a bill to allow notaries to complete trainings by video. In the 2021–22 legislative session, even the most staunchly Democratic member of the North Carolina House (Pricey Harrison) voted with the Republicans 70 percent of the time. In the senate, the most loyal Democrat (Natalie Murdock) voted with the Republicans 80 percent of the time. Most bills are just not that controversial.

So much for party polarization, some might argue.

Of course, not all bills are the Moravian cookie bill. Many bills—and with apologies to the fourth graders at Brooks Global Elementary School—particularly those with more substantive policy implications, draw much more disagreement between parties. Issues like abortion, school choice, taxation, and transgender rights may not make up the largest number of bills, but they are critical to life in North Carolina and represent a far cry from the kumbaya politics of the Moravian cookie. These salient issues are increasingly marked by partisan division and rancor.

For example, Senate Bill 20, which changed North Carolina's abortion laws in 2023, found not a single Democrat in support and nary a Republican in opposition.[4] Identical vote tallies defined House Bill 324, "Ensuring

Dignity and Nondiscrimination/Schools," which would have prohibited public schools from "promoting" a series of concepts that are sometimes grouped under the idea of "critical race theory." Just one house member (Democrat Shelly Willingham) broke with his own party on a school choice bill in 2023. The Election Day Integrity Act in 2021–22 and the Fairness in Women's Sports Act, which proposed banning transgender athletes from participating in sports, had all Republicans voting in support and just three Democrats willing to cross the aisle. And the list goes on.

This disagreement between political parties on these prominent bills, and the increasing extremism that comes as a result, is what political scientists refer to as political polarization. Politicians, of course, have a vested interest in casting the other party as more extreme while maintaining that they, and their partisan brethren, have cleaved to the moderate path. Political scientists refer to one party polarizing while the other does not as "asymmetric polarization."

The Curious Case of Tricia Cotham

This conversation about polarization and asymmetric polarization was drawn into sharp focus in 2023, when Tricia Cotham, a member of the North Carolina House representing the 112th District near Charlotte, switched from the Democratic to the Republican Party. Her party switch changed the chamber from majority Republican control to supermajority Republican control, rendering the governor's veto about as useful as a hockey puck on the beach.

Cotham had previously served in the general assembly as a Democrat from 2007 to 2017. She returned in 2022 to find what she described as a radically different partisan environment. As a result, she claimed that she was switching parties because, in the new regime, the Democratic Party wanted her to fall in line whereas the Republican Party was willing to let her be herself. The Democratic Party, in Cotham's estimation, had become too extreme and voted too often in lockstep. Her home would now be in the Republican Party, which she considered more moderate and open to dissenting opinions. Cotham was arguing that the Democrats were polarizing faster than the Republicans; she was hypothesizing that asymmetric polarization was at work.

It's easy to see where Cotham was coming from. If we apply one commonly accepted measure of state legislative voting patterns to Cotham's first term in the general assembly in 2007, she proved to be a good stand-in for an "average Democrat." About half (45 percent) of all Democrats in the chamber held more conservative opinions than she did, and the other 55 percent were more liberal.[5]

By 2020, things had changed. All but 15 percent of the 2020 Democratic delegation exhibited a more liberal voting pattern than Cotham had when she previously served. Simply put: the Democratic caucus had moved to the left. From this perspective, at least half of Cotham's hypothesis was correct—the Democrats had indeed become more liberal over time, leaving Cotham increasingly out of step with her own party.

But what about the Republicans?

While Cotham's voting record did indeed put her at odds with the majority of the Democratic Party, the same data show that she would not find a more hospitable home in the Republican Party. The Republican Party in the North Carolina House (and in the North Carolina Senate for that matter) has, in fact, steadily become more conservative over time. The average Republican in 1995 would have been a liberal outlier by 2020. With the voting record she accumulated during her previous time in office, Tricia Cotham has traded being an outlier Democrat who is more conservative than the vast majority of her Democratic caucus in 2022 for being an outlier Republican who is more liberal than the vast majority of her Republican caucus.

Although both chambers are polarized, the data indicate that the story varies slightly by chamber. Polarization in the senate has been relatively high across this entire time series, whereas the house has become polarized much more recently. Putting all this together leads clearly and unequivocally to two conclusions: (1) North Carolina state legislators are polarizing, and (2) polarization is symmetrical: both parties are polarizing.

North Carolina lawmakers can take some solace, however, in the knowledge that they are not alone in this movement toward polarization. Democratic and Republican legislators in every state in the country are polarizing and polarizing rapidly. Even state legislators in Nebraska, who run on nonpartisan ballots, are increasingly polarized across partisan lines and agree on less and less. You can attempt to dam it, restrict it, funnel it, or delay it, but partisanship, like water, will always find a path through.[6] It may not happen when it comes to the Moravian cookie, but it's happening when and where it matters.

Why Is Polarization Increasing?

The presence of polarization is easy to identify, but it is more difficult to determine its causes and even more difficult to eliminate or ameliorate it. But we have some clues. And while the mass media, geographic sorting, social media, and a host of other factors contribute, the primary cause is best seen through the demise of an odd creature who once roamed freely throughout the South: the conservative Democrat. These conservative Democrats chose their party affiliation not based on ideology but based on cultural norms and, often, the partisanship of their parents.

In 1978, more than half (56 percent) of self-identified conservatives with parents who were Democrats considered themselves Democrats. By 1994, things had changed as people followed their own ideology rather than their parents'; just 28 percent of conservatives with Democratic parents identified as Democrats.[7] Today, liberals have almost perfectly sorted themselves into the Democratic Party, and conservatives have sorted themselves into the Republican Party, regardless of their parents' party affiliation. The conservative Democrat and liberal Republican went from thriving, to endangered, to extinct in the course of about three decades.

As the people have sorted themselves, so too have the politicians. Some of this polarization has occurred through generational replacement—elected officials of a previous generation (conservative Democrats or liberal Republicans) retired or passed away and were replaced with a new generation that falls squarely in the liberal Democratic or conservative Republican orthodoxy. But other politicians have decided to sort themselves midway through their careers.

Which brings us back to Tricia Cotham.

Tricia Cotham was not the first, nor will she likely be the last, North Carolina state legislator to switch parties. State representative Paul Tine switched from being a Democrat to an unaffiliated legislator in 2015. After his switch, he caucused with the Republican majority. In making his decision, Tine said that "he wanted to stay within the moderate Democratic fold, but he felt that the party was veering too far to the left for him."[8]

Two years later, state representative Bill Brisson also switched parties, shifting from the Democratic to the Republican side of the aisle. Brisson explained, "All of my district is rural, and a lot of my constituents are. I've been getting a lot of pressure from my constituents in the past few years to change. I don't have a lot in common with the Democratic Party right now because they have become so liberal."[9]

Most notably, Michael Decker, a Republican representative from Forsyth County, created a political firestorm when he switched to the Democratic Party.[10] In doing so, Decker swung a 61–59 Republican state house majority in the 2003 legislative session to an even 60–60 tie between the two parties.

A subsequent deal allowed the Democratic leader Jim Black and Republican Richard Morgan to serve as co-Speakers for state house.[11]

Ultimately, the details surrounding the partisan switch became the basis of a criminal investigation that culminated in Decker pleading guilty to accepting a $50,000 illegal contribution from Jim Black in exchange for switching parties. Black was later convicted on corruption charges.[12]

Polarization is not the only reason for party switching, but it is a primary one. For example, there is considerable evidence that many party switchers do so because they want to run for higher office. If you find yourself in step with your current constituents but out of step with your constituents on the next step up the political ladder, you might switch parties.

Not surprisingly, some legislators switch parties after redistricting. If legislators' old districts do not look like their new districts, they might change parties to increase their odds of reelection. Others switch after a new party takes over control of the chamber. After all, if you want to pass policy, you're better off being in the majority party.

Then there is the question of ideology. Do legislators switch parties not because of progressive ambition or reelection aspirations but because they find themselves ideologically out of step with their parties? There is some evidence of ideological motivation, particularly in the American South, where conservative Democrats, once common, are now about as easy to find as a four-leaf clover at the North Pole. These conservative Democrats like Tricia Cotham may choose to exit the party for a home where they find more ideological allies.

All these explanations assume that legislators are better off if their ideology and partisanship align with those of their constituents. They assume that people will not cross party or ideological lines. They assume polarization.

What Does This All Mean for Public Policy?

The impact of this sorting of North Carolina conservatives into the Republican camp and liberals into the Democratic camp cannot be overstated. In the days when conservatives and liberals could be found within both parties, a faction of each party could find something to agree on. If a conservative-leaning bill came before the general assembly, conservative Democrats and conservative Republicans might be able to work together to pass the bill. Today, a conservative bill likely will not be well-received by the Democrats, but it will get unanimous support from the Republican Party.

Legislators know this and act accordingly. As Representative Lindsey Prather described, the reality of legislative life for Democrats in the general assembly

> feels pretty dehumanizing, to be honest. I attend every committee meeting, I ask questions, I listen to public comment. But it all feels a bit like show, knowing how the votes will end up as soon as we walk into the room. Even being asked to join a conference committee doesn't feel as exciting as it should since I know I'm just there to make things look "bipartisan." The worst is sitting on the floor listening to the impassioned speeches by my colleagues, knowing how hard they worked and how many people they spoke with about the issue. And seeing it fall along the expected party lines.[13]

Such is life in the minority party in a polarized North Carolina General Assembly.

If you want to understand gerrymandering, you could do worse than to point your GPS to the hipster enclave of West Asheville.

From 1931 to 2011, the City of Asheville anchored North Carolina's Eleventh Congressional District. Asheville was home to the district's largest newspaper and only television station, and the city also served as the district's economic and cultural center. It was your best bet for finding an art house movie, a James Beard–nominated restaurant, or a good indie rock joint. Politically and culturally, Asheville provided the liberal yin to the rest of the Eleventh's conservative yang.

As befit its purple character, the occupant of the Eleventh Congressional District seat in 2010 was Democrat Heath Shuler, an ex–football star who knew his way around a rifle range and wasn't real sure about abortion rights. Shuler's voting record ranked him as the most conservative Democrat in Congress; he even challenged Democrat Nanci Pelosi for minority leader of the House because he believed she was too liberal.[1] Shuler was an endangered species—the conservative, blue dog Democrat. He fit his district.

But that was before 2011, when Republican mapmaker Thomas Hofeller (aka the Michelangelo of redistricting) powered up his computer and clicked his way to perhaps the most effective gerrymander in US history.

Hofeller's map, which was initiated and approved by Republicans in the North Carolina General Assembly, cracked the city of Asheville at Louisiana Avenue in West Asheville and shifted most of the city to the reliably conservative Tenth District, leaving only a sliver of the Eleventh within city limits.[2] This changed the Eleventh from the most politically competitive district in the state to the most Republican district in the state overnight.[3]

As a result of Hofeller's cracking of Asheville, Shuler saw the electoral writing on the wall and decided not to run for reelection, offering the sentiment expressed by virtually every retiring politician: "I am ready to refocus my priorities and spend more time at home with my wife . . . and two young children."[4] Shuler's retirement created an open seat that was filled by a conservative Macon County real estate agent named Mark Meadows.[5]

By the time that a successful lawsuit returned Asheville to its roots in the Eleventh District, the urban-rural partisan divide had taken hold, and a Democrat would have had an easier time finding a Duke fan in the Dean Dome than winning the Eleventh—a strained metaphor drawn into sharp relief by the election of a former Chik-fil-A employee named Madison Cawthorn.

The story of the Eleventh is not unique. A similar tale could be told around the "Wilmington notch," a small heavily Democratic and African American part of Wilmington that was cracked across two state senate districts, or the campus of North Carolina State University, which was cracked across three state house districts.[6] And the list goes on. More than perhaps any other state, the map of North Carolina is littered with examples of strategic gerrymandering that have produced politically consequential results.[7]

Why Do We Do This to Ourselves?

The act of redistricting is not inherently nefarious. To move as close as possible to "one person, one vote," someone needs to draw lines that try to keep communities of interest together and ensure that each district has about the same number of people.[8] Redistricting is sown into the nature of a district system.[9]

It didn't take long for politicians to figure out that they could use the normatively agnostic redistricting process to benefit their interests and the interests of their copartisans. In predictable fashion, North Carolina was the site of the first attempt to do just that. In 1732, before the term "gerrymandering" was even coined, George Burrington, the colonial governor of North Carolina, created "new districts for the lower house of the colonial legislature out of whole cloth, while also arbitrarily altering the boundaries of the existing ones, remaking the electoral map into one that would ensure the election of those who supported his agenda."[10]

Eighty years later, Republicans in Massachusetts redistricted their state senate districts to produce an oddly shaped district that looked an awful lot like a salamander. Although he found the plan "highly disagreeable," the Republican governor Elbridge Gerry eventually conceded and signed the new map into law. And with that, the act of drawing districts to benefit your party had a name—gerrymandering.[11]

Over the next 200 years, the party in power in each state attempted to use the redistricting process to gerrymander its way to permanent power, and the party out of power, whether Democratic or Republican, responded with accusations of gerrymandering. North Carolina has been, and will likely continue to be, ground zero for these battles.[12]

The Redistricting Process in North Carolina

When it comes to redistricting, the North Carolina General Assembly wields the power. Thanks to a weak veto law, North Carolina's governor has no more control over redistricting than the cashier at the local Family Dollar. There is no commission or other party involved, and even the court's role is in question.

When it is time to redraw district lines, the general assembly draws up a series of rules to guide the process. The first draft of these rules usually includes the "traditional redistricting criteria": compactness, continuity, preservation of counties or other political subdivisions, preservation of communities of interest, preservation of cores of prior districts, and protection of incumbents.[13] The general assembly may also add other provisions, such as a ban on using race or partisan data, as it did in 2021.

The redistricting process for the North Carolina General Assembly maps (but not for the congressional maps) also includes a couple of unique rules. First, all maps must follow the "whole county provision," which says that counties can be split only to maintain population equality. Thanks to a decision in *Stephenson v. Bartlett*, legislators drawing general assembly maps also must follow the county clustering rule before a single district line is drawn.[14] This rule applies a mathematical formula to create clusters of geographically proximate counties with the proper population size.[15] It is only after this base map is produced that legislators commence drawing lines.

As long as it operates between these guardrails and does not draw the ire of the court, the general assembly can draw maps as it pleases. Its primary tools in the attempt to lock in and expand power are "cracking" and "packing."

Cracking occurs when the majority party splits concentrations of the opposing party's voters across multiple districts. This approach then reduces the opposing party's strengths in one or more districts at a time, just as the 2011 congressional district lines did by splitting Asheville.

Packing occurs when the majority party draws lines around a large concentration of the minority party's voters. This strategy results in the minority party winning one district by a large margin, while simultaneously reducing its voting power in all surrounding districts.

While no credible observer doubts the existence of cracking and packing, some argue that their effects are muted by the realities of geographic sorting. This argument holds that Democrats increasingly live near one another and Republicans increasingly live near one another. But, while Republicans are still spread across larger swaths of geography, Democrats tend to settle in dense urban centers. Thus, what may appear to be packing is nothing more than drawing compact districts that respect municipal boundaries and communities of interest. Research by political scientists demonstrates that although geographic sorting does matter, it does not explain away the power of gerrymandering to turbocharge partisan malapportionment in North Carolina.[16]

Welcome, My Friends, to the Show That Never Ends
A Brief Modern History of Gerrymandering
in North Carolina

In the 1940s, North Carolina politics was dominated by the Democratic Party, but there were pockets of Republican strength, particularly in the mountainous western part of the state. The concentration of Republicans in the west was large enough that a congressional map with a district contained solely in the mountains would have likely produced at least one Republican member of Congress. So, what did the Democrats do? They tossed out any notion of geographic cohesion and drew "bacon strip" districts that cut from west to east, pairing heavily Republican, but sparsely populated western counties with more densely populated Democratic strongholds in the Piedmont.[17] The result of this gerrymandering rendered North Carolina Republicans without a single voice in Congress from 1931 to 1953.

Similar patterns of Democratic gerrymandering continued in North Carolina for decades. The 1961 redistricting cycle, for example, produced what one scholar called an "obvious gerrymander . . . passed by the General Assembly despite strong protests from the small Republican minority, segments of the state press and even some of the Democratic legislators."[18]

In 1991, the North Carolina congressional map drawn by the Democratic legislature was pilloried by the *Wall Street Journal* as "computer-generated pornography."[19] The most egregious offender in this laughably drawn map was the Twelfth Congressional District, which stretched from Charlotte to Winston-Salem to Greensboro and into Durham. At one point, the district was so narrow that if a person opened the passenger car door on I-85, the door handle might briefly pass through a different district than the steering wheel.

But these districts are the subjects of a continuous flow of lawsuits not because of their funny shapes but rather because of what they mean for political representation. Drawing district lines to favor one party or the other is a time-tested way to gain and maintain power. Since passage of the Voting Rights Act of 1965, the empirical reality that the vast majority of African Americans vote with the Democratic Party means that questions about partisan representation are often also questions about racial representation, and vice versa.

Although the specifics of redistricting and gerrymandering vary across place and time, the one constant is that the party out of power, whether Republican or Democrat, will accuse the other of gerrymandering. In 2001, Stony Rushing, then the president of the Union County Republican Men's Club and later a congressional candidate with a penchant for dressing up like Boss Hogg, accused the Democratic majority of "gerrymandering districts and lying to get elected" and implored voters to call their local elected officials and "tell them to stop the gerrymandering and keep all Union County residents in one district."[20] The same year, GOP senators accused the Democrats of placing "a disproportionate number of Republican voters into districts represented by Republicans," thus diluting the Republican votes in the adjoining districts. Democrats assured the voters with absolutely no evidence that they had "acted in good faith."[21]

The pattern of Republicans crying gerrymandering and Democrats defending obviously unfair maps changed in 2011. The combination of a national political tide that ran counter to President Barack Obama's Democratic Party and a concerted effort by Republicans to take over state legislatures just in time for decennial redistricting resulted in massive Republican gains nationwide and in North Carolina as well.[22] Across the country, new Republican majorities drew gerrymandered districts that were even more effective than those they had suffered under for a century.[23]

There were a number of legal skirmishes over redistricting from 2011 to 2017, but the next major inflection point in North Carolina redistricting occurred in 2018, when a group of plaintiffs sued the North Carolina General Assembly, claiming that a partisan gerrymander violated their Fourteenth Amendment and equal protection rights. The *Rucho v. Common Cause* case eventually made its way to the US Supreme Court.[24] In an opinion that was the legal equivalent of a shoulder shrug, the five-to-four majority on the high court concluded that gerrymandering is a problem but not one to be solved by the federal courts. Instead, the majority opinion, written by Chief Justice John Roberts, argued that just as states are responsible for drawing their own district lines, they are also tasked with addressing the problems of gerrymandering.

And that's exactly what happened. In 2018, plaintiffs filed a case in the North Carolina courts (*Common Cause v. Lewis*), alleging that the general assembly districts drawn in 2011 were unconstitutional partisan gerrymanders.[25] Computer-generated simulations produced by expert witnesses Jowei Chen, Wes Pegden, and Jonathan Mattingly demonstrated that the odds of producing a map with such a heavily Republican advantage by chance were exceedingly small.

In addition to the usual expert witness testimony, this case also included the computer files of the aforementioned, now-deceased mapmaker Thomas Hofeller. After his death, Hofeller's daughter offered his computer to lawyers representing the Common Cause plaintiffs. Throughout the course of the trial, expert witnesses used his computer to demonstrate that Hofeller drew district lines before he was under contract to do so and that he had drawn them with remarkable precision with one goal in mind—to secure Republican supermajorities.[26] The court ruled in favor of the plaintiffs and required the maps to be redrawn.

Common Cause v. Lewis capped off a remarkable decade of redistricting litigation in North Carolina and across the country. A process that was supposed to create one state house, one state senate, and one congressional map every ten years resulted instead in the creation of four state senate maps, four state house maps, and three congressional maps in North Carolina from 2011 to 2020.

Following the decennial census of 2020, Republican mapmakers had another opportunity to draw legislative and congressional maps in 2021. And, once again, those maps were met with the ire of three separate groups of North Carolina litigants—cases that were eventually combined and heard as *Harper v. Hall*.[27] Although there were no errant hard drives, *Harper v. Hall* had its own share of twists and turns that included the delay of candidate filing (twice), accusations of improper communication between witnesses and special masters, and two rounds of legislatively drawn maps.[28] The Democratic-majority court eventually accepted the legislature's second effort at the state house and state senate maps but rejected the second effort at a congressional map. The North Carolina State Supreme Court offered its own congressional map, drawn by three special masters, that resulted in a seven-seven Democrat-Republican congressional split. All that occurred before the calendar turned to 2023.

But the end of 2022 did not mark the end of this drama. First, the newly elected Republican majority on the state supreme court reversed the previous court's opinion and rendered the maps used in 2022 "one and done"—meaning that in fall 2023, the general assembly drew up new maps for both chambers of the general assembly as well as for the congressional delegation.[29] All three maps were more advantageous for the Republicans than the previous maps. Notably, the congressional maps were expected to send at least three Democrats packing—Jeff Jackson, Wiley Nickel, and Kathy Manning. A fourth Democrat, Don Davis, faces an uncertain future at the time of this writing as his district is the lone competitive district in the state.

The legislative defendants in the *Harper v. Hall* case also brought suit against the plaintiffs (*Harper v. Hall* became *Moore v. Harper*), arguing that state courts should not have the right to intervene in the first place.[30] Election laws governing federal elections, according to the plaintiff, North Carolina Speaker of the house Tim Moore, are the purview of each state's legislature, not the courts. By telling the legislature what it could and could not do, Moore argued that the courts had violated the independent state legislature theory and overstepped their power. The case and the theory went before the US Supreme Court, where a six-to-three majority ruled against Speaker Moore and rejected a radical view of the independent state legislature theory.

The experience of North Carolina over the last two redistricting cycles reinforces how the current nationalized, hyperpartisan political moment has turbocharged the long simmering problems of redistricting in North Carolina and elsewhere. For example, Thomas Hofeller, the mapmaker with a telltale hard drive, was not a North Carolina political hack but rather a California-based national consultant who traveled from state to state, helping Republicans win.[31] The surge that propelled Republican majorities in 2010 was also not homegrown but rather part of the national initiative known as REDMAP (Redistricting Majority Project). And many of the law firms that brought suit in North Carolina were not based in the Tar Heel State but instead litigated election law across the country. In these ways and many more, the experiences of North Carolina in gerrymandering are virtually indistinguishable from the stories in Pennsylvania, Wisconsin, and elsewhere.

The razor thin majorities that define modern North Carolina politics also make the stakes of redistricting that much higher. No one can predict which party will win the next gubernatorial election, but if one party can control the district lines, it can give itself a head start in legislative elections that can pay huge dividends in terms of public policy and political power.

Moving Forward

Without effective legal or policy guardrails, gerrymandering is a fact of political life. It is a fact that was evident when the Democrats controlled the general assembly, and it is a fact that is evident now that the

Republicans are in charge. Without gerrymandering, Republican voters would have had more authentic representation in Congress and in the general assembly throughout the twentieth century and Democrats would have more authentic representation today.

Just as certain as the fact that the party in power will gerrymander to hold onto its power is the fact that the minority party will advocate for reform. Democrats may be surprised that the first person to introduce an independent redistricting bill in North Carolina was none other than Republican mega-donor Art Pope.[32] Pope has remained steadfast in his support for redistricting reform, but every year that goes by makes it more and more difficult to find Republicans who might join in this effort. Sure, there are exceptions, such as Republicans Jon Hardister's and Chuck McGrady's support of an eleven-member nonpartisan redistricting commission in 2019; but the mainstream Republican position, just like the mainstream Democratic position when the Democrats had control, is not only to oppose independent redistricting but also to challenge the very existence of independence. As Republican senator Ralph Hise quipped, "I don't believe in unicorns, fairies, or the nonpartisan commission."[33] More recently, former North Carolina GOP chair Dallas Woodhouse proclaimed on Twitter, "Any reform efforts on redistricting are dead and will not be revived."[34]

Whether Woodhouse is correct or not remains to be seen, but the evidence from other states suggests that nonpartisan commissions do in fact exist. And they can help ameliorate the problems of partisan districting. We will return to this question in the conclusion.

Part IV

Vying for Power

Other Institutional Actors in
North Carolina Government

13   The Weak North Carolina Governor

Just Enough Power to Sign the Receipt for Their Own Salary

The North Carolina governor is the most recognizable, most covered, and most prominent politician in North Carolina. A 2023 Meredith College poll found that 80 percent of North Carolinians could identify Governor Roy Cooper—more than four times the number of people who could identify Speaker of the House Tim Moore or President Pro Tem of the Senate Phil Berger.[1] That prominence seems only to be growing as gubernatorial elections become more nationalized and as the North Carolina governorship, in particular, continues to be a vehicle for national media appearances.[2] The implication of this attention is the idea that the governor matters, that the person who fills that seat and makes a home at 200 North Blount Street in Raleigh will be able to wield power and shape the state in his or her image.

To some degree, this attention is deserved. By virtue of the position's stature, when the governor talks, press gaggles follow, and the people listen. The governor is also the leader of the executive branch, has some appointment power, and can sign executive orders into law. In terms of influence over legislation, however, the governor's power is fairly limited. And, in comparison to other governors, North Carolina's governor is the weakest in the country. That is by design.

In 1776, a delegate to the North Carolina Constitutional Convention noted that the original state constitution gave the governor "just enough power to sign the receipt for his own salary."[3] Although North Carolina retired that constitution during Reconstruction and has had one more constitution in the years since (see chapter 1), the sentiment remains largely true: the North Carolina governor does not have many formal powers.

Consider the budget, the most important recurring policy item in any state. The North Carolina Constitution instructs the governor to "prepare and recommend to the General Assembly a comprehensive budget." And while every governor dutifully follows that instruction, in practice that budget recommendation does not have much power except as a relatively inexpensive doorstop.

Every odd-numbered year, the governor holds a press conference and offers a budget. The house and senate then follow suit, with one chamber going first during one budget cycle and the other going first in the next cycle. Members of the two chambers then gather in a conference committee and decide on a unified legislative budget, which is presented to the governor. The governor's power comes not in the presentation of the budget but rather at this latter stage, when the governor decides whether to sign or veto the budget. In years when the opposing party has a supermajority, that's not much power at all. Nationally, only the Idaho governor has less power over the budget than the North Carolina governor.[4]

Then there is appointment power. In most states, governors have vast power to appoint a variety of positions in state government. Until 2018, the Republican-controlled North Carolina governor could appoint about 1,500 people to various positions, a number that placed North Carolina somewhere in the middle of the pack in terms of appointment power. In 2018, the general assembly reduced the number of appointments to 300, a change that led political journalist Rob Christensen to quip, "North Carolina's governors are on their way to becoming a potted plant." Later in the same piece, Christensen suggested that while Arnold Schwarzenegger was governor of California, "the appropriate actor for North Carolina governor might be Pee-wee Herman, Sheldon Cooper, or Woody Allen." If you are not conversant in late twentieth-century Hollywood, let's just say that these three have little in common except a physique that is best compared to a string bean. The 2023 legislative session saw even more attempts to wrest appointment power from the governor, further weakening an office that was compared to Pee-wee Herman just five years before.[5]

While these factors point to a weak North Carolina governor, the real story of gubernatorial power (or lack thereof) in North Carolina can be found in the veto, the sine qua non of gubernatorial power. The veto in state government works similarly to the president's veto: if a bill reaches the governor's desk, the governor can choose to sign it, let it become law without signing it, or veto it. A veto returns the bill to the legislature where the legislators can attempt to override the veto or let it sit dormant, never to become law. Without the veto, governors have no formal power to stop legislation. Today the governor of North Carolina has veto power; but as we will see, the process to give the office this most basic power was long and arduous and resulted in one of the weakest vetoes in the country. The history of the veto says much about the place of the governor in North Carolina politics and about how short-term partisan interests can sometimes run afoul of good government.

The Gubernatorial Veto

It is almost impossible to overstate how late North Carolina was to the veto party. Most states adopted the executive veto when they were admitted to the Union. By 1910, North Carolina was the only state that had not adopted the veto. It would be another eighty-six years before the governor of North Carolina would gain this most basic executive power.

The process to give the North Carolina governor veto power was not just a long one, it was a controversial and confusing one that bypassed a half-dozen potential opportunities to adopt a veto. A bill was proposed in the general assembly and passed out of the senate as early as 1925 that would have given the governor the veto power, but it never made it out of the house chamber.[6] In 1933, an entirely new constitution that included the veto was proposed and even passed the general assembly but never made it into law because of a technicality.

There were various attempts made to introduce a veto in the 1940s and 1950s, but the next concerted effort took place in 1965, when the *Charlotte Observer* editorial board argued that "good government is better with a gubernatorial veto." According to the *Observer*, "The absence of the veto in North Carolina is noted in college classrooms all over the country with the interest that one regards a man with a gap in his front teeth." The notion that the lack of veto made North Carolina stand out—and not in a good way—clearly gained favor with the 1967 Constitution Committee that recommended that the veto be included in the new constitution. Once again, however, the supporters of the veto were thwarted by a skeptical general assembly that didn't want to lose any grip on power.

Forces began to mobilize for the veto once again in 1977. In a legislative session preview, the *News and Observer* noted that one of Governor Hunt's primary goals was to lobby "forcefully for gubernatorial veto power."[7] Predictably, members of the general assembly did not agree with this goal, fearing that "the veto [would] sap them of the power they so dearly hold."[8]

In 1981, former governor Bob Scott weighed in on the veto, stating, "The gubernatorial veto will be needed to preserve of system of checks and balances and to counterbalance a general assembly that is growing in power as well as in size."[9] Governor Jim Martin took up the veto mantle in 1985 in his State of the State address, despite knowing that he was facing long odds. According to Martin, "Our state reptile is the turtle, and you never get anywhere unless you stick your neck out."

Republicans in the general assembly, who had been frozen out of legislative power for more than a century, tended to favor the veto. Democrats, including Henson Barnes, the chair of the North Carolina Senate Judiciary Committee, however, were steadfast in their opposition to it. According to Barnes, "The first legislature swore never again would the people of North Carolina be subjected to the whims of one man."[10] In 1987, similar battle lines were drawn, with the Republicans, including Governor Martin, supporting veto authority and the Democrats in opposition. Democratic Speaker Liston Ramsey characterized the ongoing fight as one where the minority party was simply attempting to gain power: "Give me power, give me power, give me power—that's what he's saying."[11] During that battle, the *News and Observer* featured a political cartoon with the headline "Governor v. Legislature." Governor Martin was depicted riding an elephant, charging toward the legislative building, which sat atop "veto hill." Arrows were shown flying from the legislative building toward a defiant Martin.[12]

Every year from 1990 to 1994, the senate passed bills to establish the veto, and every year they were dead on arrival in the house. In 1995, however, things began to change as Republican fortunes improved in the state, as was highlighted by the Republican takeover of the senate. As a result, Democrats seemed to be coming to grips with the reality that they would not maintain a legislative majority in perpetuity. They reevaluated. Joining the other forty-nine states in offering the governor a legislative veto might not be such a bad idea after all.

Three different veto bills were on the floor at various times during the 1995–96 session. While all three would have given the governor veto power that could be overridden by a three-fifths vote in the general assembly, one included line-item veto power, one included language that would have given the general assembly the power to confirm a transportation board, and one did not include language for either and instead proposed only a straightforward veto. Republicans favored line-item veto power, but Democrats, ever aware of their partisan advantage in the legislature, did not want to give the governor this more expansive power.

It is this final bill, Senate Bill 3, that ultimately passed (46–3 in the senate; 97–18 in the house). Because it involved a constitutional change, the veto then had to go to a vote of the people where it passed overwhelmingly, garnering 3 out of every 4 votes cast and securing a majority of the vote in all 100 North Carolina counties.

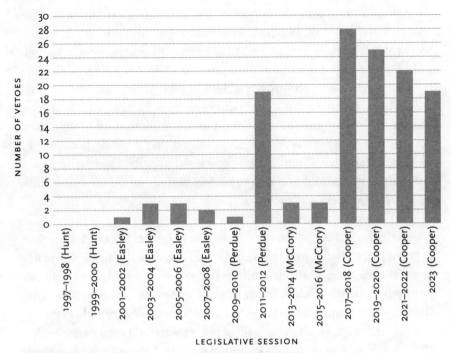

Graph 13.1. Vetoes in North Carolina by legislative session, 1997–2023.
Source: Data on vetoes from North Carolina Legislative Library, "North Carolina Veto History and Statistics, 1997–2023," accessed March 25, 2024, https://sites.ncleg.gov /library/wp-content/uploads/sites/5/2023/03/VetoStats.pdf. Analysis and graph by author.
Note: North Carolina governors did not have the veto power until 1997. The graph includes every veto cast in the state from its inception through 2023. Years indicate the legislative session. Names in parentheses indicate the governor at the time.

Ironically, the chief sponsor of this bill was none other than Democrat Roy Cooper, who would occupy the governor's office two decades later and use his veto power more often than all other North Carolina governors combined (see graph 13.1), but who would frequently be frustrated by his inability to affect Republican redistricting proposals. Cooper's bill gave the governor a "narrowly tailored veto" that did not include a line-item veto—an additional responsibility that would, according to Cooper, have "give[n] our governor too much power."[13] Today, North Carolina is one of only six states in the country without the line-item veto.[14]

The veto that was passed also did not apply uniformly to all bills; constitutional amendments, local bills, and redistricting bills were immune from the governor's veto pen. The impacts of a veto applying to redistricting are reviewed in chapter 12, and the ins and outs of constitutional amendments are discussed in chapter 1. Local bills, however, deserve some more attention.

Local bills in the North Carolina General Assembly have traditionally been thought of as noncontroversial bills that apply to a small geographic area. Think disannexations, occupancy tax changes, and the like. Given their relatively uncontroversial roots, it makes sense that when legislators drew up the gubernatorial veto, they dictated that it would not apply to local bills. It was not so much that they wanted to protect legislative power but that the system did not need to be gummed up with these penny-ante bills. Just pass them and move on.

The rules governing local bills are a bit curious—at least at first glance. Local bills must affect fifteen counties or fewer, they cannot affect more than 51 percent of the state, and they cannot be about some oddly specific policy areas. For example, local bills cannot relate to ferries or bridges, cemeteries, juror pay, regulating labor, trade, mining or manufacturing, or changing the name of a municipality. Otherwise, the parameters are wide open.

In recent years, local bills are still used for their traditional purposes, but they have also been increasingly used to shift the levers of power in North Carolina politics. Consider the recently passed House Bill 88, which turned elections for boards of education in Ashe, Cabarrus, Henderson, McDowell, and Mitchell Counties from nonpartisan into partisan affairs. There are, of course, good reasons for this change (partisan elections tend to have higher turnout than nonpartisan elections), but there will also likely be partisan effects as the voters in these majority Republican counties will now have a partisan cue when they go to vote, lessening the chance that a Democrat is elected, and making it all but impossible for unaffiliated candidates to find their way to elected office.

So, today the North Carolina governor, like all governors, has the power to veto legislation, but that power is extremely weak. According to one scale of gubernatorial power, only Indiana has a less-powerful gubernatorial veto. Even the veto threshold runs counter to the governor's interest in North Carolina. In the majority of states, the legislature can override with two-thirds of the legislature in agreement; in North Carolina that threshold is just three-fifths.

In all, the story of the gubernatorial veto provides two important lessons for observers of North Carolina politics. First, North Carolina government was created with an eye toward establishing a strong legislature and a weak executive. The governor did accumulate some power in the intervening years, but despite two new constitutions, it took North Carolinians more than two centuries after statehood to give the governor this most basic executive power. And even after the century-long struggle to achieve veto power concluded, North Carolina remains a state dominated not by the executive but by the legislative branch.

The battle over the governor's veto also highlights the oldest battle in politics—the battle over power. Before the rise of hyperpartisanship and during the one-party Democratic South, it was the legislative branch that did not want to cede power to the executive branch. As Republicans slowly gained power in the executive branch, Republican legislators became more amenable to the possibility of a veto. But it was not until the Republicans had gained one chamber of the legislature and the executive branch was returned to Democratic control that the Democrats agreed to give the people a right to vote on the question of the gubernatorial veto.

Gubernatorial Succession

The veto is not the only constitutional change to affect the governor's duties. Prior to 1978, North Carolina was one of only seven states that limited the governor from running for a second successive term, a fact described at the time as one "that makes North Carolina either unique or backward, depending on whether one listens to anti- or pro-succession forces."[15] The anti-succession forces argued that it would make the governor, meant to be the less-powerful branch, too powerful, whereas the pro-succession advocates argued that the governor had virtually no power in the current system; the governor was a lame-duck from day one.

Similar to the push for the veto, the decision to allow the governor to run for reelection was a long time coming. Then governor Luther H. Hodges started the push in 1954, and every governor who followed him supported the idea of a second term. Even Cy Young–award winner and North Carolina native Jim "Catfish" Hunter weighed in with support for gubernatorial succession.[16]

The general assembly, always wary of the expansion of executive power, opposed the idea for decades, as did prominent politicians like US senator Sam Ervin. Gubernatorial succession finally became law on November 8, 1977, when Amendment III narrowly passed a vote of the people, with support from 52 percent of those who voted. The measure failed to gain majority support in about a third of North Carolina counties (thirty-two), including most of the Republican stronghold counties in the western part of the state.

The law had immediate impact when Governor Jim Hunt ran for a second term and was reelected with 62 percent of the vote. Hunt then served *another* two terms, garnering the majority of the votes in 1992 and 1996, serving a total of sixteen years in office, the longest of any governor in North Carolina history. Since Hunt's initial term, every North Carolina governor has served a second term with the exception of Beverly Perdue, who chose not to pursue a second term as governor, and Pat McCrory, who lost his reelection bid to Democratic attorney general Roy Cooper.

Council of State

In case there were not already enough constraints on executive power in North Carolina, the governor also has nine additional members of the council of state to contend with. The governor, lieutenant governor, secretary of state, state auditor, treasurer, superintendent of public instruction, attorney general, commissioner of agriculture, commissioner of labor, and commissioner of insurance together make up the North Carolina Council of State. Only two other states divide executive authority among this many popularly elected positions.[17]

This large council of state, which owes its origins to the British monarchy, creates problems for the governor, both in executing policy and in creating unrealistic expectations for what it can accomplish. As Governor Robert Scott explained to political scientist Jack Fleer, "The governor has . . . the expectations of people out there. They think the governor is the Ayatollah of everything, but he's of course not responsible for the departments of agriculture or labor or the auditor, all of those, even though many people out across the state think he can run that, too."[18]

In addition to the problems of fragmentation and outsized expectations, the large elected council of state creates confusion among voters as well. I promise you there's a difference between the jobs of the auditor and the treasurer. I also promise you that few people in the state, apart from the auditor and treasurer themselves, could tell you the nature of that difference. Perhaps for that reason, there tends to be very little turnover in council of state offices in North Carolina. Incumbency, always an advantage in any elected office, is magnified when voters do not know much.

Conclusion

Being the governor of North Carolina is difficult, not because the job comes with a tremendous amount of power but rather because the average North Carolinian (mistakenly) believes that it does. The governor is in the unique and regrettable position of taking the blame for what goes poorly in the state, without having the power to fix it. Virtually locked out of policymaking power, the governor must instead wield power outside the legislative arena. The governor can make some policy through executive orders and still have some power over appointments, although the number of those appointments shrinks with each legislative session.

This essential quandary of the governor, like so many other things, is made much more difficult in the nationalized, polarized, and competitive political environment of North Carolina. A competitive environment means that almost regardless of the action in question, the governor will draw the ire of half of the state's population. Further, the competitive nature of the state means that when the governor is of a different party than the general assembly, the legislative branch will use every tool at its disposal to strike quickly, while the iron is hot, and the majorities are in its favor. There just aren't many tools in the governor's toolbox.

14   North Carolina Elects Judges
But Appointing Them Won't Make
Them Any Less Political

The 2016 election for the North Carolina Supreme Court associate justice featured incumbent Bob Edmunds versus challenger Michael Morgan. It was a competitive and hard-fought race. And it was, at least on paper, nonpartisan. When North Carolina voters went to the ballot box, they were presented with the choice between Edmunds and Morgan without any indication as to either candidate's partisanship.

The political class, however, knew the score and attempted to communicate it to those who did not speak in political shorthand. The *News and Observer* referred to the "Republican majority" on the court and argued that the election would "determine the ideological balance of the court and whether the court [would] test the legislature's right-wing adventures or encourage them."[1] The Democratic Party threw its money and endorsements behind Morgan, while the Republicans were steadfast in their support of Edmunds.

Once the votes were counted, it became clear that Morgan won and won big. He garnered 54.5 percent of the vote—practically a landslide in North Carolina terms. In an even bigger surprise, he won in over three-quarters of the state's hundred counties. He won in the Piedmont, the west and the east. He won in Democratic strongholds like Mecklenburg, Durham, and Guilford, and he won in unexpected places like Republican strongholds Clay and Pender Counties.

It was a surprising victory made even more surprising by the larger political environment. The 2016 election was marked by red MAGA hats and a Donald Trump victory in North Carolina. Trump won the aforementioned Clay County with over 73 percent of the vote; and he won Pender County with over 63 percent of the vote. Republican Richard Burr won handily in a US Senate race against Democrat Deborah Ross, and the Republicans cleaned up in legislative races. In the midst of a red wave, Democrat Mike Morgan somehow surfed to easy victory.

But how?

The Republicans, who had control of the general assembly, thought they knew the answer. Certainly Clay County voters must not have known that a vote for Morgan over Edmunds was a vote for a liberal over a conservative incumbent. It must have been the nonpartisan ballot. If voters had more information, perhaps they would have made a different decision—one consistent with, rather than in opposition to, the red wave; a decision that, in an alternate universe, would have resulted in an Edmunds victory.

Armed with supermajority control, the 2016 general assembly set about turning judicial elections in North Carolina into partisan affairs. A legislative fix could make sure this would not happen again. So, five weeks after Morgan won reelection, the Republican supermajority passed Senate Bill 4. Lame-duck Republican governor Pat McCrory quickly signed it into law and with the stroke of a pen, judicial elections in North Carolina became explicitly partisan affairs once again.[2]

Six years later, North Carolina voters were once again presented with choices for the state supreme court, but this time the partisan label was in full view on the ballot. The result: the Republicans won both seats and gained majority control of the state supreme court. The newly constituted court soon agreed to rehear a few cases that had previously been decided counter to the opinion of the newly seated Republican majority. In one notable example, the court reheard the *Harper v. Hall* redistricting case and ruled that the previous court was wrong in concluding that the Republican-drawn maps were illegal partisan gerrymanders.[3] In another, it overturned the previous Democratic-majority court's opinion on voter ID, ensuring that voters throughout North Carolina would be asked to present an ID before casting a vote.[4] Whether these are good or bad changes is, of course, in the eye of the beholder. But one thing both sides can agree on is that the makeup of the North Carolina bench matters.

The effects of partisan change on the state supreme court cannot be overstated. Study after study demonstrates that despite protestations to the contrary, state supreme court justices rule in ideologically predictable ways. Judges may claim to be above partisan politics, but at least in terms of how they decide their cases, they can be understood as partisans—just like state legislators, governors, and county commissioners.

A Brief History of Judicial Selection in North Carolina

Given the importance of the judiciary and the inherently political nature of their jobs, it should not be a surprise that the 2016 change is the most recent example of politicians tweaking the rules for judicial selection.

Prior to 2004, judges in North Carolina ran on partisan ballots. The 2004 change was intended to reduce the partisanship of the judiciary and reduce the politicization of the courts. The bill that made that change also came in tandem with a change to public financing.[5] The evidence suggests that, while perhaps well-intentioned, removing the partisan label did not rid judicial elections of their political implications. It did have an effect on the electorate, however.

One primary effect of nonpartisan elections is that they increase the incidence of ballot roll-off, that is, the tendency for voters to fill out their ballot for some seats and not for others. If a voter cast votes for president, US Senate, and Congress but skips over an election for dogcatcher, that would be ballot roll-off. In partisan elections, even for relatively low-profile offices like state judges, ballot roll-off tends to be very low. In partisan judicial elections in 1996, 1998, 2000, and 2002, ballot roll-off never exceeded 8.5 percent of all votes. In the first election after nonpartisan elections were reintroduced in North Carolina, over one-fifth of the people who cast a vote for president did not cast a vote for state supreme court justice! When the state moved back to partisan elections in 2018, roll-off returned to the single digits.

Do We Have to Elect Judges?

All fifty states elect members of Congress, US senators, governors, and state legislators. And with the exception of the Nebraska Legislature, all states elect candidates for those offices on partisan ballots. The judiciary is different.

In some states, governors appoint state supreme court justices with virtually no constraints. In other states, the governor has the ultimate power of appointment, but there is a commission that provides the governor with a list of potential candidates. In a third set of states, justices are appointed by the state legislature.

Then there are the states that elect judges—some through partisan elections, some through nonpartisan elections, and some, like North Carolina, bounce back and forth between the two like a pickleball in a retirement community. Not surprisingly, many reform advocates have taken aim at judicial elections as the problem, offering their elimination as the solution to what ails the judiciary. It's an idea that briefs well.

And there are advantages. Eliminating judicial elections would eliminate some of the money from politics. Judges would no longer have to raise money from donors.[6] Citizens would not have their college football season interrupted with ads for judicial elections, and the postal carriers would carry a little less of a load on their backs without the weight of fliers for North Carolina's judicial contests.

What this would not do, however, is eliminate partisanship. Political scientists Chris Bonneau and Melinda Gann Hall have probably done more research on judicial elections than anyone else alive, and they come to one consistent conclusion in their work: judicial elections are not perfect, but they are better than the alternatives. If judges are appointed, for example, they will be even more beholden to the party networks than they are in an election. And the people of the state will have no ability to weigh in, either in support or in opposition, on the judges. Judges in an appointment system exist outside of reach of citizen feedback but not beyond the reach of politics.[7] Anyone who doubts this should consider the US Supreme Court and ask themselves: Are any of those justices divorced from politics?

Perhaps the solution for North Carolinians looking for a more responsive judiciary is not to insulate the courts further from the public but to embrace, and perhaps even enhance, the electoral connection further.

Looking Forward

The war over the details of judicial selection is not likely to end anytime soon. Even in a legislature-first state like North Carolina, the courts have enacted important policies that influence every part of the government from taxes to representation to health care to education. At the same time, judges decide cases in ideologically consistent ways. Sure, there are exceptions, but particularly in the most salient cases, Republican and Democratic justices view the law differently. Both political parties know this. And, in a competitive, polarized, and nationalized environment, they act accordingly. As a result, elections for North Carolina's judiciary are only going to become more high profile, more expensive, and more consequential.

Local Politics in a Nationalized Environment
Vertical Federalism in North Carolina Politics

Across the street from the Western Carolina University campus in Cullowhee, North Carolina, is half a square mile known as the Village of Forest Hills. To the eye, Forest Hills looks like every other subdivision you've ever seen. There's a sign marking its boundaries perched at the intersection of its two primary streets, South Country Club Drive and North Country Club Drive. The 335 residents live in fairly uniform ranch-style houses built in the same era, all on nearly identical lots. There are no stop lights, and there's not a commercial business to be found.[1]

Cullowhee is, at least by comparison, quite large. With a population 23 times greater than Forest Hills, a land area almost 8 times greater, a comprehensive university of more than 11,000 students, a few businesses, and half a dozen or so stop lights, Cullowhee comes a lot closer to most people's idea of a town than Forest Hills does. According to the state of North Carolina, however, the Village of Forest Hills is a municipality, whereas Cullowhee is not.

Since its incorporation in 1997, the Village of Forest Hills has had all the trappings of government. There's a mayor and four councillors, a charter, dozens of ordinances and codes that specify, among other things, what citizens may do with their property. Cullowhee, by comparison, is a "Census Designated Area." There is no mayor of Cullowhee, no council, and there are no ordinances or laws, beyond what is prescribed by the county. Cullowhee is not a town, a village, or a city but rather a state of mind.

A Typology of Local Governments in North Carolina

What we refer to as "local government" in North Carolina is really a confusing patchwork of thousands of entities with generally distinct, but sometimes overlapping, powers. There are counties, municipalities, special districts, school districts, and just when you thought you had them all nailed down, you can add regional councils of government to the mix. It's a lot to keep track of.

Despite key differences, all these local governments are increasingly important, increasingly watched, and increasingly defined by the forces of polarization, competition, and nationalization. Gone are the days of a relatively nonpartisan local government that existed outside the hurricane of American politics. Even in elections that are technically nonpartisan, political parties are now involved. County commission meetings still discuss property taxes and zoning, but now they may also talk about diversity, equity, and inclusion (DEI) initiatives. Even school board meetings, once only newsworthy for their discussions of the local school calendar, are increasingly visited by national political entrepreneurs promoting book banning. Local governments matter—in North Carolina and elsewhere. And for that reason, we need to better understand the various organizations that fall under the local government umbrella in North Carolina.

COUNTIES

It is seated deep in the folklore of North Carolina that there are 100 counties in the state. Every square inch of the state rests within a county, and county borders have remained unchanged since 1911, when Avery and Hoke became the ninety-ninth and one-hundredth counties in the state. If you live in North Carolina, you live in a county.

The original purpose of a county was to act like a franchise of the state— the county was conceived as a means to accomplish state business closer to home. All North Carolina counties employ tax collectors, administer elections, and have sheriffs who, along with their deputies and county criminal justice system, execute the state's laws. Like most political institutions, however, the power and responsibilities of counties began to grow over time. According to the UNC School of Government's indispensable *County and Municipal Government in North Carolina*, "Around the middle of the twentieth century, citizens living outside cities began to request some of the governmental services characteristic of cities but not of counties. They wanted community water or sewer systems, organized fire protection, and recreational spaces or programs. They wanted to be able to dispose of their trash in some way other than dumping or burning. And they wanted the protection of zoning."[2]

Counties were the local authorities to take on these responsibilities. Although there is variation across counties in the specifics of how, where, and to what extent they supply these services, there are a baker's dozen functions exclusive to counties in North Carolina.

These functions, as well as another four dozen or so functions shared by municipalities and counties, are overseen by 100 independent board of county commissioners, all of whom are elected in partisan elections. All county boards have 9 or fewer members who serve terms of 2 or 4 years.

Some are elected by district; others countywide. That basic structure holds constant across counties despite dramatic differences in county population and size. Wake and Mecklenburg Counties have over a million residents each, whereas Tyrell, Hyde, Graham, and Jones counties are home to fewer than 10,000 people each. The 2 largest counties in the state have more constituents than the 64 smallest counties combined, yet in terms of county-level elected officials, they are treated roughly the same.

It is often said that the US Senate is the most malapportioned legislative body in the world.[3] Although county commissions do not constitute one legislative body, in terms of the number of constituents per representative, malapportionment in the US Senate pales in comparison to malapportionment in North Carolina counties.

MUNICIPALITIES

Whereas the structure and distribution of counties in North Carolina is fairly straightforward, municipalities are much more complicated. There are 552 municipalities in North Carolina, a number that does not provide quite the resonance of 100 counties. Most municipalities are contained within a single county, but there are 14 counties that defy this rule. High Point is particularly notable as portions of it rest in 4 counties—Guilford, Davidson, Forsyth, and Randolph.

Municipalities in North Carolina can take on 3 possible names—town, city, or village—but all have the same statutory authority. And while you might assume that cities are bigger than towns, there is no rule that specifies this. For example, the Town of Cary is home to over 176,000 people and is the seventh largest municipality in the state of North Carolina.

The relationship between municipalities and counties also varies dramatically depending on the county. At the extremes, there are no municipalities in Currituck or Hyde Counties, whereas 94 percent of the population of Mecklenburg County resides in a municipality. Statewide, slightly more than half of North Carolina citizens live in a municipality.

In terms of services, municipalities are solely responsible for cemeteries, communications services, electric and gas systems, sidewalks, street lighting, streets, and traffic engineering. And municipalities share responsibilities with counties for several dozen functions ranging from animal shelters to watershed improvement.

Municipal governments in North Carolina have a variety of different structures. Some have partisan councils, others are nonpartisan. Some elect members in districts, others at large. Some have relatively small councils, while others have council sizes in the double-digits. Most importantly, some operate under the mayor-council system, while others operate under the council-manager system.

In the council-manager system, which comprises the majority of municipalities in North Carolina, an appointed manager is charged with overseeing the day-to-day operations of the city, whereas the elected officials are meant to deal with the policy aspects of the municipality. The idea is that managers are insulated from politics, although there's no way to escape politics entirely. In fact, managers who are registered Republicans are more likely to be appointed by Republican boards, and registered Democrats are more likely to be appointed by Democratic boards, while competitive local governments tend to hire managers who are registered as unaffiliated.[4]

SPECIAL DISTRICTS AND SCHOOL BOARDS

Some, but not all, North Carolinians reside in special districts or school districts that may or may not conform to county or municipal lines. There are just under 300 special districts across the state, and they come in all shapes and sizes. Some are governed by elected boards, some by appointed boards. Some are big, some are small. These special districts are responsible for things such as airport authorities, water and sewer authorities, and the like.

The work of school boards is more straightforward: they oversee the work of schools in their districts. More specifically, they make sure that each school has the requisite number of contact hours with students; they set policies within the district; they hire, fire, and maintain personnel authority over the superintendent; they oversee the school district's budget; and they ensure that facilities are up to snuff. But how they do that work, where they do that work, and who's involved are much more complicated questions.

There are 115 school boards spread across the state of North Carolina. Most align with county lines; some do not. For example, the City of Asheville maintains its own school district, as does Buncombe County, where the city is located. Each school board has an average of 6.6 seats for a total of 759 school board seats spread across the state. No school board has fewer than 5 or more than 11 members.[5] Some school boards hold elections in even-numbered years, whereas some hold elections in odd-numbered years. Odd-year elections are beset by anemic voter turnout and voter confusion. A 2023 primary in Charlotte saw just 4 percent of all registered voters turn out to vote![6]

Another example of low voter turnout and confusion came in a recent election for the nonpartisan Jackson County School Board in District 2. After the May 17, 2022, election, challenger Lisa Buchanan had garnered 43 percent of the vote in District 2, whereas incumbent Abigail Clayton won 37 percent of the vote. A third candidate brought in the remaining 20 percent. So, you might think that Buchanan would be declared the winner, right? Wrong. Jackson County has a little-known local law that says that the winning candidate must garner at least 50 percent of the vote or else the second-place candidate can call for a runoff. The problem was, few in Jackson County seemed to know that rule, not even the county board of elections.

But somehow Clayton did know it, and she called for a runoff. According to the *Sylva Herald*, "Though a nonpartisan race on paper, the context took a hard partisan turn with the local Democratic Party backing Clayton and the Republican Party backing Buchanan."[7] Clayton won the runoff with 8 percent of registered voters in the county turning out.

Home Rule: Absence Makes the Heart Grow Fonder

Perhaps the most important single thing to know about local government in North Carolina is that North Carolina is not a home rule state.[8] And, while not unique to North Carolina, this fact combines with other aspects of the state to reinforce the reality that nationalization and polarization define even the smallest governments in North Carolina.

So what is home rule power? For an example, see Article XVIII, Section 3 of the Ohio Constitution: "Municipalities shall have authority to exercise all powers of local self-government and to adopt and enforce within their limits such local police, sanitary and other similar regulations, as are not in conflict with general laws."

The idea behind home rule is fairly simple: the state government should leave the local governments alone unless they violate the state constitution or state laws or infringe upon the right of another municipality to do the same.

Local governments in North Carolina are granted power not through a broad grant of constitutional power, as in the case of Ohio, but rather through individual statutes on specific areas of government. In practice, that means that the state government in North Carolina has much more power to tell local governments what to do and how to do it.[9]

It also means that there is an ongoing tension between local and state governments about who has the power to act. This vertical power tension has increasingly defined fights in North Carolina politics. In 2016, for example, the City of Charlotte passed an ordinance that said, among other things, that people could use bathrooms that matched their gender identity, regardless of the sex they were assigned on their birth certificate. In retaliation, the North Carolina General Assembly then passed the soon-to-be-infamous "bathroom bill" (House Bill 2) that dictated that municipalities such as Charlotte did not have the right to make that kind of determination. The bathroom bill that made national headlines was ultimately a bill about whether municipalities or state government holds the power. And it was a bill that likely would not have been passed were North Carolina a home rule state.

Looking Forward

Battles over vertical power are likely only to intensify in the coming years as the forces of nationalization, competition, and polarization combine to turn local governments from bodies that are out of the partisan spotlight to ones that are squarely in the middle. The general assembly has shown an increasing tendency to use the lack of home rule power in North Carolina to exert power on local bodies. As Canton mayor Zeb Smathers told me:

> Somewhere along the way, the political winds switched to become more abrasive toward these small towns. From ETJs [extra-territorial jurisdictions] to partisan elections it seems to be a constant. Every session all of us in some ways seem to be having to swat off things that want to poke and prod and take power away. Even though it's understood that the closest level of government, the most responsive, is local government. I am not asking for the power to be brought to the doors of my town hall. I just think, if you're an elected official in Raleigh and you want to strengthen the state. If you're not truly giving opportunities for local governments to have the resources, then you're missing a huge opportunity.[10]

At least for the time being, that tension will continue.

CONCLUSION
Toward a Better North Carolina

Nothing lasts forever in politics, and certainly the themes, ideas, and tensions highlighted in this book are no exception. At some point the march of history will change the state in important and unforeseen ways. But in the short run, the three trends that define current North Carolina politics—nationalization, competition, and polarization—are unlikely to change. And, if the last few years are any indication, their effects are accelerating, rather than slowing down. Astute observers of our politics will therefore accept these three forces as a fact of life for the foreseeable future. Reform must work with, rather than against, these prevailing winds.

Prospects for Reform

In 1967, the *Asheville Citizen Times* made the case that the Constitution of 1868 needed to be scrapped as it had served the state from "the horse and buggy to the jet airplane," and, as a result, it could not "cope adequately with 20th Century problems." The question remains, as we look at a constitution that has governed us from the beginnings of the color television to social media: Can it cope adequately with twenty-first-century problems? Do we have the institutions and a political system that fit the times? And particularly in a time when partisanship defines everything from the kind of car you drive to what kind of beer you drink, is reform even possible?

Here, I outline five potential reforms to improve North Carolina politics and offer one road that is best not taken. While all these reforms would take political will to accomplish, none is dead on arrival, either. And while I believe that all five of these would improve the state, this list, much like this book, should be considered the starting point for conversations, not the end point.

ELIMINATE THE LITERACY TEST

North Carolina needs to eliminate the literacy test from the state constitution. As described in chapters 1 and 4 of this book, Article VI, Section 4 of the state constitution says in clear language: "Every person presenting himself for registration shall be able to read and write any section of the

Constitution in the English language." While the literacy test has not been enforced in decades, its presence in our state's constitution reinforces in word, if not in deed, that the right to vote in North Carolina is contingent upon this racist vestige of the Jim Crow South—that the past is not even past in North Carolina politics.

Because it is enshrined in the state constitution, the threshold for eliminating the literacy test is higher than it would be for other issues. At least 60 percent of the membership of both houses of the general assembly must vote to place the question on the ballot, and the majority of voters must then vote to eliminate the language.

Ridding the state constitution of the literacy test is not a new idea. In 1969, Henry Frye, the first African American to serve in the general assembly after 1900, successfully placed the elimination of the literacy test on the legislative agenda. It passed through the general assembly with flying colors, leaving Frye "jubilant" at the prospect of its passage.[1]

Unfortunately, North Carolina voters did not agree. Elimination of the literacy test was the only one of seven ballot amendments rejected in the 1970 election (just 44 percent of North Carolinians voted to remove the literacy test language from the state constitution). Since then, it has come up for elimination every few years.

In 2013 and 2019, the North Carolina House of Representatives passed bills to eliminate the literacy test, but the senate never took a vote. In 2021, the idea was introduced once again, but despite a bipartisan list of cosponsors, it never made it to a floor vote. The 2023 legislative session looked like another good opportunity for repeal. All the major players, including the most powerful Republican in Raleigh, Majority Leader Phil Berger, were on board.[2] But that bill, like all the previous attempts at repeal, died in the legislative process.

It is almost impossible to find a credible political observer, whether liberal or conservative, who will argue that keeping the literacy test is good public policy. Yet there it remains.

The folklore suggests that the powers that be in Raleigh want to eliminate the literacy test but that they fear that the voters might not agree. After all, what would be a more visible black eye on the state than if the citizens voted to keep a policy that is almost universally accepted as racist and unenforceable?

For a time, polling supported this concern. A May 2021 Civitas poll indicated that just 39 percent of North Carolina registered voters would vote to repeal "the requirement that every person presenting himself for registration shall be able to read and write any section of the Constitution in the English language."

But there are some recent rays of hope for those who want to eliminate the literacy test. Using slightly different wording than the Civitas poll, a 2022 poll commissioned by the North Carolina Bar Association found that 55 percent of likely North Carolina voters support repealing the literacy test. Respondents who were reminded of the law's historical roots, however, were even more supportive of repeal. After hearing that the literacy test "was added to the North Carolina constitution in 1900, together with a poll tax, to deprive Black voters the right to vote," and that "this law is not enforced and some people would like to see it officially repealed," 61 percent supported repeal.

Perhaps the wording of the amendment is key. Perhaps times are changing. Regardless, we need to put it to a vote of the people and find out.

PROFESSIONALIZE THE GENERAL ASSEMBLY

The North Carolina General Assembly has the vast majority of the power in North Carolina politics, but it does not have the resources to conduct its duties. This was true in the middle of the twentieth century when reformers advocated for more professionalism in the general assembly, and it is even more true today in a nationalized, competitive, and polarized North Carolina. The state would be better off with a more professional legislature.

It would be convenient to believe the fiction that a less professional legislature is closer to the people and more responsive to their needs, but all available evidence suggests the opposite. If you give people increasing responsibilities but do not give them the tools to do the job well, they will use every tool at their disposal to complete the task but have little to no incentive or ability to do the task well. This is certainly the case in the North Carolina General Assembly. Further, interest groups and lobbyists become more important with a relatively unprofessional legislature, increasing the influence of a group of unelected people who, while not the scoundrels they are made out to be, are insulated from reward or punishment at the ballot box.

Something needs to change.

The most obvious solution would be to increase legislative salary. Legislators are understandably reticent to do to this, but as demonstrated in chapter 10, it is possible to move public opinion on this point. Further, a reform that would not just increase salary but place legislative salary in the hands of an independent commission that would adjust salary up (and down), based on the economy and the demands of the job, might just garner enough public support. The messaging has to be right, but it is far from impossible.

A related reform would be to consider the proposal suggested by Senator Jim Perry. Senator Perry noted the increasingly lengthy legislative sessions and the unpredictability of legislative service and suggested that constitutional limits on sessions, as used in many states, would have the potential to produce more realistic expectations of legislative service.[3] I agree.

STRENGTHEN THE GOVERNOR'S VETO

The governor in North Carolina has almost comically little power over public policy in the state of North Carolina, yet the average North Carolinian looks upon the governor as the chief policymaker. This creates an almost untenable situation for any occupant of the governor's mansion—Democrat or Republican. The institution did gain some power with the implementation of the gubernatorial veto, but as discussed in chapter 13, the specifics of the veto power still make it extremely difficult for the governor to provide a yin to the legislature's yang. The governor's power has been reduced even further in the intervening years as the appointment power of the office has been stripped to virtually nothing.

While we should all be wary of gubernatorial power run amok, the current tools at the governor's disposal are laughably few. As a result, the citizens of North Carolina would be much better off if the governor's toolbox held a few more tools. The most obvious one, and the one that would put North Carolina most in alignment with the rest of the country, is to expand the veto power to include the line-item veto.

Different states implement the line-item veto in different ways, but all allow the governor to eliminate parts of a bill and accept others. Giving the North Carolina governor the line-item veto would reduce the power of the legislature to place "poison pill" provisions in bills that are unrelated to the main content of the bill. It would also help the governor have a bit more power to shape policy outcomes. More healthy interbranch competition would be a good thing for North Carolina, regardless of the partisan dynamics at play.

The other specifics of the gubernatorial veto—no power over local bills, constitutional amendments, or redistricting—are also ripe for revision. Local bills are increasingly used by the general assembly to bypass gubernatorial oversight, and the specific nature of these bills makes them unlikely to be covered by the state's press. The legislature—whether in Republican or Democratic control—should not be able to pass any kind of law without checks. Although I prefer an independent redistricting commission (more on that in a few pages), if that reform cannot happen, it would only make sense to give the governor more power over this increasingly important process.

ELIMINATE OFF-YEAR ELECTIONS

As established in chapter 6, North Carolina elections are a confusing patchwork of rules, dates, and people. Some of this confusion is unavoidable and perhaps even positive. After all, few would want to eliminate primary elections and have party elites choose our nominees. Nonetheless, there are a few things we can do to eliminate some of the confusion and fatigue. One of these is to eliminate odd-year elections.

Consider 2023. On September 12, 2023, the cities of Charlotte and Sanford held elections for 10 seats on their city councils (7 for Charlotte, 3 for Sanford). On October 10, elections were held for another 41 seats across the state of North Carolina. And November 7 saw 1,062 more seats up for election. Those elections took place in 93 counties, but in only certain municipalities within those counties. Confused yet? I am. And so are most voters.

The result of all this confusion is that voters may not even know that an election is taking place, resulting in abysmally low voter turnout. This low turnout makes tight elections more likely. For example, in the town of Sylva, North Carolina, which elects town councillors in off-year elections, two of the five members of council were elected by a coin toss! To make matters even worse, the people who do show up to vote in off-year elections look little like the electorate as a whole. Interest groups have an increased impact in these off-year elections because it is easier to nudge the electorate in one direction or another when people are less engaged and knowledgeable.[4] These negative effects are seen beyond the ballot box; representatives elected in off-year elections pass policy more favorable to special interests than those elected in a normal cycle.

And then there is the issue of cost. Elections are not free, and off-year elections require additional expenditures by county boards of elections—expenditures that may reduce the amount of money available to run even-year elections.

Some may argue that eliminating odd-year elections in North Carolina will create more nationalized local politics, but as has been demonstrated over and over again in the pages of this book, North Carolina politics is already nationalized. National groups already do work to gain favor through odd-year elections and in local politics. We already lost that battle.

There is no question that eliminating odd-year elections would increase voter turnout, reduce the influence of local interest groups, and reduce the overall cost of running elections in North Carolina. And here is the best part: there's not a clear partisan winner at play. It is time to eliminate odd-year elections in North Carolina.

INDEPENDENT REDISTRICTING COMMISSION

I saved the most politically difficult reform for last: an independent redistricting commission for North Carolina. You are probably thinking that Republicans in North Carolina will never go for this. After all, I closed out chapter 12 with a quote from former chair of the North Carolina Republican Party Dallas Woodhouse stating almost exactly that. And, at least in the short run, Woodhouse is right. But I do believe there is a time when reform may be possible; the key is to act then. But first, let's pierce the fiction that independence isn't possible.

A dozen states have redistricting commissions, but only some truly qualify as "independent." Independent commissions are more than advisors to a legislative body; their opinion carries the day. Independent commissions must also not simply be partisan committees in disguise; the legislature or other political body cannot simply have carte blanche to appoint them. Washington, Iowa, and California all have slightly different commissions that qualify as independent. And enough time has passed since their creation that we can see how they have performed.

The scholarship on independent redistricting commissions is increasingly clear. Compared to districts drawn in traditionally partisan manner, independent redistricting commissions (IRCs) draw districts that are more competitive and compact.[5] Further, IRC-drawn districts are more likely to preserve the cores of prior districts and split fewer political subdivisions, both resulting in less voter confusion.[6] Altogether, IRCs "are not a magic bullet, [but] they are the best option for redistricting that allows for transparency over backroom negotiations and can, hopefully, help restore some faith in our democratic institutions."[7]

Examining the totality of circumstances around redistricting in all fifty states in 2020, a group of political scientists echoes the conclusion that, while not a cure-all, IRCs offer the best chance to achieve fair maps and reduce the influence of partisanship run amok. "These commissions generally produce less biased and more competitive plans than when one party controls the process. . . . Though commissions are not always perfect, these results recommend the approach as something more states should consider for the best redistricting cycle. They can be an especially powerful reform when accompanied by explicit rules requiring them to draw fair maps that give everyone an equal voice in the political process."[8]

So, IRCs can work. How do we get the political will to create them? First let's remind ourselves that independent redistricting is popular. Sure, it is slightly more popular among Democrats than among Republicans in North Carolina, but no one likes gerrymandering—a fact borne out in study after study. Experimental research shows that with the exception of the strongest partisans, people will choose fairness over partisan gains when given the option.[9]

Knowing this, redistricting advocates need to do what they can to disentangle their messaging from partisan considerations. Redistricting reform will work only when people do not see one party as winning and the other as losing from the new arrangement. On the heels of a century of Democratic-controlled legislature, the Democrats weren't going to give up control. Likewise, in the case of a "red North Carolina," Republicans in the general assembly will never give up power over redistricting. Faced with the reality of a "purple North Carolina," where either party could be in control in the future and in which it could very well (once again) be Democrats doing the gerrymandering, perhaps change is possible.

One tool is to make sure to have true bipartisan actors working to support redistricting efforts. Art Pope, Jon Hardister, John Hood, and Chuck McGrady are all prominent Republicans who have, at various times, supported redistricting reforms in North Carolina. Democrats who want change had best be prepared to work with them.

Separating IRCs from partisan considerations also means that the timing must be right. Leading into the 2021 round of redistricting, for example, it was clear that the Republicans would control the general assembly and the redistricting process in North Carolina; any change was considered a partisan loss for Republicans. And, of course, prior to the 2001 round of redistricting, Democrats would not listen to Republican representative Art Pope, who was proposing his own independent commission. Change, therefore, must occur as far away as possible from the next decennial cycle, but also as distant as possible from the last cycle where the winners and losers are known and clear.[10] The sweet spot, therefore, sits smack in the middle of the decade. That sweet spot is now.

THE ROAD BEST NOT TAKEN: TERM LIMITS

Some may be curious why I am not advocating for term limits. After all, term limits are popular with the public. A McLaughlin and Associates survey found that 82 percent of the public supports term limits. A 2013 Gallup poll came to a similar conclusion—75 percent of the people surveyed supported term limits for members of the US House and Senate. Various state polls also indicate strong support for term limits. The problem is that term limits do not solve the problems they were meant to solve. They introduce new ones.

Various state governments have been tinkering with legislative term limits for years. Fifteen states currently have term limits for their state legislatures: Maine, California, Colorado, Arkansas, Michigan, Florida, Ohio, South Dakota, Montana, Arizona, Missouri, Oklahoma, Nebraska, Louisiana, and Nevada.[11] By comparing various outcomes before and after term limits in these states, political scientists have learned a great deal about the effects of term limits. By and large, the news is not positive for term-limit advocates.

Part of the problem rests in the decline in legislative expertise that follows the implementation of term limits. When experienced politicians are relieved of their duties, they are replaced by new legislators who may have trouble finding the copier or figuring out where the good coffee is, much less understanding the intricacies of health care policy, the pros and cons of school choice, or whether energy deregulation produces better outcomes.

To make matters worse, when legislators lack information, there is a group that is always ready to provide interested information to legislators—lobbyists. After term limits were implemented in Michigan, "the ties between lobbyists and legislators" became closer than they were before. At the same time, state senators elected after term limits were *less* likely to seek advice and information from local officials. In the words of political scientists Marjorie Sarbaugh-Thompson and Lyke Thompson, "Without this street-level perspective legislators are deprived of information about how policies affect day-to-day life in their local communities. This has potentially profound effects for the state and its citizens."[12]

One of the promises of term limits is that they might relieve legislatures of the demographic biases that pervade our electoral system. Unfortunately, that promise remains unrealized. Term-limited legislatures are no more diverse in terms of race, gender, or economic class than non-term-limited legislatures. Further, term limits do not result in significantly younger legislators.[13]

Implementing term limits does succeed in "throwing the bums out," but they are only replaced by a different group of bums who look awfully similar to the ones who were just relieved of their duties.

To add insult to injury, Sarbaugh-Thompson and Thompson find that the "biggest difference between the new (pre-term limit) and old (post-term limit) breeds of legislator is that the post-term limits breed is vastly more politically ambitious than their predecessors."[14] If you elect people with the guarantee that they will be fired in a few years, they will enter office with an exit plan already in place. In politics, that exit plan means they will be angling for higher office immediately, instead of focusing on the work of the state.

In terms of policymaking, the evidence also lines up in opposition to term limits. Term-limited legislatures pass policies that are less reflective of public opinion than non-term-limited legislatures. In addition, whereas committees provide a measure of expertise and specialization in non-term-limited states, that expertise and domain-knowledge is diminished when legislators are term limited.[15]

Term limits are an idea that briefs well. Who wouldn't jump at the opportunity to replace the current crop of legislators with one that is more diverse, considers more perspectives, and isn't motivated by reelection? The problem is that while term limits do indeed increase turnover, there is no mechanism to ensure that the new crop of legislators will be more other-regarding, representative, or responsible than the ones who just left.

Ultimately, elections remain the best way we have to hold our politicians accountable. We should strengthen the electoral connection, rather than weaken it by mandating term limits.

Conclusion
None of these reforms will be easy to pass, particularly given that North Carolina does not have an initiative process. Even the reform that has the most bipartisan backing—eliminating the literacy test—has been discussed for a half century, but the stain on the state's constitution remains today. Still, reform is possible.

As demonstrated throughout this book, North Carolina politics has changed over the years. Everything—from the balance of power between the institutions, to the role of local governments, to how and where we vote, to the factors that affect our voting patterns—has changed. And things will change again. Advocates for change must be informed on the issues, understand the structure of North Carolina government and the realities of North Carolina politics, and be prepared to strike when the time is right.

An Information Guide to North Carolina Politics

This book is meant to provide readers with the basics—the anatomy of North Carolina politics, as indicated in the title. I hope that in your own way you will attempt to put some flesh on those bones over the coming days, months, and years. For the students forced to read this for a class (sorry!), that may mean more research. For others, you may attempt to run for office or work in or around North Carolina politics yourself. For the largest number of readers, however, I expect you will do neither. Instead, my hope is that you can use the anatomy lesson of this book to become a better and more active citizen and participant in the state's politics. It is easy to get sucked into the daily ticktock of national politics (as I write these words, Congressman George Santos might or might not be expelled from office for a variety of transgressions—from the mundane to the downright bizarre), but the reality of American politics today is that state government is where the action is.

The problem is that we are awash in information about national politics, while information on state politics is more difficult to come by. To help combat that problem, I present below a resource guide for North Carolina politics. It includes everything from data sources to podcasts. Given the sheer number of newspapers and journalists in the state, I do not list every outlet, but I do make some suggestions. An expanded and updated version of this guide is available on my website at www .chriscooperwcu.com/anatomy.

Books
Overviews of North Carolina Politics and Government
Beyle, Thad L., and Merle Black, eds. *Politics and Policy in North Carolina.* New York: Ardent Media, 1975.
[Beyle and Black went on to become two of the most well-respected observers of southern politics. Beyle's introductory chapter gives a good sense of the tensions that continue to define North Carolina politics—and includes the first mention I can find of the phrase "paradox of North Carolina politics".]

Christensen, Rob. *The Paradox of Tar Heel Politics: The Personalities, Elections, and Events That Shapes Modern North Carolina.* 2nd ed. Chapel Hill: University of North Carolina Press, 2010.
[Christensen is the dean emeritus of the North Carolina Capital Press Corps, and his book gives a rich sense of the people who made the state's politics. The paperback edition came out just as the general assembly was about to transition to Republican power.]

Cooper, Christopher A., and H. Gibbs Knotts, eds. *The New Politics of North Carolina.* Chapel Hill: University of North Carolina Press, 2008.
[This is an edited volume covering the major institutions and topics in North Carolina politics and government. Chapters are written by leading political scientists throughout the state.]

Eamon, Tom. *The Making of a Southern Democracy: North Carolina Politics from Kerr Scott to Pat McCrory.* Chapel Hill: University of North Carolina Press, 2014.
[A native of Kinston, North Carolina, Eamon is a longtime professor of political science at East Carolina University and one of the smartest observers of the state's politics. This book is an encyclopedic tour of the political history of the state from the twentieth century through the early twenty-first century.]

Fleer, Jack D. *North Carolina Government and Politics.* Lincoln: University of Nebraska Press, 1994.
[Fleer, a (now retired) professor of political science at Wake Forest University, wrote this book as part of a series with the University of Nebraska Press that included profiles of most US states. It is in many ways an update of his 1968 book.]

———. *North Carolina Politics: An Introduction.* Chapel Hill: University of North Carolina Press, 1968.
[Fleer's papers, which include research for this book as well as his other books, are available at the Z. Smith Reynolds Library at Wake Forest University.]

Luebke, Paul. *Tar Heel Politics: Myths and Realities.* Chapel Hill: University of North Carolina Press, 1990.
[Luebke, a sociologist at UNC-Greensboro and a Democratic member of the general assembly, argues that the central tension in North Carolina politics is between modernizers and traditionalists.]

———. *Tar Heel Politics 2000.* Chapel Hill: University of North Carolina Press, 1998.
[An update of Luebke's 1990 book.]

Rankin, Robert S. *The Government and Administration of North Carolina*. New York: Cromwell, 1955.
[This is an early textbook of North Carolina government. Rankin was a well-respected political scientist at Duke University.]
Wagner, Paul W. *North Carolina: The State and Its Government*. New York: Oxford University Press 1947.
[Wagner was a political science professor at UNC Chapel Hill. This slim volume is the earliest textbook of North Carolina government that I can find.]

Books about Specific Aspects of North Carolina Politics and Government

Baumgartner, Frank R., Derek A. Epp, and Kelsey Shoub. *Suspect Citizens: What 20 Million Traffic Stops Tell Us about Policing and Race*. New York: Cambridge University Press, 2018.
[Baumgartner, Epp, and Shoub examine every traffic stop in North Carolina from 2002 to 2016 and find tremendous disparities by race.]
Bitzer, J. Michael. *Redistricting and Gerrymandering in North Carolina: Battlelines in the Tar Heel State*. London: Palgrave, 2021.
[An authoritative, well-researched, and complete history of redistricting and gerrymandering in North Carolina by one the most astute observers of the state's politics.]
Bluestein, Frada S., ed. *County and Municipal Government in North Carolina*. Chapel Hill: University of North Carolina Press, 2014.
[This is the best source on local government in North Carolina. Each chapter is written by an expert who teaches at the UNC School of Government.]
Christensen, Rob. *The Rise and Fall of the Branchhead Boys: North Carolina's Scott Family and the Era of Progressive Politics*. Chapel Hill: University of North Carolina Press, 2019.
[A compelling and historically grounded book about the first family of North Carolina politics: the Scotts.]
Corriher, Billy. *Usurpers: How Voters Stopped the Takeover of North Carolina's Courts*. Self-published, 2021.
[An analysis of the battle over North Carolina's courts and voting rights.]
Cunningham, David. *Klansville, U.S.A.: The Rise and Fall of the Civil Rights–Era Ku Klux Klan*. New York: Oxford University Press, 2012.
[An exhaustively researched book on the role of the Klan in North Carolina and the political ramifications today.]

Fleer, Jack D. *Governors Speak*. Lanham, MD: University Press of
America, 2007.
[An exploration of the changing power of the North Carolina
governor from Terry Sanford through Jim Hunt.]

Graff, Michael, and Nick Ochsner. *The Vote Collectors: The True Story of
the Scamsters, Politicians, and Preachers behind the Nation's Greatest
Electoral Fraud*. Chapel Hill: University of North Carolina Press,
2021.
[This one is a page-turner. The top-line takeaway is that it examines
the "nation's greatest electoral fraud," conducted in North Carolina's
Ninth Congressional District. But it is really a book about place,
politics, history, and the ways in which the three meet.]

Hood, John. *Catalyst: Jim Martin and the Rise of North Carolina
Republicans*. Winston-Salem, NC: John F. Blair Publisher, 2015.
[John Hood, one of the leading free-market conservative voices in
the state, offers a look at how Jim Martin was integral to Republican
ascendency in North Carolina.]

Leloudis, James L., and Robert R. Korstad. *Fragile Democracy: The
Struggle over Race and Voting Rights in North Carolina*. Chapel Hill:
University of North Carolina Press, 2020.
[An overview and analysis of the battle over voting rights in North
Carolina by two leading historians.]

Matthews, Donald R. *North Carolina Votes*. Chapel Hill: University of
North Carolina Press, 1962.
[This book includes 304 tables of election returns for president
(1868–1960), governor (1868–1930), and US senator in North Carolina
(1914–30).]

Nichol, Gene R. *Indecent Assembly: The North Carolina Legislature's
Blueprint for the War on Democracy and Inequality*. Durham, NC:
Blair, 2020.
[A scathing look at the North Carolina General Assembly under
Republican control. The author is a professor of law at UNC, a vocal
progressive, and a frequent critic of the general assembly.]

Orth, John V., and Paul Martin Newby. *The North Carolina State
Constitution*. 2nd ed. New York: Oxford University Press, 2013.
[The best source on the North Carolina Constitution—provides both
legal and historical analysis. The book is a collaboration between a law
professor (Orth) and the current chief justice of the North Carolina
Supreme Court (Newby).]

Book Chapters

There are scores of books about the politics of the South and electoral politics more generally that include North Carolina as one of the state-specific chapters. Here is a list from 2013 to 2023. A list going back farther and updated regularly can be found at www.chriscooperwcu /anatomy.

Bitzer, J. Michael. "North Carolina: A Deeply Divided Partisan State." In *The New Politics of the Old South: An Introduction to Southern Politics*, 7th ed., edited by Charles S. Bullock and Mark J. Rozell, 101–26. Langham, MD: Rowman and Littlefield, 2022.

———. "North Carolina: Even More Evenly Divided in 2020." In *The 2020 Presidential Election in the South*, edited by Scott E. Buchanan and Branwell Dubose Kapeluck, 223–44. Langham, MD: Rowman and Littlefield, 2021.

Bitzer, J. Michael, and Charles Prysby. "North Carolina: Up and Down the Tar Heel Political Roller Coaster." In *The 2016 Presidential Election in the South*, edited by Scott E. Buchanan and Branwell DuBose Kapeluck, 156–96. Fayetteville: University of Arkansas Press, 2018.

Campbell, Karl E. "Tar Heel Politics in the 20th Century: The Rise and Fall of the Progressive Plutocracy." In *Reinterpreting North Carolina History*, edited by Larry E. Tise and Jefrey J. Crow, 241–68. Chapel Hill: University of North Carolina Press, 2017.

Cooper, Christopher A., and H. Gibbs Knotts. "The Bluest Red State in America: Exploring North Carolina's Political Past, Present, and Future." In *Presidential Swing States: Why Only Ten Matter*, edited by David Schultz and Stacy Hunter Hecht, 111–30. Boston: Lexington Press, 2015.

———. "North Carolina: Still Swingin' in the South." In *Presidential Swing States*, 2nd ed., edited by David Schultz and Rafael Jacob, 203–22. Boston: Lexington Press, 2019.

———. "Reliably Purple: The 2020 Presidential Election in North Carolina." In *Presidential Swing States*, 3rd ed., edited by David Schultz and Rafael Jacob, 79–96. Boston: Lexington Press, 2022.

Kropf, Martha, and JoEllen V. Pope. "Election Costs: A Study of North Carolina." In *The Future of Election Administration*, edited by Mitchell Brown, Kathleen Hale, and Bridgett A. King, 185–99. New York: Springer, 2019.

Lang, Robert E. "South Atlantic: Georgia and North Carolina." In *The Shifting Urban-Rural Divide*, edited by David F. Damore, Robert E. Lang, and Karen Danielsen, 129–70. Washington, DC: Brookings Institution Press, 2020.

Myers, Adam S. "The 2014 Senate and 2012 Presidential Elections in North Carolina: A Microgeographical Comparison." In *Races, Reforms, and Policy: Implications of the 2014 Midterm Elections*, edited by Christopher J. Galdieri, Tauna S. Sisco, and Jennifer C. Lucas, 64–77. Akron, OH: University of Akron Press, 2017.

Prysby, Charles. "North Carolina: No Longer Federal Red and State Blue?" In *Second Verse, Same as the First: The 2012 Presidential Election in the South*, edited by Scott E. Buchanan and Branwell DuBose Kapeluck, 171–84. Fayetteville: University of Arkansas Press, 2014.

———. "North Carolina: The Shifting Sands of Tar Heel Politics." In *The New Politics of the Old South*, 5th ed., edited by Charles Bullock III and Mark J. Rozell, 157–80. Landham, MD: Rowman and Littlefield, 2014.

Prysby, Charles, and J. Michael Bitzer. "North Carolina: A Growing Partisan Divide." In *The New Politics of the Old South*, 6th ed., edited by Charles Bullock III and Mark J. Rozell, 186–213. Landham, MD: Rowman and Littlefield 2018.

Tervo, Carolina. "Why Republicans Went Hard Right in North Carolina." In *Upending American Politics: Polarizing Parties, Ideological Elites, and Citizen Activists from the Tea Party to the Anti-Trump Resistance*, edited by Theda Skocpol and Caroline Tervo, 53–77. New York: Oxford University Press, 2020.

Wilkinson, Betia Cutaia. "The 2016 Latino Vote in North Carolina." In *Latinos and the 2016 Election: Latino Resistance and the Election of Donald Trump*, edited by Gabriel R. Sanchez, Luis R. Fraga, and Ricardo Ramirez, 149–65. East Lansing: Michigan State University Press, 2020.

Peer-Reviewed Journal Articles

Peer-reviewed journal articles in political science do not usually examine North Carolina politics in isolation, but sometimes people use North Carolina as a case to illustrate broader concepts in American politics. Here is a list of peer-reviewed journal articles from 2013 to 2023 that use some aspect of North Carolina politics as a key or the key case. An updated list appears online at www.chriscooperwcu.com/anatomy.

Bitzer, Michael, Christopher A. Cooper, Whitney Ross Manzo, and Susan Roberts. "Growing and Distinct: The Unaffiliated Voter as Unmoored Voter." *Social Science Quarterly* 103, no. 7 (2022): 1587–601.

Bitzer, Michael, Tyler Dukes, and Christopher A. Cooper. "A Turnout Effect, a Substitution Effect, or Both? Changes in Distance to the Early Voting Site and Voter Turnout." *Election Law Journal* 22, no. 3 (2023): 278–85.

Burnett, Craig M., and Christopher R. Prentice. "An Exploration of How Partisanship Impacts Council Manager Systems." *Politics and Policy* 46, no. 3 (2018): 392–415.

Carter, Daniel, Zah Hunter, Dan Teague, Gregory Herschlag, and Jonathan Mattingly. "Optimal Legislative County Clustering in North Carolina." *Statistics and Public Policy* 7, no. 1 (2020): 19–29.

Cooper, Christopher A. "Innumeracy and State Legislative Salaries." *Public Opinion Quarterly* 85, no. 1 (2021): 147–60.

Gibson, Nadine Suzanne. "Moving Forward or Backsliding: A Causal Inference Analysis of the Effects of the Shelby Decision in North Carolina." *American Politics Research* 48, no. 5 (2020): 649–62.

Greenberger, Michael. "A Method to Detect Whether Countywide Vote Centers Are Located Optimally: The Case of North Carolina." *Election Law Journal* 22, no. 2 (2023): 105–16.

Hazelton, Morgan L. W., Jacob M. Montgomery, and Brendan Nyhan. "Does Public Financing Affect Judicial Behavior? Evidence from the North Carolina Supreme Court." *American Politics Research* 44, no. 4 (2016): 587–617.

Herron, Michael C. "Mail-in Absentee Ballot Anomalies in North Carolina's 9th Congressional District." *Election Law Journal* 18, no. 3 (2019): 191–213.

Herron, Michael C., and Daniel A. Smith. "Race, Shelby County, and the Voter Information Verification Act in North Carolina." *Florida State University Law Review* 43 (2017). https://ir.law.fsu.edu/lr/vol43/iss2/5.

Herschlag, Gregory, Han Suung Kang, Justin Luo, Christy Vaughn Graves, Sachet Bangia, Robert Ravier, and Jonathan C. Mattingly. "Quantifying Gerrymandering in North Carolina." *Statistics and Public Policy* 7, no. 1 (2020): 30–38.

Kropf, Martha. "North Carolina Election Reform Ten Years after the Help America Vote Act." *Election Law Journal* 12, no. 2 (2013): 179–89.

Kropf, Martha, JoEllen V. Pope, Mary Jo Shepherd, and Zachary Mohr. "Making Every Vote Count: The Important Role of Managerial Capacity in Achieving Better Election Administration Outcomes." *Public Administration Review* 80, no. 5 (2020): 733–42.

Merivaki, Thessalia, and Daniel A. Smith. "A Failsafe for Voters: Cast and Rejected Provisional Ballots in North Carolina." *Political Research Quarterly* 73, no. 1 (2020): 65–78.

Michael E. Shepherd, Adriane Fresh, Nick Eubank, and Joshua D. Clinton. "The Politics of Locating Polling Places: Race and Partisanship in North Carolina Election Administration, 2008–2016." *Election Law Journal* 20, no. 2 (2021): 155–77.

Mohr, Zachary, JoEllen V. Pope, Martha E. Kropf, and Mary Jo Shepherd. "Strategic Spending: Does Politics Influence Election Administration Expenditure?" *American Journal of Political Science* 63, no, 2 (2019): 427–38.

Shi, Ying. "Cross-Cutting Messages and Voter Turnout: Evidence from a Same-Sex Marriage Amendment." *Political Communication* 33, no. 3 (2015): 433–59.

Smith, Jacob F. H., and Neil Weinberg. "The Elevator Effect: Advertising, Priming, and the Rise of Cherie Berry." *American Politics Research* 44, no. 3 (2016): 496–522.

Suttmann-Lea, Mara, and Thessalia Merivaki. "Don't Drown the Message: The Effects of Voter Education on Mail Ballot Acceptance in North Carolina." *Journal of Election Administration, Research, and Practice* 1, no. 2 (2022): 69–95.

Walker, Hannah L., Michael C. Herron, and Daniel A. Smith. "Early Voting Changes and Voter Turnout: North Carolina in the 2016 General Election." *Political Behavior* 41 (2019): 841–69.

Data Sources

CAMPAIGN FINANCE

Campaign finance for federal offices: Lots of ways to access these data from the Federal Election Commission on this site. Your best bet is to poke around and find the method that works for your purposes. www.fec.gov/data/elections/?state=&cycle=2022&election_full =true.

Campaign finance reports for state and local candidates in North Carolina: You can search for campaign receipts or expenditures by the candidate or campaign committee. https://cf.ncsbe.gov/CFOrgLkup/.

Campaign finance information in an easy to digest format: Lots of good campaign finance information and data. www.opensecrets.org/.

Civitas Action scores: These data are maintained by Civitas Action, a conservative 501c(4) organization. Civitas Action scores legislators on a scale of 0 to 100, with a 100 representing a more conservative legislator ("most supportive to freedom," in the organization's words), and a 0 representing a more liberal voting record ("least supportive of freedom," in its terms). Despite the fact that they are produced by a think tank with an ideological perspective, these scores are reliable and correlate well with other measures such as the Shor-McCarty scores referenced last in this section. https://civitasaction.org.

Legislative business ratings: Individual legislator ratings from the North Carolina Free Enterprise Foundation (NCFREE). The closer the rating is to 100, the more aligned that legislator was with the principles of free enterprise during the selected session of the general assembly. Ratings are available in odd-numbered years from 2009 to present. https://ncfree.org/research/legislative-business-ratings/.

Legislative effectiveness: This website has not been updated since 2016, but the North Carolina Center for Public Policy Research used to conduct a survey about the most "effective" legislators in North Carolina. The website has archived the results from 1998, 2004, 2015, and 2016. https://nccppr.org/category/legislative-rankings/.

Lobbyist influence: Every two years from 2004 to 2014, the North Carolina Center for Public Policy Research conducted surveys to determine lobbyist influence in North Carolina. The past results are archived on this website. https://nccppr.org/category/lobbyist -rankings/.

NFIB scores for North Carolina: Similar to the Civitas Action scores, the National Federation of Independent Businesses identifies important issues and places them on a percent scale (100 percent means the legislator voted with the NFIB-preferred position 100 percent of the time). www.nfib.com/north-carolina/voting-record/.

NOMINATE scores: The go-to source for voting behavior of members of Congress. You can download datasets or just go to specific members of Congress. https://voteview.com.

Shor-McCarty ideology data: This is the standard political science measure for state legislator ideology. It includes estimated ideology for every state legislator and state legislative chamber in America from 1993 to 2020. https://dataverse.harvard.edu/dataverse/bshor.

OFFICEHOLDING

County commission partisanship from the North Carolina Association of County Commissioners: An underutilized but extremely helpful resource. The organization has county-level officeholding numbers from 2002 to the present and statewide numbers from 1974 to the present. The data include partisanship, race, and gender. www.ncacc .org/research-and-publications/research/county-elections/.

State legislative partisanship from the National Conference of State Legislatures: Includes data for all fifty states from 2009 to the present. www.ncsl.org/research/about-state-legislatures/partisan-composition.

Women in office resources from the Center for American Women and Politics at Rutgers University: The source for gender and politics data. It includes women serving in Congress, statewide office, and state legislatures in easily accessible formats from 1975 to the present. Lots of ways to search the data. https://cawpdata.rutgers.edu/.

POLICY

Correlates of State Policy dataset: Not North Carolina–specific, but this dataset (which includes some cool, easy-to-navigate visualization features if you are not comfortable with spreadsheets) has over 2,000 variables for all 50 states, beginning in 1900. https://cspp.ippsr.msu .edu/cspp/.

REDISTRICTING

North Carolina congressional maps, 1789–present: I put these together from various sources. www.chriscooperwcu.com/nc-politics-resources.

North Carolina General Assembly redistricting data: This is the official NCGA site for redistricting data and information. https://ncleg.gov /Redistricting.

VOTING AND ELECTIONS

Candidate lists: Lists of candidates running for office (current and some past elections). www.ncsbe.gov/results-data/candidate-lists#candidate -files.

Provisional and absentee data: A great way to follow who votes early and absentee in North Carolina. www.ncsbe.gov/results-data/absentee -and-provisional-data.

Voter history: A dataset with all registered voters in the state, with indicators for whether they voted in the last ten elections, along with their methods of voting (early in person, mail, or Election Day). You can link this dataset with the one listed in the previous entry by using the NCID variable to create a powerful tool with which to better understand the North Carolina electorate. www.ncsbe.gov/results -data/voter-history-data.

Voter registration data: A dataset with every registered voter in the state (over 7 million records!), along with a host of demographic and geographic indicators. www.ncsbe.gov/results-data/voter-registration -data.

Less comfortable with datasets and just want the basics?

Civitas Partisan Index (CPI): The John Locke Foundation has a measure of partisan lean for general assembly districts, using the results of a host of North Carolina elections. These data, like the Daily Kos data, are generated by an organization with an ideological perspective, but the data are reliable and useful. www.johnlocke.org/what-are-the -partisan-leanings-of-court-ordered-legislative-districts/.

District partisan lean: The Cook Political Report is the go-to resource for congressional district partisan lean (what it calls the Cook Partisan Voting Index, or PVI). www.cookpolitical.com/cook-pvi.

Election results: An easy to use drop-down that allows you to examine election results (including results by county and by method of voting) for all elections from 1992 to the present. https://er.ncsbe.gov/.

Election results by congressional and state legislative district: The Daily Kos measure is particularly helpful because it provides results based on various iterations of the district lines—so, for example, how did the Eleventh Congressional District vote for president in 2020 based on current district lines versus previous district lines? www.dailykos.com/stories/2018/2/21/1742660/-The-ultimate-Daily -Kos-Elections-guide-to-all-of-our-data-sets.

Ideology by district and county: The American Ideology Project has "public preference estimates" for every county and every congressional and state legislative district in the country, using data from 2006 to 2021. https://americanideologyproject.com/.

Look up any voter: If you simply want to look up the voter registration and voter history for an individual voter, here's an easy link: https://vt.ncsbe.gov/RegLkup/.

Two-party presidential vote share in North Carolina by county, 1950–present: I put this spreadsheet together with data from various editions of the *North Carolina Manual* and other sources: www.chriscooperwcu.com/nc-politics-resources.

Voter registration statistics by county: Straightforward snapshots of voter registration statistics by county at various time periods. https://vt.ncsbe.gov/RegStat/.

Voter turnout by election: Voter turnout already computed for a variety of elections. www.ncsbe.gov/results-data/voter-turnout.

State-level voter turnout by election, 1980–present: Michael McDonald at the University of Florida keeps these data by state (including, but not limited to North Carolina). Make sure to read his explanation of the advantages of using voting eligible population (VEP) as opposed to voting age population (VAP). www.electproject.org/election-data/voter-turnout-data.

MISCELLANY

If you want to find data and it is not in one of the places listed in the previous sections, you may need to comb through some hard-copy records. Here are some good places to start:

North Carolina Government 1585–1974: A Narrative and Statistical History: Published in 1975 by the North Carolina Department of Secretary of State. It is a revision and update of the 1913 *North Carolina Manual*.

North Carolina House and Senate Journals: The primary record of the work of the general assembly. https://statelibrary.ncdcr.libguides.com/LegPubs/Journals.

North Carolina Manual: A treasure trove of great data on North Carolina politics and government. It was published biannually by the secretary of state from 1903 to 2011. Most research libraries have hard copies. You can find archived copies here: www.carolana.com/NC/NC_Manuals/home.html.

Polling in North Carolina

ACADEMIC POLLING

East Carolina University Poll: https://surveyresearch.ecu.edu/ecu-poll/.
Elon Poll: www.elon.edu/u/elon-poll/.
High Point University Poll: www.highpoint.edu/src/hpupoll/.
Meredith Poll: www.meredith.edu/meredith-poll/.

PRIVATE POLLING

Public Policy Polling: Generally considered a left-leaning polling firm but
still reliable and accurate. The firm does work across the country, but
as you might expect from a North Carolina–based polling firm, it does
a good job keeping up with public opinion in the Tar Heel State.

THINK-TANK POLLING

Carolina Forward: A left-leaning, progressive organization that does
polling in North Carolina.
John Locke Foundation: A conservative organization that does polling in
North Carolina once a month.

Podcasts

Like catching up on politics while driving, mowing the lawn, at the gym,
or on a run? We are fortunate to have a number of podcasts that focus
mostly on North Carolina politics. A few of my favorites include the
following:

Charlotte Talks: Long-running interview show at WFAE in Charlotte. Not
exclusively North Carolina–related, and not always political, but lots
of content on North Carolina politics.
Do Politics Better: Run by lobbyists Brian Lewis and Skye David, this
podcast gives a good sense of the inner workings of the general
assembly and how policy is really made. Somehow they manage to
keep the mood relatively light and positive—I still haven't figured out
how they do that, week after week.
Due South: Leoneda Inge and Jeff Tiberii host this engaging daily
show about politics, culture, and society in the South. Lots of North
Carolina politics content, but pay particular attention to the Friday
news roundup.
NC Capitol Wrap: Another terrific podcast—this one is from WRAL.
Great insight on all things North Carolina politics, particularly

insightful on issues surrounding the general assembly and legislative politics.

Tying It Together with Tim Boyum: Boyum is a mainstay in the North Carolina politics world, and this podcast is worth listening to whether he is profiling a recent policy issue on the floor of the general assembly or talking to a tree farmer.

Under the Dome: The original source for North Carolina politics coverage. The print version of *Under the Dome* has been a fixture in North Carolina politics from long before I came along. The podcast features a weekly roundup of North Carolina politics from reporters at the Raleigh *News and Observer* that is worth a listen.

WUNC Politics Podcast: Put out by Colin Campbell and the folks at WUNC, this is a great review of what's happened and a forward-thinking look at what's to come.

General Media Sources, Blogs, and Newsletters

If you want to keep up with local or state politics in North Carolina, there is no better place to start than with your local media. Although the sheer number of newspapers, radio stations, and TV stations in the state makes it impossible for me to list them all, this should not obscure the central point that *there is no better way to follow politics in North Carolina than to follow local and state media*. In addition to daily newspapers, there is some great reporting at local, small-town weeklies, and at local TV stations. North Carolina also has a strong network of NPR affiliates that are worth listening to (and contributing to). In addition to traditional local media, we have unique statewide online outlets including *The Assembly*, a magazine that explores various aspects of North Carolina politics, Carolina Public Press, and NC Health News. Spectrum News also has statewide television programming, some of which is available online. Loretta Boniti from Spectrum News hosts *In Focus*, a thirty-minute public affairs program that often has North Carolina politics content, interviews, and insights. *Capital Tonight*, a mainstay of North Carolina politics also makes many of its interviews available online.

If you want to know the state of thought from the conservative end of the spectrum, check out the John Locke Foundation and its respective publications. On the liberal end of things, try NC Policy Watch or Carolina Forward. North Carolina also has active voting rights groups, including the League of Women Voters of North Carolina and Common

Cause North Carolina. The Public School Forum puts out an education policy primer every year, and the Martin Center for Academic Renewal focuses on higher education (mostly, but not exclusively, in North Carolina) from a conservative perspective.

Used properly, social media can be a good way to follow what's going on in North Carolina politics. There are too many helpful accounts to list, so I won't attempt to do so here. Your best bet is to search the hashtags #ncpol (for North Carolina politics) and #ncga (for the North Carolina General Assembly). You can also follow specific congressional districts by typing #nc and the district number (for example, #nc11 to follow North Carolina's Eleventh Congressional District). You will probably start to notice accounts you like (and don't like) and can choose to follow specific folks accordingly. My recommendation would be to begin with journalists who cover state politics (or cover the part of the state you care about most).

North Carolina also has a number of good newsletters, blogs, and Substacks that provide perspective on North Carolina politics. Here are a few:

Anderson Alerts: A North Carolina politics Substack from freelance journalist Bryan Anderson. https://andersonalerts.substack.com/.

Carolina Demography: Not always explicitly "political," but a must read if you are interested in the ways demography interacts with politics and public policy in North Carolina. www.ncdemography.org/blog/.

Inside Politics: Weekly newsletter from WFAE political reporter Steve Harrison. www.wfae.org/inside-politics-newsletter.

Legislative Reporting Service Daily Bulletin Online: A helpful daily update about how individual bills are moving through the North Carolina General Assembly. https://lrs.sog.unc.edu/.

Longleaf Politics: Smart analysis of the state's politics from a conservative-leaning journalist. In some ways, the conservative yin to *Politics NC*'s liberal yang (see *Politics NC* entry in this section). www .longleafpol.com/.

NC Insider: A terrific daily compendium of stories about North Carolina government and politics. It also includes bill tracking and more. This newsletter requires a paid subscription. www.ncinsider.com/.

NC Local: A weekly email newsletter about local news in North Carolina. https://nclocalnewsworkshop.org/.

NC Tribune: A daily subscription newsletter that compiles stories about North Carolina politics and government. It also provides some reporting of its own, but it requires a paid subscription. https://nctribune.com/.

North Carolina Rabbit Hole: Not always political, but always worth reading. www.ncrabbithole.com/.

Old North State Politics: A public scholarship blog by four political scientists: Michael Bitzer, Whitney Ross Manzo, Susan Roberts, and myself. www.oldnorthstatepolitics.com/.

Politics NC: Thomas Mills, a Democratic operative and public affairs consultant/writer keeps this North Carolina–based Substack. https://politicsnc.substack.com/.

Quantifying Gerrymandering: Jonathan Mattingly and his team of mathematicians at Duke University maintain a helpful blog on all things redistricting. Lots of North Carolina content. https://sites.duke.edu/quantifyinggerrymandering/.

Notes

Introduction

1. I hate to begin this book with the passive voice, but no one I've asked remembers who moved the fubar meter that day.

2. I'll leave it to you to figure out what fubar stands for, although I will tell you that the last four letters stand for "Up Beyond All Recognition." But beware: if you Google it to find out what the first letter stands for, you'll soon find out that fubar is NSFW (not safe for work). To find where the fubar meter rests today, check its Twitter account: @NCGA_FUBAR. The tweet on June 8, 2011, 11:55 p.m., read, "Let's see, we're passing bills that rewrite the state's voting laws at three minutes to midnight? FUBAR AT 10. Beers all around. #ncga." https://x.com/NCGA_FUBAR/status/78671534088138752?s=20.

3. Editorial Board, "The Decline of North Carolina," *New York Times*, July 9, 2013.

4. Stephen Moore, "Why Are North Carolina Liberals So @&%*! Angry? If It's Monday, It Must Be Another Protest against Tax-Cutting Republicans," *Wall Street Journal*, July 19, 2013.

5. Levitsky and Ziblatt, *How Democracies Die*, 208–9.

6. In 2013, *The Daily Show* featured an interview with Buncombe County Republican Don Yelton who said (when referring to the "monster bill"), "If it hurts a bunch of college kids that's [*sic*] too lazy to get off their bohunkus and get a photo ID, so be it. If it hurts the whites, so be it. If it hurts a bunch of lazy blacks that wants the government to give them everything, so be it." This interview was later cited in a Fourth Circuit opinion that overturned the state's voter ID law. See Jonathan Drew and Emery P. Dalesio, "Appeals Court Decision Strikes Down NC Voter ID Case," *Asheville (NC) Citizen Times*, July 29, 2016.

7. Luebke, *Tar Heel Politics*; Luebke, *Tar Heel Politics 2000*.

8. Dan Kane and J. Andrew Curliss, "Black Ally Decker Is Sentenced to 4 Years," *Charlotte Observer*, April 27, 2007.

9. Lee, *Insecure Majorities*. Lee primarily uses examples and data from the US Congress, although chapter 8 focuses on state legislatures. For a similar argument, see Koger and Lebo, *Strategic Party Government*.

10. Lee, *Insecure Majorities*, 197.

11. In one bit, Noah says, "When Governor McCrory says 'Ninth Largest State,' he makes it seem like it's his catchphrase—which apparently it is. . . . Somewhere, the governor of the 10th largest state is there like 'damn you McCrory, quit rubbing it in we're doing our best.' And then he's taking a golden number 9 out of his cabinet and he rubs it, saying '*someday, someday*.'" *Daily Show with Trevor Noah*, season 2016.

12. Schultz and Jacob, *Presidential Swing States*.

13. O'Neill, *All Politics Is Local*.

14. Hopkins *Increasingly United States*.

15. Prysby, "No Longer Federal Red."

16. Maybe they're better considered "chapterettes."

Chapter 1

1. Brown and Pope, "Measuring and Manipulating Constitutional Evaluations."

2. Dinan, *American State Constitutional Tradition*.

3. Dinan, *State Constitutional Policies*.

4. Dinan, *American State Constitutional Tradition*.

5. Orth and Newby, *North Carolina State Constitution*, 4.

6. Rankin, *Government and Administration*, 16.

7. Orth, *North Carolina State Constitution*, 3.

8. US Congress, "An Act to Provide."

9. In a notable departure from the call for a convention, however, the majority of voters in thirty-four of the eighty-nine counties that cast votes voted "no" on the soon-to-be-ratified constitution. North Carolina Department of the Secretary of State, *North Carolina Manual of 1913*, 1016–18.

10. Orth and Newby, *North Carolina State Constitution*.

11. Rankin, *Government and Administration*; Orth, *North Carolina State Constitution with History and Commentary*; Sanders, "Our Constitution."

12. Orth, *North Carolina State Constitution*, 25.

13. North Carolina State Constitution Study Commission, *Report of the North Carolina State*, 144.

14. Waynick and Moore, "Constitutional Revision"; Rankin, *Government and Administration*, 23.

15. "Moore Calls for Study of N.C. Constitution," *High Point (NC) Enterprise*, October 27, 1967.

16. I am not throwing shade here. Eure referred to himself as the "the oldest rat in the Democratic barn" because he served as secretary of state for so long (thirty-one years). Miles Lawton, "Celebrating 'Oldest Rat in the Barn': Historic Marker Honors Eure," *Chowan Herald* (Edenton, NC), September 30, 2019.

17. "A Politician Opposes Constitutional," *Asheville (NC) Citizen Times*, November 11, 1967.

18. North Carolina State Constitution Study Commission, *Report of the North Carolina State*.

19. Orth, *North Carolina State Constitution*, 32.

20. "Tar Heel Editors Speak: Poll Reflects Disfavor for Four-Year Terms," *News and Observer* (Raleigh, NC), November 29, 1981.

21. Most notably by the recent *Moore v. Harper* case (*Moore v. Harper*, 143 S. Ct. 2065, 216 L. Ed. 2d 729 [2023]).

Chapter 2

1. "Ford Visits State Fair in Pitch for NC Votes," *Winston-Salem (NC) Journal*, October 24, 1976.

2. "Whistle-Stoppers," editorial, *High Point (NC) Enterprise*, October 21, 1976.

3. "Details Mapped for Carter Visit," *Asheville (NC) Citizen Times*, June 26, 1976.

4. "Ford Visits State Fair."

5. George Gallup, "Ford, Carter in Virtual Tie," *News and Observer* (Raleigh, NC), November 2, 1972.

6. Jim Hummel, "North Carolina Called Key in Presidential Race," *Daily Tar Heel* (Chapel Hill, NC), August 25, 1980.

7. Karen Dunn, "Candidates Target N.C. as Crucial 'Swing State,'" *Daily Tar Heel* (Chapel Hill, NC), October 14, 1988; Rob Christensen, "Mrs. Bush Calls Husband 'Most Qualified,'" *News and Observer* (Raleigh, NC), September 3, 1992; Under the Dome, "N.C. Merits a Visit by Both Doles," *News and Observer* (Raleigh, NC), June 13, 1996.

8. Peter Wallsten and Jen Pilla, "Edwards Placed on Gore's Short List," *Charlotte Observer*, August 4, 2000.

9. Frederick Schouten and Chuck Raasch, "Ten Things to Know about John Edwards," *Daily Journal* (Wilmington, NC), July 7, 2004.

10. Ryan Teague Beckwith, "Clinton Accused of Writing Off North Carolina," *Charlotte Observer*, March 12, 2008.

11. WTVD, "President Trump Returning to North Carolina 1 Day after Biden's First Visit," ABC News, September 21, 2020, https://abc11.com/trump-charlotte -rally-president-in-north-carolina-nc-healthcare/6485962/.

12. Cooper and Knotts, "Reliably Purple."

13. Link, *Righteous Warrior*.

14. Christensen, *Paradox of Tar Heels Politics*, 3.

15. Noel, *Political Ideologies*. In this chapter, ideology is presented in a traditional liberal (left) to conservative (right) framework. It is important to note that many of the most prominent commentators of North Carolina politics have resisted this idea. In *Tar Heel Politics 2000*, Paul Luebke eschewed the liberal/conservative view of North Carolina politics, opting instead for the terms "traditionalism" and "modernism."

16. Heath Shuler was a football player turned real estate agent, turned member of Congress, turned lobbyist for Duke Energy, turned part-time assistant football coach, and is now a lobbyist working for BakerHostetler, a prominent law firm and lobbying group. When Shuler represented North Carolina's Eleventh Congressional district from 2007 to 2013, he was the most conservative Democrat in Congress. See voteview.com, s.v. "Shuler, Heath," accessed March 23, 2024, https://voteview.com/person/20737/heath-shuler. He recently moved to Tennessee.

17. Jodi Enda, "When Republicans Were Blue and Democrats Were Red: The Era of Color-Coded Political Parties Is More Recent Than You Might Think," *Smithsonian Magazine*, October 31, 2012.

18. Jensen, "Congress Less Popular Than Cockroaches." Unfortunately for our once esteemed members of Congress, cockroaches have recently overtaken them in the court of public opinion.

19. Erikson, Wright, and McIver, *Statehouse Democracy*.

20. Tausanovitch and Warshaw, "Measuring Constituent Policy Preferences."

21. Berry et al., "Measuring Citizen and Government Ideology."

22. Morris, *Movers and Stayers*.

23. Caughey and Warshaw, "Dynamics of State Policy Liberalism."

24. Luebke, *Tar Heel Politics 2000*, 23.

25. You can also be forgiven if I lost you at multilevel regression and poststratification.

26. Presidential elections also have the benefit of not being subject to redistricting.

27. G. Bluestein, *Flipped*.

28. A November 2023 Meredith poll showed that the likely 2024 general election matchup of Trump and Biden was a toss-up with neither candidate ahead of the margin of error. Likewise, the likely gubernatorial matchup of Democrat Josh Stein and Republican Mark Robinson was similarly deadlocked.

Chapter 3

1. Williams, "Murphy to Manteo."

2. I've lobbied for the phrase "Hothouse to Hatteras" to better encapsulate the true east and west end of the state. Thus far, my lobbying efforts have gone unrealized.

3. Key, *Southern Politics*, 219.

4. Fleer, *North Carolina Government*; Luebke, *Tar Heel Politics 2000*; Eamon, *Making of a Southern Democracy*.

5. Rankin, *Government and Administration*.

6. Remember that these patterns, while extremely important, represent the average county, not the average voter.

7. Delli Carpini, Keeter, and Kennamer, "Effects of the News Media Environment"; Rogers, *Accountability in State Legislatures*.

8. Silbermann, "Gender Roles."

9. Zeb Smathers, interview by the author, June 30, 2023; Hood and McKee, *Rural Republican Realignment*.

10. US Census Bureau, "Nation's Urban and Rural Populations."

11. J. Michael Bitzer, "What Precinct Polarization Might Tell Us about NC's Politics before Redistricting Kicks Off," *Old North State Politics* (blog), August 6, 2021, www.oldnorthstatepolitics.com/2021/08/precinct-polarization-and -redistricting.html.

Chapter 4

1. Caleb Crain, "What a White-Supremacist Coup Looks Like," *New Yorker*, April 27, 2020.

2. For the definitive account of the Wilmington Massacre, see David Zucchino's Pulitzer Prize–winning book, *Wilmington's Lie*.

3. Lilly Knoepp, "Macon County Group Remembers Mitchell Mozeley on the Anniversary of His Lynching," Blue Ridge Public Radio, November 10,

2021, www.bpr.org/news/2021-11-10/macon-county-group-remembers-mitchell
-mozeley-on-the-anniversary-of-his-lynching.

4. Acharya, Blackwell, and Sen, *Deep Roots*.

5. Cunningham, *Klansville, U.S.A.* But see Morris, "Partisan Politics in the
21st Century South."

6. Faulkner, *Requiem for a Nun*.

7. Elmore, "Human, John Adams."

8. Cunningham, *Klansville, U.S.A.*

9. Florida was the only other southern state with partial coverage.

10. Bullock, Gaddie, and Wert, *Rise and Fall of the Voting Rights Act*.

11. Hood, Kidd, and Morris, *Rational Southerner*.

12. Maxwell and Shields, *Long Southern Strategy*.

13. Charlotte, NC, became the focal point for the busing debate. Smith, *Boom
for Whom?*

14. Lamis, *Two-Party South*, 8. This is perhaps the most infamous quote in the
history of southern politics. The full quote includes racial slurs, so I don't include
it here in its entirety.

15. Luebke, *Tar Heel Politics 2000*; Leloudis and Korstad, *Fragile Democracy*.

16. Frank James, "Political Pro with Race-Baiting Past Doesn't See It in
Romney's Welfare Charge," National Public Radio, September 10, 2012, www
.npr.org/sections/itsallpolitics/2012/09/10/160885683/political-pro-with-race
-baiting-past-doesnt-see-it-in-romneys-welfare-charge.

17. *Shelby County v. Holder*, 570 U.S. 529 (2013).

18. Leloudis and Korstad, *Fragile Democracy*.

19. Covington, *Henry Frye*, 102.

20. Sullivan, "Even at the Turning of the Tide"; Bullock et al., "Election of
African American State Legislators"; Cooper, "Multimember Districts in State
Legislatures."

21. Sullivan, "Even at the Turning of the Tide."

22. Sullivan, "Even at the Turning of the Tide."

23. Rebecca Waler, "Flyers Containing 'False, Hurtful' Statements Posted
ahead of Fletcher Mayoral Race," *Blue Ridge Now* (Hendersonville, NC),
November 1, 2021.

24. Preston Blakely, interview by the author, June 23, 2023.

25. Grose, *Congress in Black and White*. Grose finds, however, that roll-call
votes of white and Black people who represent similarly situated districts are not
distinct.

26. Jordan, "Black Legislators."

27. Rankin, *Government and Administration*; Bass and DeVries,
Transformation of Southern Politics; Fleer, *North Carolina Government*; Eamon,
Making of a Southern Democracy.

28. Luebke, *Tar Heel Politics 2000*, 133.

29. Danny McComas, interview by the author, October 10, 2023.

30. Barreto, Collingwood, and Manzano, "New Measure."

31. Bullock et al., *South and the Transformation of U.S. Politics*; Wilkinson, "North Carolina Latinos," 150 (quote).

32. Henry Gargan, "State's 1st Indian-American Legislator Takes Oath of Office," *News and Observer* (Raleigh, NC), January 15, 2017.

33. Avi Bajpai, "Teaching Asian American History in NC Schools, and Other Global Goals of the New AAPI Caucus," *News and Observer* (Raleigh, NC), May 23, 2023.

34. Berden and Masuoka, "Growing Political Force."

35. Lynn Bonner, "First Asian American Women Elected to the NC Legislature," NC Newsline, November 17, 2022, https://ncnewsline.com/briefs/first-asian-american-women-elected-to-the-nc-legislature/.

36. Herrick and Mendez, "American Indian Party Identification."

37. Fraga, *Turnout Gap*.

Chapter 5

1. She was the first woman ever nominated to a legislative seat in the South. She didn't even have the legal authority to hold elective office in North Carolina until the general assembly gave that right to women two months before her election.

2. "A Divergence from Precedent," *Charlotte News*, June 8, 1920.

3. Lindsey Prather, interview by the author, June 6, 2023.

4. Pitkin, *Concept of Representation*.

5. Frances McKusick, "Rep. Jane Pratt Popular Southern Gentlewoman," *Herald Sun* (Durham, NC), August 29, 1946.

6. McDaniel, "Historic All-Women City Council."

7. Trent Brown, "Durham Voters Elect County's 1st All-Female Board and 1st Muslim Woman Commissioner," *News and Observer* (Raleigh, NC), March 9, 2020.

8. E. Shaw and Tesfaselassie, *Status of Women*.

9. Karen Kedrowski, interview by the author, June 15, 2023.

10. Holman, "Women in Local Government"; Holman, "Sex and the City"; Caiazza, "Women's Representation in Elected Office."

11. Swers, *Difference Women Make*; Bratton, "Critical Mass Theory Revisited"; Tolleson-Rinehart, "Do Women Leaders Make a Difference?"

12. Nickelson and Jansa, "Descriptive Representation and Innovation."

13. Richardson and Freeman, "Gender Differences in Constituency Services"; Holman, *Women in Politics in the American City*.

14. Kathlene, "Power and Influence in State Legislative Policymaking."

15. Atkeson and Carrillo, "More Is Better."

16. Jones, "Descriptive Representation of Gender."

17. Sarah Kliff, "The Research Is Clear: Electing More Women Changes How Government Works," Vox, March 8, 2017, www.vox.com/2016/7/27/12266378/electing-women-congress-hillary-clinton.

18. Bos et al., "This One's for the Boys," 488.

19. Bos et al., "This One's for the Boys," 497.

20. Fox and Lawless, *It Takes a Candidate*.

21. Lawless, *Becoming a Candidate*.

22. Lillian's List, "About," accessed March 20, 2024, https://lillianslist.org /about/.

23. Arceneaux, "Gender Gap."

24. Hogan, "Influence of State and District Conditions."

25. Cooper, "Multimember Districts and State Legislatures."

26. Prather, interview, June 6, 2023.

27. E. Shaw and Tesfaselassie, *Status of Women*.

Chapter 6

1. Steve Harrison, "Here's Another 50th out of 50 Ranking for Charlotte: Voting," WFAE, September 18, 2023, www.wfae.org/politics/2023-09-18/heres -another-50th-out-of-50-ranking-for-charlotte-voting.

2. "Senate Would Put Ban on Cures for 'Incurable Ills,'" *Wilmington (NC) Morning Star*, January 28, 1917.

3. Charles Duncan, "Intimidation, Interference: Election Officials Report 21 Incidents in N.C. Midterms," Spectrum News, November 11, 2023, https:// spectrumlocalnews.com/nc/charlotte/2022-elections/2022/11/11/intimidation --interference--elections-officials-report-21-incidents-in-n-c--midterms.

4. Chris Arnold, "Death Threats and Harassment: 2024 Election Workers Are Already Scared," National Public Radio, June 23, 2023, www.npr.org/2023/06 /23/1183931372/death-threats-and-harassment-2024-election-workers-already -are-scared.

5. By law, noncitizens, felons who are completing their sentences, and a small number of people who are mentally incapacitated cannot vote.

6. D. Shaw and Petrocik, *Turnout Myth*.

7. Gerry Cohen, personal correspondence with the author, June 30, 2023.

8. Most local elections provide the possibility for one-stop voting, but a few counties have held out and do not allow for this option.

9. Allen Smith, "GOP Unveils Program to Get Republicans Voting Early: We Need 'Change of Culture,'" NBC News, June 7, 2023, www.nbcnews.com/politics /2024-election/gop-unveils-program-get-republicans-voting-early-change -culture-rcna88162.

10. Hasen, *Voting Wars*.

11. Laura Lee and Jordan Wilkie, "Inside the 'Election Integrity' Efforts Targeting North Carolina," *The Assembly*, October 11, 2022, www.theassemblync .com/politics/elections/north-carolina-election-integrity/.

12. Josh Dawsey and Amy Gardner, "Top GOP Lawyer Describes Ease of Campus Voting in Private Pitch to RNC," *Washington Post*, April 20, 2023.

Chapter 7

1. More commonly known as primaries and caucuses.

2. House Bill 48 reads, "All persons who are recorded on the registration books as 'Independent' or 'No Party' designees, as of the date of ratification of

this fact, shall be presumed to be recorded as 'Unaffiliated' unless and until such persons request, in the manner provided by law, that their registration record be changed."

3. Rob Christensen, "Democratic, GOP Leaders Split an Opening Primaries in N.C.," *News and Observer* (Raleigh, NC), December 12, 1986.

4. Although a voter could not "vote in the primary of more than one party on the same day."

5. Tim Funk, "GOP Primaries Open to Unaffiliated Voters," *Charlotte Observer*, June 24, 1987.

6. Rob Christensen, "Parties Gear up to Run in '96," *News and Observer* (Raleigh, NC), September 17, 1995.

7. The specifics of third-party registration vary over time. Today North Carolina has three registered third parties: the Libertarian, the Green, and the No Labels parties.

8. Wade Rawlins, "Independents' Day Is Here," *News and Observer* (Raleigh, NC), July 29, 1996.

9. Yes, this is a euphemism for death.

10. Hood and McKee, *Rural Republican Realignment*; Hood and McKee, "What Made Carolina Blue?"

11. Specht, "Woodhouse Says GOP Is Winning."

12. Christopher A. Cooper and Michael Bitzer, "Democrats Are Voting in GOP Primaries. Did They Sink Madison Cawthorn?," *Washington Post*, June 16, 2022.

13. Bitzer et al., "Growing and Distinct."

14. Jeff Rose, interview by the author, December 2, 2020.

Chapter 8

1. Jennifer Moxley, interview by the author, January 2, 2023. Moxley told me that another unaffiliated candidate, Michael Zytkow, knocked on so many doors in his effort to get on the ballot that he lost forty pounds.

2. Bill Arthur, "McDuffie Pins Hopes on Petitions," *Charlotte Observer*, May 6, 1978. McDuffie was quite a character. At one point he got into a fight with an editorial cartoonist that was reminiscent of Dan Quayle's fight with the fictitious Murphy Brown. According to Phil Whitesell, "He also once dumped a bagful of chicken feathers on the floor of the City Council chamber to make a point." Phil Whitesell, "Democrats in Senate Race Snub Unaffiliated McDuffie," *Charlotte News*, November 4, 1978.

3. Whitesell, "Democrats in Senate Race."

4. Gail Smith, "A Flair for Showmanship: NC Sen. Jim McDuffie's Colorful Political Career Often Found before Center Stage," *Charlotte Observer*, February 9, 1985.

5. Her legislative record included a bill to make strawberry the state fruit: WFAE, "The 'Berry' True Story of How One Bill Became a Law," April 23, 2019, www.wfae.org/local-news/2019-04-23/the-berry-true-story-of-how-one-bill -became-a-law. Foon Rhee, "A First: Candidate Not Tied to Party Wins House Seat," *Charlotte Observer*, November 8, 1990.

6. Even that is a bit misleading. Jones served in the 2010–11 session as an unaffiliated candidate but was reelected to four subsequent terms as a Republican.

7. Is this correct? Probably. But without a master list it's impossible to know for sure. Debnam later switched to the Republican Party.

8. North Carolina State Board of Elections, "Unaffiliated Candidates for Elections in 2022," revised May 5, 2022, https://s3.amazonaws.com/dl.ncsbe.gov /Candidate%20Filing/2022_Fact_Sheet_Petition_Unaffiliated_Candidate.pdf.

9. North Carolina State Board of Elections, "Unaffiliated Candidate Petitions," accessed March 17, 2024, www.ncsbe.gov/candidates/petitions/Unaffiliated -candidate-petitions.

10. The signature rules have changed over the years. In 1991, the North Carolina General Assembly reduced the requirement from 10 percent to 4 percent. It was later reduced to 2 percent and was reduced, further still, to its current level (1.5 percent) in 2017.

11. Lilly Knoepp, "There Are 2.5 Million Unaffiliated Voters in North Carolina. So Why Aren't There More Unaffiliated Candidates?," Blue Ridge Public Radio, September 29, 2022, www.bpr.org/bpr-news/2022-09-29/there-are-2-5-million -Unaffiliated-voters-in-north-carolina-so-why-arent-there-more-Unaffiliated -candidates.

12. WFAE, "Independent Zytkow Petitions His Way onto City Council Ballot," September 25, 2013, www.wfae.org/local-news/2013-09-25/independent-zytkow -petitions-his-way-onto-city-council-ballot.

13. Any candidate can be an unaffiliated candidate; a person's voter registration does not affect one's eligibility to be an unaffiliated candidate. Given the process I describe in the text, however, it should not be surprising that few partisans think that the grass is greener on the unaffiliated side.

14. Tamas and Hindman, "Ballot Access Laws."

15. Well, they have read Duverger, *Political Parties*, or they have read enough about Duverger to pretend that they read Duverger and get away with it.

16. The same political scientists who took offense at the last note (of course they've read Duverger!) are likely thinking that there is reason to question Duverger's law. Although they are correct (see, in particular, Dunleavy and Diwaker, "Analyzing Multiparty Competition"), even the Duverger naysayers acknowledge that the central finding applies in the American political context.

17. If you got that implicit Stuart Smalley reference, I'm assuming you are above the age of forty.

Chapter 9

1. Blair Reeves, interview by the author, June 8, 2023.

2. Joe Stewart, interview by the author, June 15, 2023.

3. The number of lobbyists in North Carolina grew dramatically from the late 1960s to the late 1980s, but it has remained fairly stable since. For example, there were 151 registered lobbyists in 1969 compared to 840 in 1991. Fleer, *North Carolina Government*.

4. Payson, *When Cities Lobby*.

5. Thanks to journalist Andrew Jones, who collected and shared this information while reporting for the *Asheville Citizen Times*. He currently works for the *Asheville Watchdog*.

6. Payson, *When Cities Lobby*, 3.

7. Stewart, interview.

8. Kingdon, *Agendas, Alternatives, and Public Policies*.

9. Stewart, interview.

10. Kollman, *Outside Lobbying*.

11. "New Group in Raleigh to Keep Eye on State," *News and Observer* (Raleigh, NC), March 4, 1977.

12. Under the Dome, "Conservatives Plan a New Think Tank," *News and Observer* (Raleigh, NC), January 11, 1990.

13. See the American Legislative Exchange Council homepage, https://alec .org/.

14. Hertel-Fernandez, "Who Passes Businesses' 'Model Bills'?"

15. Hertel-Fernandez and Skocpol, "How the Right Trounced Liberals"; Hertel-Fernandez, "Explaining Liberal Policy Woes"; Hertel-Fernandez, *State Capture*.

16. Reeves, interview.

17. Sam Brody and Roger Sollenberger. "Inside the Relentless Campaign to Ruin Madison Cawthorn," Daily Beast, May 10, 2022, www.thedailybeast.com /inside-the-relentless-campaign-to-ruin-madison-cawthorn.

Chapter 10

1. When the building opened, the interior walls were described as "rough, simply gray cast stone. They are unadorned with no tablets, inscriptions, memorials, murals or sculpture." William A. Shires, "North Carolina's Legislative Building Completed," *Daily Times-News* (Burlington, NC), February 1, 1963.

2. Anthony Paletta, "The Most Hated of Architects: On Edward Durell Stone," *Los Angeles Review of Books*, January 30, 2013, https://lareviewofbooks.org /article/the-most-hated-of-architects-on-edward-durrell-stone/#!. Stone also designed, among other buildings, the Museum of Modern Art in New York City, the Kennedy Center in Washington, DC, and Busch Stadium in St. Louis.

3. Squire, *Evolution of American Legislatures*, 291.

4. The text of the 1946 Amendment reads: "For the duration of both regular and special sessions the members shall receive, in addition to the salaries herein provided for, the sum of ten dollars per day for each day not to exceed sixty days in any one session in commutation for expenses incurred for travel to and from their homes to the seat of government, subsistence, and other necessary expenses." The text of the 1948 Amendment reads: "Fixing salaries of members of the General Assembly at twelve hundred dollars ($1,200.00) and Presiding Officers at fifteen hundred dollars ($1,500.00) and fixing salaries for Extra sessions at two hundred and fifty dollars ($250.00) and three hundred dollars ($300.00) respectively."

5. The text of the amendment reads as follows:

> The members of the General Assembly for the term for which they have been elected shall receive as a compensation for their services the sum of fifteen dollars ($15.00) per day for each day of their session, for a period not exceeding ninety days; and should they remain longer in session they shall serve without compensation. The compensation of the presiding officers of the two houses shall be twenty dollars ($20.00) per day for a period not exceeding ninety days. Should an extra session of the General Assembly be called, the members and presiding officers shall receive a like rate of compensation for a period not exceeding twenty-five days.

6. The text reads: "Amending Section 28 of Article II of the Constitution establishing procedure for fixing compensation for members and officers of the General Assembly, and denying benefit of any increase in compensation to members of the session which enacts it."

7. A terrific review and update of the Citizens Conference on State Legislatures and John Burns's *The Sometime Governments* as it relates to North Carolina politics can be found in Gerry Cohen's master's thesis, "Legislative Reform in North Carolina." If you ask anyone who works in or around North Carolina politics about Gerry, you will find that they are no more than six degrees removed from working with him. He is the Kevin Bacon of North Carolina politics.

8. Grumm, "Effects of Legislative Structure," 309.

9. In addition to their salary, they receive $104 a day for a per diem, a mileage reimbursement, retirement, and health benefits.

10. Jim Perry, personal correspondence with the author, June 27, 2023.

11. Prather, interview by the author, June 1, 2023.

12. Williamson, Morris, and Risk, "Institutional Variation."

13. Quoted in Cullen, "Pay Problem." See also Squire, "Legislative Professionalism."

14. Prather, interview, June 1, 2023.

15. Former North Carolina House member Brian Turner had a unique solution to this problem. He attached a camper to the back of his Chevy Suburban and lived out of his camper while the general assembly was in session.

16. Cooper, "Innumeracy and State Legislative Salaries." I also found similar numbers in California, New Hampshire, and Wisconsin.

17. The correction did not work in California, however. Even Californians have a limit to what they will pay their legislators.

18. Fortunato, McCain, and Schiff, "Public Support for Professional Legislatures."

Chapter 11

1. Local Palate, "Traditional Moravian Cookies," October 6, 2022, https://thelocalpalate.com/recipes/traditional-moravian-cookies.

2. Although it's similar to the German Lebkuchen cookie.

3. The North Carolina Senate wasn't so keen on the idea, however. Like the sad bill from *Schoolhouse Rock!*, they let it die in committee. The senate doesn't like symbolic bills.

4. This bill also illustrates the power of "gut and amend." The original bill was not about abortion but rather about the safe surrender of infants when they are abused. North Carolina State Senate, "Safe Surrender Infants/Safe Sleep Prog. Funds," Senate Bill DRS15010-Nba-4, General Assembly of North Carolina, Session 2023, www.ncleg.gov/Sessions/2023/Bills/Senate/PDF/S20v0.pdf.

5. These data come from Shor, "Individual State Legislator."

6. Masket, *Inevitable Party.*

7. Abramowitz and Saunders, "Ideological Realignment."

8. Jessica Jones, "Why Did OBX State Rep Paul Tin Change His Affiliation to Independent?," WUNC, January 18, 2015, www.wunc.org/politics/2015-01-08/why-did-obx-state-rep-paul-tine-change-his-affiliation-to-independent.

9. Jon Evans, "Veteran State Lawmaker Brisson Changing Parties, Joining GOP," WECT News, October 25, 2017, www.wect.com/story/36679552/veteran-state-lawmaker-brisson-changing-parties-joining-gop/.

10. Mark Binker, "Forsyth Legislator Switches Parties: Mike Decker's Switch Creates a 60–60 Tie in the North Carolina House," *News and Record* (Greensboro, NC), January 24, 2003.

11. Kane and Curliss, "Black Ally Decker Is Sentenced."

12. The bribe, as North Carolina politics veterans know, took place in a Salisbury, North Carolina, IHOP restaurant bathroom (sometimes truth really is stranger than fiction).

13. Prather, interview by the author, June 1, 2023.

Chapter 12

1. This conclusion comes from his NOMINATE score, a commonly accepted measure of congressional ideology. See Voteview.com, s.v. "Shuler, Heath," accessed March 23, 2024, https://voteview.com/person/20737/heath-shuler.

2. For more on the twists and turns of this particular gerrymander, see North Carolina treasure Jeremy Markovich's description in *Politico*. Jeremy Markovich, "I Ran the Worst 5K of My Life So I Could Explain Gerrymandering to You," *Politico*, November 15, 2017, www.politico.com/magazine/story/2017/11/15/gerrymandering-5k-asheville-north-carolina-215829/.

3. I measure competitiveness here by the percent of voters in the old and new districts who supported John McCain (the previous Republican presidential candidate) for president.

4. John Boyle, "Shuler Won't Run for Re-Election," *Asheville (NC) Citizen Times*, February 3, 2012, A1. Like Babe Ruth calling his shot, Larry Ford, chair of the Republican Party in Rutherford County, predicted exactly what would happen to the district and to Shuler when the new district lines were drawn: "Heath Shuler is toast." Campbell Robertson, "Shuler Seeks Party Shift to Right," *News and Observer* (Raleigh, NC), November 14, 2010, B7.

5. Meadows would go on to serve three terms in Congress, cofound the conservative Freedom Caucus, and serve as chief of staff to President Trump.

6. Cooper, "Expert Report," submitted in *Harper v. Hall*.

7. Bitzer, *Redistricting and Gerrymandering*.

8. "Someone" is doing a lot of work in that sentence. More on that later. This all assumes a district rather than an at-large system.

9. This is a not-so-thinly veiled reference to James Madison's notion in "Federalist No. 10" that "faction is sown into the nature of man."

10. Seabrook, *One Person, One Vote*, 22.

11. Seabrook, *One Person, One Vote*, 22. To add insult to injury, not only is Gerry's name forever associated with a pejorative term but we're mispronouncing it (he pronounced it with a hard *G*).

12. Bitzer, *Redistricting and Gerrymandering*.

13. National Conference of State Legislatures, *Redistricting Law 2020*, 80. While these criteria are assumed and accepted in the vast majority of states, the inclusion of incumbency protection and preservation of cores of prior district do "lock in" much of the previous district lines.

14. Aka the Stephenson rule from *Stephenson v. Bartlett*, 355 N.C. 279, 560 S.E.2d 550 (N.C. 2002).

15. Cooper et al., "NC General Assembly County Clustering."

16. Keena et al, *Gerrymandering the States*; Rodden, *Why Cities Lose*.

17. Key, *Southern Politics*.

18. Orr, "Persistence of the Gerrymander."

19. "Political Pornography," *Wall Street Journal*, September 9, 1991.

20. Isaac Stanley-Becker, "Gun Enthusiast and Real-Life 'Boss Hogg' Seizes GOP Mantle in Congressional Race Tainted by Fraud," *Washington Post*, February 27, 2019; Stony Rushing, "Voters, Beware Liberals and Gerrymandering," Letters to the Editor, *Charlotte Observer*, September 13, 2001.

21. "Senate Approves New Boundaries for Chamber," *Rocky Mount (NC) Telegram*, September 21, 2001.

22. This was not specific to Obama. One of the most consistent trends in American politics is that the president's party loses seats in the first midterm election. This effort was known as REDMAP (Redistricting Majority Project). Seabrook, *One Person, One Vote*, 6–7.

23. Keena et al., *Gerrymandering the States*.

24. *Rucho v. Common Cause*, 139 S. Ct. 2484, 204 L. Ed. 2d 931 (2019).

25. *Common Cause v. Lewis*, 358 F. Supp. 3d 505 (E.D.N.C. 2019).

26. Cooper, "Rebuttal Report," submitted in *Common Cause v. Lewis*.

27. *Harper v. Hall*, 380 N.C. 314 (N.C. 2022).

28. A special master is someone the court appoints to do something the court can't do for itself; the special master has expertise or knowledge the court believes it does not have. In this context, special masters are people who are called on to draw new district lines.

29. The congressional maps were always meant to be used only for one election.

30. *Harper v. Hall*, 380 N.C. 314 (N.C. 2022); *Moore v. Harper*, 143 S. Ct. 2065, 216 L. Ed. 2d 729 (2023).

31. David Daley, "The Secret Files of the Mastermind of Modern Republican Gerrymandering," *New Yorker*, September 6, 2019.

32. Pope's bill (House Bill 318) would have included nine people: three appointed by the governor and two each by the supreme court, house Speaker, and senate president pro tem. No more than one appointee per office could be affiliated with the same political party, except for the governor, who would be required to have one out of three appointees from the same political party. In practical terms, in 2024 that would have resulted in a five (Democrat) and four (Republican) commission. Ruth Sheehan, "Governing by the Rule of Me," *News and Observer* (Raleigh, NC), November 29, 2001, 7.

33. Dan Way, "Senate Committee Approves Redistricting Map," *Carolina Journal* (Raleigh, NC), August 27, 2017.

34. Dallas Woodhouse (@DallasWoodhouse), Twitter, April 17, 2013, 8:50 a.m., https://twitter.com/DallasWoodhouse/status/1647945507547824129.

Chapter 13

1. Meredith Poll, November 2023.

2. Sievert and McKee, "Nationalization in U.S. Senate."

3. "Veto Power, Succession Needed for Strong Governor," *Daily Tar Heel* (Chapel Hill, NC), March 23, 1977.

4. Although the governors of twenty-one other states have about the same budget power as the North Carolina governor.

5. See, for example, Associated Press, "North Carolina House Committee OKs Bill to Shift Appointments on Boards Away from Governor," May 30, 2023, https://apnews.com/article/north-carolina-commissions-appointments-governor-legislature-8be560eb0c293f80516ab8dad10c6c5f.

6. "Gubernatorial Veto Endorsed," *Daily Tar Heel* (Chapel Hill, NC), November 10, 1925.

7. Martin Donsky, "Legislators' Independence Could be Put to Test," *News and Observer* (Raleigh, NC), January 9, 1977.

8. "Veto Power, Succession Needed for Strong Governor."

9. "Scott Backs Veto Power," *Asheville (NC) Citizen Times*, April 23, 1981.

10. Katherine White, "Gubernatorial Veto Bill Has Powerful Senate Foe," *Charlotte Observer*, February 28, 1985.

11. "Martin Renews His Push for Veto," *Winston-Salem (NC) Journal*, April 16, 1987.

12. "Governor v. Legislature," *News and Observer* (Raleigh, NC), June 14, 1987.

13. Andrea M. Cashion, "Veto Issue Is Primed for Public Vote: Cooper's Veto Bill Passes Judiciary Committee," *Rocky Mount (NC) Telegram*, February 1, 1995.

14. Lauth, "Other Six."

15. Carol Wilson Utley, "Gubernatorial Succession Issue Provides Emotions," *High Point (NC) Enterprise*, November 6, 1977.

16. "Arnie for Governor," *News and Record* (Greensboro, NC), November 30, 1977.

17. Fleer, *North Carolina Government*.

18. Fleer, *North Carolia Government*, 280.

Chapter 14

1. "Morgan for Supreme Court," *News and Observer* (Raleigh, NC), October 26, 2016.

2. Anne Blythe, "North Carolina Lawmakers Create Partisan Election Process for Courts That Review Their Laws," *News and Observer* (Raleigh, NC), December 17, 2016.

3. *Harper v. Hall*, 380 N.C. 314 (N.C. 2022).

4. *N.C. State Conference of the NAACP v. McCrory*, 831 F.3d 204 (4th Cir. 2016). See also Charles Duncan, "N.C. Supreme Court Reverses Voter ID Ruling," Spectrum News, April 28, 2023, https://spectrumlocalnews.com/nc/charlotte /news/2023/04/28/n-c—supreme-court-reverses-voter-id-ruling.

5. Eric Dyer, "Lawmakers Approve Bill Altering Judicial Elections," *News and Observer* (Raleigh, NC), October 2, 2002.

6. Corriher, "Partisan Judicial Elections."

7. Bonneau and Hall, *In Defense of Judicial Elections*.

Chapter 15

1. Forest Hills is small, but in case you think I'm choosing the most extreme example, seventy-nine municipalities have fewer registered voters than Forest Hills. Fontana Dam, located in Graham County, is the smallest with thirteen total registered voters.

2. F. Bluestein, *County and Municipal Government*, 5.

3. Lee and Oppenheimer, *Sizing Up the Senate*.

4. Burnett and Prentice, "Exploration of How Partisanship Impacts Council Manager Systems."

5. Drescher, "Politics of North Carolina's School Boards."

6. Steve Harrison, "NC GOP Elections Board Members Resign in Protest over Mail Ballot Changes," WFAE, November 24, 2020, www.wfae.org/politics/2020 -09-24/2-nc-gop-elections-board-members-resign-in-protest-over-mail-ballot -changes.

7. "Clayton Retains School Board Seat in Runoff Context," *Sylva (NC) Herald*, July 27, 2022.

8. Bluestein, "Is North Carolina a Dillon's Rule State?"

9. Some have argued that because it is not a home rule state that North Carolina must be a Dillon's Rule state. As UNC School of Government faculty member Frayda Bluestein reminds us, that is not true. She maintains that comparing home rule and Dillon's Rule states "would be like comparing the 49ers vs. the Yankees." Home rule and Dillon's Rule are "distinct legal concepts." F. Bluestein, *County and Municipal Government*, 5.

10. Zeb Smathers, interview by the author, June 30, 2023.

Conclusion

1. Rod Cockshutt, "Literacy Test Ban Now Goes to Voters," *News and Observer* (Raleigh, NC), June 21, 1969.

2. Hannah Schoenbaum, "North Carolina Lawmakers again Seeking Literacy Test Repeal," Associated Press, March 1, 2023, https://apnews.com/article/north-carolina-literacy-test-repeal-constitution-b48b06f86c266offa865db4573172799.

3. Perry, interview with author.

4. Anzia, *Timing and Turnout*; F. Bluestein, *County and Municipal Government*.

5. Edwards et al., "Independent Redistricting Commissions."

6. Edwards et al., "Institutional Control."

7. Sadhwani, "Independent Redistricting."

8. Warshaw, McGhee, and Migurski, "Districts for a New Decade," 447.

9. McCarthy, "Limits of Partisanship."

10. Although the specifics of our proposals are different, the argument that the timing is ideal for redistricting reform is echoed in a piece by Andy Jackson at the conservative John Locke Foundation. Jackson, "Now That We're Done."

11. National Conference of State Legislatures, *Redistricting Law 2020*.

12. Sarbaugh-Thompson and Thompson, *Implementing Term Limits*.

13. Carey, Niemi, and Powell, *Term Limits in State Legislatures*.

14. Carey, Niemi, and Powell, *Term Limits in State Legislatures*, 287.

15. Kousser, *Term Limits*.

Bibliography

Newspapers and Periodicals

Asheville (NC) Citizen Times

Blue Ridge Now (Hendersonville, NC)

Carolina Journal (Raleigh, NC)

Charlotte News

Charlotte Observer

Chowan Herald (Edenton, NC)

Daily Journal (Wilmington, NC)

Daily Tar Heel (Chapel Hill, NC)

Daily Times-News (Burlington, NC)

Herald Sun (Durham, NC)

High Point (NC) Enterprise

Los Angeles Review of Books

News and Observer (Raleigh, NC)

News and Record (Greensboro, NC)

New Yorker

New York Times

Pensacola (FL) News Journal

Smithsonian Magazine

Sylva (NC) Herald

Rocky Mount (NC) Telegram

Wall Street Journal

Washington Post

Wilmington (NC) Morning Star

Winston-Salem (NC) Journal

Interviews and Correspondence

Blakely, Preston. Interview by the author. June 23, 2023.

Cohen, Gerry. Personal correspondence with the author. June 30, 2023.

Kedrowski, Karen. Interview by the author. June 15, 2023.

McComas, Danny. Interview by the author. October 10, 2023.

Moxley, Jennifer. Interview by the author. January 2, 2023.

Perry, Jim. Personal correspondence with the author. June 27, 2023.

Prather, Lindsey. Interview by the author. June 1, 6, 2023.

Reeves, Blair. Interview by the author. June 8, 2023.

Rose, Jeff. Interview by the author. December 2, 2020.

Smathers, Zeb. Interview by the author. June 30, 2023.

Stewart, Joe. Interview by the author. June 15, 2023.

Court Cases and Associated Reports

Common Cause v. Lewis, 358 F. Supp. 3d 505 (E.D.N.C. 2019).

Cooper, Christopher A. "Expert Report on North Carolina's General Assembly Districts." Submitted in *Harper v. Hall*, 18: VCS 014001 (April 8, 2019).

———. "Rebuttal Report of Christopher A. Cooper, PhD." Submitted in *Common Cause v. Lewis*, 18: VCS 014001 (June 7, 2019).

Harper v. Hall, 380 N.C. 314 (N.C. 2022).

Moore v. Harper, 143 S. Ct. 2065, 216 L. Ed. 2d 729 (2023).

N.C. State Conference of the NAACP v. McCrory, 831 F.3d 204 (4th Cir. 2016).

Rucho v. Common Cause, 139 S. Ct. 2484, 204 L. Ed. 2d 931 (2019).

Shelby County v. Holder, 570 U.S. 529 (2013).

Stephenson v. Bartlett, 355 N.C. 279, 560 S.E.2d 550 (N.C. 2002).

Other Published Sources

Abramowitz, Alan, and Kyle Saunders. "Ideological Realignment in the U.S. Electorate." *Journal of Politics* 60, no. 3 (1998): 634–52.

Acharya, Avidit, Matthew Blackwell, and Maya Sen. *Deep Roots: How Slavery Still Shapes Southern Politics.* Princeton, NJ: Princeton University Press, 2018.

Anzia, Sarah. *Timing and Turnout: How Off Cycle Elections Favor Organized Groups.* Chicago: University of Chicago Press, 2013.

Arceneaux, Kevin. "The Gender Gap in State Legislative Representation: New Data to Tackle an Old Question." *Political Research Quarterly* 54, no. 1 (2001): 143–60.

Atkeson, Lonna R., and Mary Carrillo. "More Is Better: The Influence of Collective Female Descriptive Representation on External Efficacy." *Politics and Gender* 3, no. 1 (2007): 79–101.

Barreto, Matt A., Loren Collingwood, and Sylvia Manzano. "A New Measure of Group Influence in Presidential Elections: Assessing Latino Influence in 2008." *Political Research Quarterly* 63, no. 4 (2010): 908–21.

Bass, Jack, and Walter DeVries. *The Transformation of Southern Politics: Social Change and Political Consequence Since 1945.* Athens: University of Georgia Press, 1976.

Berden, Edward, and Natalie Masuoka. "A Growing Political Force: Asian Americans in the 2022 Election." In *The Red Ripple: The 2022 Midterm Elections and What They Mean for 2024*, edited by Larry J. Sabato, Kyle Kondik, Carah Ong Whaley, and J. Miles Coleman, 171–84. Lanham, MD: Rowman and Littlefield, 2023.

Berry, William D., Evan J. Ringquist, Richard C. Fording, and Russell L. Hanson. "Measuring Citizen and Government Ideology in the American States, 1960–1993." *American Journal of Political Science* 42, no. 1 (1998): 327–48.

Bitzer, J. Michael. *Redistricting and Gerrymandering in North Carolina: Battlelines in the Tar Heel State.* Cham, Switzerland: Palgrave, 2021.

Bitzer, J. Michael, Christopher A. Cooper, Whitney Ross Manzo, and Susan Roberts. "Growing and Distinct: The Unaffiliated Voter and American Politics." *Social Science Quarterly* 103, no. 7 (2022): 1587–601.

Bluestein, Frayda. *County and Municipal Government in North Carolina.* 2nd ed. Chapel Hill: University of North Carolina School of Government, 2015.

———. "Is North Carolina a Dillon's Rule State?" *Coates' Canons NC Local Government Law* (blog), October 24, 2012. https://canons.sog.unc.edu/2012/10/is-north-carolina-a-dillons-rule-state/.

Bluestein, Greg. *Flipped: How Georgia Turned Purple and Broke the Monopoly on Republican Power.* New York: Viking, 2012.

Bonneau, Chris W., and Melinda Gann Hall. *In Defense of Judicial Elections.* New York: Routledge, 2009.

Bos, Angela L., Jill S. Greenlee, Mirya R. Holman, Zoe M. Oxley, and J. Celeste Lay. "This One's for the Boys: How Gendered Political Socialization Limits

Girls' Political Ambition and Interest." *American Political Science Review* 116, no. 2 (2022): 484–501.

Bratton, Kathleen A. "Critical Mass Theory Revisited: The Behavior and Success of Token Women in State Legislatures." *Politics and Gender* 1, no. 1 (2005): 97–125.

Brown, Adam R., and Jeremy C. Pope. "Measuring and Manipulating Constitutional Evaluations in the States: Legitimacy versus Veneration." *American Politics Research* 47, no. 5 (2019): 1135–61.

Bullock, Charles S. III, Ronald Keith Gaddie, and Justin J. Wert. *The Rise and Fall of the Voting Rights Act*. Norman: University of Oklahoma Press, 2016.

Bullock, Charles S. III, William D. Hicks, M. V. Hood III, Seth C. McKee, and Daniel A. Smith. "The Election of African American State Legislators in the Modern South." *Legislative Studies Quarterly* 45, no. 4 (2020): 581–608.

Bullock, Charles S. III, Susan A. MacManus, Jeremy D. Mayer, and Mark J. Rozell. *The South and the Transformation of U.S. Politics*. New York: Oxford University Press, 2019.

Burnett, Craig M., and Christopher R. Prentice. "An Exploration of How Partisanship Impacts Council Manager Systems." *Politics and Policy* 46, no. 3 (2018): 392–415.

Caiazza, Amy. "Does Women's Representation in Elected Office Lead to Women-Friendly Policy? Analysis of State-Level Data." *Women and Politics* 26, no. 1 (2004): 35–70.

Carey, John M., Richard G. Niemi, and Lynda W. Powell. *Term Limits in State Legislatures*. Ann Arbor: University of Michigan Press, 2000.

Caughey, Devin, and Christopher S. Warshaw. "The Dynamics of State Policy Liberalism, 1936–2014." *Journal of Politics* 79, no. 4 (2016): 899–913.

Christensen, Rob. *The Paradox of Tar Heel Politics: The Personalities, Elections, and Events That Shaped Modern North Carolina*. Chapel Hill: University of North Carolina Press, 2008.

Citizens Conference on State Legislatures and John Burns. *The Sometime Governments: A Critical Study of the 50 American Legislatures*. New York: Bantam Books, 1971.

Cohen, Gerry F. "Legislative Reform in North Carolina, Case Study 1971–2004: Of Actions on the Recommendations in the Sometimes Governments; A Study of the 50 American Legislatures." MA thesis, University of North Carolina, Chapel Hill, 2004.

Cooper, Christopher A. "Innumeracy and State Legislative Salaries." *Public Opinion Quarterly* 85, no. 1 (2021): 147–60.

——. "Multimember Districts and State Legislatures." In *Democracy in the States: Experiments in Election Reform*, edited by Bruce E. Cain, Todd Donovan, and Caroline J. Tolbert, 134–46. Washington, DC: Brookings Institution Press, 2008.

Cooper, Christopher A., Blake Esselstyn, Gregory Herschlag, Jonathan Mattingly, and Rebecca Tippett. "NC General Assembly County

Clustering from the 2020 Census." August 2020. https://sites.duke.edu
/quantifyinggerrymandering/files/2021/08/countyClusters2020.pdf.

Cooper, Christopher A., and H. Gibbs Knotts. "Reliably Purple: The 2020
Presidential Election in North Carolina." In *Presidential Swing States*, 3rd ed.,
edited by David Schultz and Rafael Jacob, 79–96. Boston: Lexington Press,
2022.

Corriher, Billy. "Partisan Judicial Elections and the Distorting Influence of
Campaign Cash." Center for American Progress, October 25, 2012. www
.americanprogress.org/article/partisan-judicial-elections-and-the-distorting
-influence-of-campaign-cash/.

Covington, Howard E., Jr. *Henry Frye: North Carolina's First African American
Chief Justice.* Jefferson, NC: MacFarland, 2013.

Cullen, Morgan. "Pay Problem: January 2011." National Conference of State
Legislatures, January 11, 2011. www.ncsl.org/labor-and-employment/pay
-problem-january-2011.

Cunningham, David. *Klansville, U.S.A: The Rise and Fall of the Civil Rights-Era
Ku Klux Klan.* New York: Oxford University Press, 2013.

The Daily Show with Trevor Noah. Season 2016, no. 2785. Aired May 16, 2016, on
Comedy Central, 33 minutes.

David Leip's Atlas of US Presidential Elections. "2020 Presidential General
Election Results: North Carolina." Accessed February 6, 2024. https://
uselectionatlas.org/RESULTS/.

Delli Carpini, Michael X., Scott Keeter, and J. David Kennamer. The Effects of
the News Media Environment on Citizen Knowledge of State Politics and
Government. *Journalism and Mass Communication Quarterly* 71, no. 2
(1994): 443–56.

Dinan, John C. *The American State Constitution Tradition.* New York: Oxford
University Press, 2006.

———. *State Constitutional Politics: Governing by Amendment.* Chicago:
University of Chicago Press, 2018.

Drescher, Dean. 2022. "The Politics of North Carolina's School Boards." EdNC,
October 24, 2022. www.ednc.org/the-politics-of-north-carolinas-school
-boards/.

Dunleavy, Patrick, and Rekha Diwaker. "Analyzing Multiparty Competition in
Plurality Rule Elections." *Party Politics* 19, no. 6 (2013): 855–66.

Duverger, Maurice. *Political Parties: Their Organization and Activity in the
Modern State.* New York: Wiley, 1951.

Eamon, Tom. *The Making of a Southern Democracy: North Carolina Politics
from Kerr Scott to Pat McCrory.* Chapel Hill: University of North Carolina
Press, 2014.

Edwards, Barry C., Michael Crespin, Ryan D. Williamson, and Maxwell Palmer.
"Institutional Control of Redistricting and the Geography of Representation."
Journal of Politics 79, no. 2 (2017): 722–26.

Edwards, Barry C., Angel Sanchez, Tyler Yeargain, Michael Crespin, and Jessica Hayden. "Can Independent Redistricting Commissions Lead Us Out of the Political Thicket?" *Albany Government Law Review* 9, no. 2 (2016): 288–340.

Elmore, Joseph E. "Hyman, John Adams." NCPedia, 1988. www.ncpedia.org /biography/hyman-john-adams.

Erikson, Robert S., Gerald C. Wright, and John P. McIver. *Statehouse Democracy: Public Opinion and Policy in the American States*. New York: Cambridge University Press, 1993.

Faulkner, William. *Requiem for a Nun*. New York: Random House, 1951.

Fleer, Jack. *North Carolina Government and Politics*. Lincoln: University of Nebraska Press, 1994.

Fording, Richard. "Updated Measures of Citizen and Government Ideology." Last updated June 18, 2018. https://rcfording.wordpress.com/state-ideology-data/.

Fortunato, David, Josh McCain, and Kaylyn Jackson Schiff. "Public Support for Professional Legislatures." *State Politics and Policy Quarterly* 23, no. 3 (2023): 327–39.

Fox, Richard L., and Jennifer L. Lawless. *It Takes a Candidate: Why Women Don't Run for Office*. New York: Cambridge University Press, 2005.

Fraga, Bernard. *The Turnout Gap: Race, Ethnicity, and Political Inequality in a Diversifying America*. New York: Cambridge University Press, 2018.

Grose, Christian. *Congress in Black and White: Race and Representation in Washington and at Home*. New York: Cambridge University Press, 2011.

Grumm, John G. "The Effects of Legislative Structure on Legislative Performance." In *State and Urban Politics: Readings in Comparative Public Policy*, edited by Richard I. Hofferbert and Ira Sharkansky, 298–322. Boston: Little Brown, 1971.

Hasen, Richard L. *The Voting Wars: From Florida 2000 to the Next Election Meltdown*. New Haven, CT: Yale University Press, 2013.

Herrick, Rebekah, and Jeanette Mendez. "American Indian Party Identification: Why American Indians Tend to be Democrats." *Politics Groups and Identities* 8, no. 2 (2020): 275–92.

Hertel-Fernandez, Alexander. "Explaining Liberal Policy Woes in the States: The Role of Donors." *PS: Political Science and Politics* 49, no. 3 (2016): 461–65.

———. *State Capture: How Conservative Activists, Big Businesses, and Wealthy Donors Reshaped the American States—and the Nation*. New York: Oxford University Press, 2019.

———. "Who Passes Businesses' 'Model Bills'? Policy Capacity and Corporate Influence in U.S. State Politics." *Perspectives on Politics* 12, no. 2 (2014): 582–602.

Hertel-Fernandez, Alexander, and Theda Skocpol. "How the Right Trounced Liberals in the States." *Democracy: A Journal of Ideas* 39 (Winter 2016). https://democracyjournal.org/magazine/39/how-the-right-trounced-liberals -in-the-states/.

Hogan, Robert E. "The Influence of State and District Conditions on the Representation of Women in State Legislatures." *American Politics Research* 29, no. 1 (2001): 4–24.

Holman, Mirya R. "Sex and the City: Female Leaders and Spending on Social Welfare Programs in U.S. Municipalities." *Journal of Urban Affairs* 36, no. 4 (2014): 701–15.

———. "Women in Local Government: What We Know and Where We Go from Here." *State and Local Government Review* 49, no. 4 (2017): 285–96.

———. *Women in Politics in the American City*. Philadelphia: Temple University Press, 2015.

Hood, M. V., III, Quentin Kidd, and Irwin Morris. *The Rational Southerner: Black Mobilization, Republican Growth, and the Partisan Transformation of the American South*. New York: Oxford University Press, 2012.

Hood, M. V., III, and Seth C. McKee. *Rural Republican Realignment in the Modern South: The Untold Story*. Columbia: University of South Carolina Press, 2022.

———. "What Made Carolina Blue? In-Migration and the 2008 North Carolina Presidential Vote." *American Politics Research* 38, no. 2 (2010): 266–302.

Hopkins, Daniel J. *The Increasingly United States: How and Why American Political Behavior Nationalized*. Chicago: University of Chicago Press, 2018.

Jackson, Andy. "Now That We're Done with Redistricting, Let's Talk about Redistricting Reform." John Locke Foundation, November 16, 2023. www.johnlocke.org/now-that-were-done-with-redistricting-lets-talk-about-redistricting-reform/.

Jensen, Tom. "Congress Less Popular Than Cockroaches, Traffic Jams." *Public Policy Polling*, January 8, 2013. www.publicpolicypolling.com/polls/congress-less-popular-than-cockroaches-traffic-jams/.

Jones, Philip E. "Does the Descriptive Representation of Gender Influence Accountability for Substantive Representation." *Politics and Gender* 10, no. 2 (2014): 175–99.

Jordan, Milton C. "Black Legislators: From Political Novelty to Political Force." *North Carolina Insight* 12 (December 1989): 40–58.

Kathlene, Lyn. "Power and Influence in State Legislative Policymaking: The Interaction of Gender and Position in Committee Hearing Debates." *American Political Science Review* 88, no. 3 (1994): 560–76.

Keena, Alex, Michael Latner, Anthony J. McGann, and Charles Anthony Smith. *Gerrymandering the States: Partisanship, Race, and the Transformation of American Federalism*. New York: Cambridge, 2021.

Key, V. O., Jr. *Southern Politics in State and Nation*. Knoxville: University of Tennessee Press, 1949.

Kingdon, John W. *Agendas, Alternatives, and Public Policies*. Updated 2nd ed. Boston: Pearson, 2011.

Koger, Gregory, and Matthew J. Lebo. *Strategic Party Government: Why Winning Trumps Ideology*. Chicago: University of Chicago Press, 2017.

Kollman, Ken. *Outside Lobbying: Public Opinion and Interest Group Strategies.* Princeton, NJ: Princeton University Press, 1998.

Kousser, Thad. *Term Limits and the Dismantling of State Legislative Professionalism.* New York: Cambridge University Press, 2010.

Lamis, Alexander P. *The Two-Party South.* New York: Oxford University Press, 1990.

Lauth, Thomas. "The Other Six: Governors without the Line-Item Veto." *Public Budgeting and Finance* 36, no. 4 (2016): 26–49.

Lawless, Jennifer L. *Becoming a Candidate: Political Ambition and the Decision to Run.* New York: Cambridge University Press, 2012.

Lee, Frances E. *Insecure Majorities: Congress and the Perpetual Campaign.* Chicago: University of Chicago Press, 2016.

Lee, Frances E., and Bruce Ian Oppenheimer. *Sizing Up the Senate: The Unequal Consequences of Equal Representation.* Chicago: University of Chicago Press, 1989.

Leloudis, James L., and Robert R. Korstad. *Fragile Democracy: The Struggle over Race and Voting Rights in North Carolina.* Chapel Hill: University of North Carolina Press, 2020.

Levitsky, Steven, and Daniel Ziblatt. *How Democracies Die.* New York: Crown, 2018.

Link, William. *Righteous Warrior: Jesse Helms and the Rise of Modern Conservatism.* New York: St. Martin's Press, 2008.

Luebke, Paul. *Tar Heel Politics: Myths and Reality.* Chapel Hill: University of North Carolina Press, 1990.

———. *Tar Heel Politics 2000.* Chapel Hill: University of North Carolina Press, 1998.

Madison, James. "Federalist No. 10: The Utility of the Union as a Safeguard against Domestic Faction and Insurrection (continued)." The Federalist Papers. *Daily Advertiser* (New York), November 22, 1787.

Masket, Seth. *The Inevitable Party: Why Attempts to Kill the Party System Fail and How They Weaken Democracy.* New York: Oxford University Press, 2016.

Maxwell, Angie, and Todd Shields. *The Long Southern Strategy: How Chasing White Voters in the South Changed American Politics.* New York: Oxford University Press, 2021.

McCarthy, Devin. "Limits of Partisanship in Citizen Preferences on Redistricting." *Election Law Journal* 21, no. 2 (2022): 155–70.

McDaniel, Polly. "Historic All-Woman City Council to Lead Asheville's Government." City of Asheville, press release, December 2, 2020. www.ashevillenc.gov/news/historic-all-woman-city-council-to-lead-ashevilles-government/.

Meredith Poll. "An In-Depth Examination of North Carolina Voter Attitudes on Important Current Issues." November 1–5, 2023. https://c7p4g5i9.rocketcdn.me/wp-content/uploads/2023/11/Meredith-Poll-Report-November-2023.docx.pdf.

Morris, Irwin. *Movers and Stayers: The Partisan Transformation of 21st Century Southern Politics*. New York: Oxford University Press, 2021.

——. "Partisan Politics in the 21st Century South: The Fading Impact of Antebellum Slavery." *American Politics Research* 50, no. 6 (2022): 743–51.

National Conference of State Legislatures. *Redistricting Law 2020*. Denver: NCSL, 2020.

Nickelson, Jack, and Joshua M. Jansa. "Descriptive Representation and Innovation in American Legislatures." *Political Research Quarterly* 76, no. 4 (2023): 2018–35.

Noel, Hans. *Political Ideologies and Political Parties in America*. New York: Cambridge University Press, 2013.

North Carolina Department of the Secretary of State. *North Carolina Manual of 1913*. Edited by R. D. W. Connor. Raleigh, NC: North Carolina Historical Commission, 1913.

——. *North Carolina Manual of 1973*. Edited by John L. Cheney Jr. Raleigh, NC: Thad Eure, Secretary of State, 1973.

——. *North Carolina Manual of 1977*. Edited by John L. Cheney Jr. Raleigh, NC: Thad Eure, Secretary of State, 1977.

——. *North Carolina Manual of 1979–1980*. Edited by John L. Cheney Jr. Raleigh, NC: Thad Eure, Secretary of State, 1979.

——. *North Carolina Manual of 1981–1982*. Edited by John L. Cheney Jr. Raleigh, NC: Thad Eure, Secretary of State, 1981.

——. *North Carolina Manual of 1983–1984*. Edited by John L. Cheney Jr. Raleigh, NC: Thad Eure, Secretary of State, 1983.

——. *North Carolina Manual of 1985–1986*. Edited by John L. Cheney Jr. Raleigh, NC: Thad Eure, Secretary of State, 1985.

——. *North Carolina Manual of 1987–1988*. Edited by John L. Cheney Jr. Raleigh, NC: Thad Eure, Secretary of State, 1987.

——. *North Carolina Manual of 1989–1990*. Edited by John L. Cheney Jr. Raleigh, NC: Rufus L. Edmisten, Secretary of State, 1989.

——. *North Carolina Manual of 1991–1992*. Edited by Julie W. Snee. Raleigh, NC: Rufus L. Edmisten, Secretary of State, 1991.

——. *North Carolina Manual of 1993–1994*. Edited by Lisa A. Marcus. Raleigh, NC: Rufus L. Edmisten, Secretary of State, 1993.

——. *North Carolina Manual of 1995–1996*. Edited by Lisa A. Marcus. Raleigh, NC: Rufus L. Edmisten, Secretary of State, 1995.

——. *North Carolina Manual of 1997–1998*. Edited by Sam Stowe. Raleigh, NC: Elaine F. Marshall, Secretary of State, 1997.

——. *North Carolina Manual of 1999–2000*. Edited by Sam Stowe. Raleigh, NC: Elaine F. Marshall, Secretary of State, 1999.

——. *North Carolina Manual of 2001–2002*. Edited by Sam Stowe. Raleigh, NC: Elaine F. Marshall, Secretary of State, 2001.

——. *North Carolina Manual of 2003–2004*. Edited by Saw Stowe. Raleigh, NC: Elaine F. Marshall, Secretary of State, 2003.

———. *North Carolina Manual of 2005–2006.* Edited by Sam Stowe. Raleigh, NC: Elaine F. Marshall, Secretary of State, 2005.

———. *North Carolina Manual of 2007–2008.* Edited by Sam Stowe. Raleigh, NC: Elaine F. Marshall, Secretary of State, 2007.

———. *North Carolina Manual of 2009–2010.* Edited by Liz Proctor. Raleigh, NC: Elaine F. Marshall, Secretary of State, 2009.

———. *North Carolina Manual of 2011–2012.* Edited by Liz Proctor. Raleigh, NC: Elaine F. Marshall, Secretary of State, 2011.

North Carolina State Board of Elections. "Voter Registration Data," s.v. "Statewide Voter Registration (ZIP)." Last modified November 18, 2023. www .ncsbe.gov/results-data/voter-registration-data.

North Carolina State Constitution Study Commission. *Report of the North Carolina State Constitution Study Commission to the North Carolina State Bar and the North Carolina Bar Association.* Raleigh, NC: The Commission, 1968. https://archive.org/details/reportofnorthcaroonort/page/n7/mode/2up.

O'Neill, Tip. *All Politics Is Local and Other Rules of the Game.* New York: Adams Media Group, 1995.

Orr, Douglas M, Jr. "The Persistence of the Gerrymander in North Carolina Congressional Redistricting." *Southeastern Geographer* 9, no. 2 (1969): 39–54.

Orth, John V. *The North Carolina State Constitution.* New York: Oxford University Press, 2011.

———. *The North Carolina State Constitution with History and Commentary.* Chapel Hill: University of North Carolina Press, 1993.

Orth, John V., and Paul Martin Newby. *The North Carolina State Constitution.* 2nd ed. New York: Oxford University Press, 2013.

Payson, Julia. *When Citizens Lobby: How Local Governments Compete for Power in State Politics.* New York: Oxford University Press, 2021.

Pitkin, Hanna Fenichel. *The Concept of Representation.* Berkeley: University of California Press, 1972.

Prysby, Charles. "No Longer Federal Red and State Blue?" In *Second Verse, Same as the First: The 2012 Presidential Election in the South,* edited by Scott E. Buchanan and Branwell DuBose Kapeluck, 171–84. Fayetteville: University of Arkansas Press, 2014.

Rankin, Robert S. *The Government and Administration of North Carolina.* New York: Thomas Y. Crowell, 1955.

Richardson, Lilliard E., Jr., and Patricia K. Freeman. "Gender Differences in Constituency Services among State Legislators." *Political Research Quarterly* 48, no. 1 (1995): 169–79.

Rodden, Jonathan. *Why Cities Lose: The Deep Rootes of the Urban-Rural Divide.* New York: Basic Books, 2019.

Rogers, Steven. *Accountability in State Legislatures.* Chicago: University of Chicago Press, 2023.

Sadhwani, Sara. "Independent Redistricting: An Insider's View." *The Forum* 20, no. 3–4 (2022): 357–70.

Sanders, John L. "Our Constitutions: An Historical Perspective." North Carolina
Legislative Library. Accessed March 17, 2024. https://chrome-extension://
efaidnbmnnnibpcajpcglclefindmkaj/https://www.sosnc.gov/static_forms
/publications/North_Carolina_Constitution_Our_Co.pdf.

Sarbaugh-Thompson, Marjorie, and Lyke Thompson. *Implementing Term
Limits: The Case of the Michigan Legislature.* Ann Arbor: University of
Michigan Press, 2017.

Schultz, David, and Rafael Jacob. *Presidential Swing States.* 3rd ed. Lanham,
MD: Rowman and Littlefield, 2022.

Seabrook, Nicholas. *One Person, One Vote: A Surprising History of
Gerrymandering in America.* New York: Pantheon, 2022.

Shaw, Daron R., and John R. Petrocik. *The Turnout Myth: Voting Rates and
Partisan Outcomes in American National Elections.* New York: Oxford
University Press, 2020.

Shaw, Elise, and Adiam Tesfaselassie. *The Status of Women in North Carolina:
Political Participation.* Washington, DC: Institute for Women's Policy
Research, 2020.

Shor, Boris. "Individual State Legislator Shor-McCarty Ideology Data, April 2023
Update." Harvard Dataverse (V1, UNF:6:UqRjMSqS2n8oRe3iqJoJwA==
[fileUNF]). Accessed June 3, 2023. https://doi.org/10.7910/DVN/NWSYOS.

Sievert, Joel, and Seth C. McKee. "Nationalization in U.S. Senate and
Gubernatorial Elections." *American Politics Research* 47, no. 5 (2018):
1055–80.

Silbermann, Rachel. "Gender Roles, Work-Life Balance, and Running for Office."
Quarterly Journal of Political Science 10, no. 2 (2015): 123–53.

Smith, Stephen. *Boom for Whom? Desegregation, Education, and Development.*
Albany: University Press of New York, 2004.

Specht, Paul. "Woodhouse Says GOP Is Winning Unaffiliated Voters in NC."
Politifact.com. September 27, 2017. www.politifact.com/factchecks/2017/sep
/27/dallas-woodhouse/woodhouse-says-gop-winning-Unaffiliated-voters-nc/.

Squire, Peverill. *The Evolution of American Legislatures: Colonies, Territories,
and States, 1619–2009.* Ann Arbor: University of Michigan Press, 2012.

———. "Legislative Professionalism and Membership Diversity in State
Legislatures." *Legislative Studies Quarterly* 17, no. 1 (1992): 69–79.

Sullivan, Brenda. "Even at the Turning of the Tide: An Analysis of the North
Carolina Legislative Black Caucus." *Journal of Black Studies* 30, no. 6 (2000):
815–38.

Swers, Michele L. *The Difference Women Make: The Policy Impact of Women in
Congress.* Chicago, University of Chicago Press, 2002.

Tamas, Bernard, and Matthew Dean Hindman. "Ballot Access Laws and the
Decline of American Third-Parties." *Election Law Journal* 13, no. 2 (2014):
260–76.

Tausanovitch, Chris, and Christopher Warshaw. "Measuring Constituent Policy
Preferences in Congress, States Legislatures, and Cities." *Journal of Politics*
75, no. 2 (2013): 330–42.

————. "Subnational Ideology and Presidential Vote Estimates (v2022)." Harvard Dataverse (V1, UNF:6:h3CHNRumBxPs42QMveTROg== [fileUNF]). Accessed June 3, 2023. https://doi.org/10.7910/DVN/BQKU4M.

Tolleson-Rinehart, Susan. "Do Women Leaders Make a Difference?" In *Gender and Policymaking: Studies of Women in Office*, edited by D. Dodson, 93–102. New Brunswick, NJ: Center for the American Woman and Politics, Eagleton Institute of Politics, Rutgers, State University of New Jersey, 1991.

US Census Bureau. "Nation's Urban and Rural Populations Shift Following Census." December 29, 2022. www.census.gov/newsroom/press-releases/2022/urban-rural-populations.html.

US Congress. "An Act to Provide for the More Efficient Government of the Rebel States." *Statutes at Large*, 39th Cong., 2nd Sess. (1867).

Warshaw, Christopher, Eric McGhee, and Michael Migurski. "Districts for a New Decade—Partisan Outcomes and Racial Representation in the 2021–22 Redistricting Cycle." *Publius: The Journal of Federalism* 52, no. 3 (2022): 428–51.

Waynick, Capus M., and L. I. Moore. "Constitutional Revision: Not Dead but Sleeping." *Popular Government*, November 1934, 16–26.

Wilkinson, Betina Cutaia. "North Carolina Latinos: An Emerging, Influence Electorate in the South." In *Latinos and the 2012 Elections: The New Face of the American Voter*, edited by Gabriel R. Sanchez, 149–65. East Lansing: Michigan State University Press, 2015.

Williams, Wiley J. "Murphy to Manteo." NCPedia, 2006. www.ncpedia.org/manteo-murphy.

Williamson, Ryan, John C. Morris, and Jonathan M. Fisk. "Institutional Variation, Professionalism, and State Implementation Choices: An Examination of Investment in Water Quality across the 50 States." *American Review of Public Administration* 51, no. 6 (2021): 436–48.

Zucchino, David. *Wilmington's Lie: The Murderous Coup of 1898 and the Rise of White Supremacy*. New York: Grove, 2020.

Index

Page numbers in italics refer to illustrations.

and, 61, 68; of gubernatorial elections, 119; impact of, on governor's power, 126–27, 142–43; interest groups and, 91, 92; of judicial elections, 131; legislative professionalization and, 140; of local politics, 5, 36–37, 77, 84, 85, 92, 132–37; outlook for, 18, 138; racial differences and, 48; redistricting and, 115; women and, 57

National Rifle Association (NRA), 86

Native Americans, 47

NCCPPR, 89–90

N.C. State Conference of the NAACP v. McCrory, 129

Nebraska, 100, 105, 146; Nebraska Legislature, 130

Nevada, 146; Nevada Legislature, 56

Newby, Paul, 6

New Hampshire, 101, 175n16

New Hanover County, 33, 35, 45, 73

News and Observer, 17, 71, 121, 122, 128

news outlets, 90–91

New York Times, 1–2

Nickel, Wiley, 115

Nineteenth Amendment (US), 49

Noah, Trevor, 4, 165n11

Noel, Hans, 22

No Labels (party), 172n7

NOMINATE scores, 176n1 (chap. 12)

nomination contests, 69, 71, 72

nonpartisan elections, 124, 128–31

nonpartisan redistricting commissions. *See* independent redistricting commissions (IRCs)

nonpartisanship: of commissions, 116; of boards of education, 124, 133, 136; of judges, 128–31; nonpartisan ballots, 105; of think tanks, 90–91

Northampton County, 30, 40, 46

North Carolina Association of County Commissioners, 54

North Carolina Center for Public Policy Research (NCCPPR), 89–90

North Carolina Central University, 44

North Carolina Constitution, 11; of 1868, 12, 13, *14*, 15, 166n9; of 1971, 15, *15*, 16–18, *17*; original, 12

North Carolina Council of State, 12, 15, 50, 126

North Carolina Elections Integrity Team (NCEIT), 68

North Carolina General Assembly: and absentee voting, 65–66; Asian Americans in, 46; Black people in, 39, 42, 43–44, 140; and constitutional amendment process, 18–19; descriptive representation in, 53–54; and gerrymandering, 109, 112–13, 114–15; Indigenous peoples in, 47; Latinx people in, 45; and literacy test, 140; lobbyists and, 86–88; party switching in, 104–5, 106–7, 173n7; polarization in, 103–8; power of, in Constitution of 1868, 13; power of, in Constitution of 1971, 16; power of, in original constitution, 12; professionalism in, 95–96, 98–99, 100–101, 141–42; racial politics in, 41; Republican policies in, 1–2, 22, 24–25, 109, 128–30; role of, in election administration, 61, 66, 70; role of, in redistricting policies, 111, 145; unaffiliated candidates in, 79–80; vs. power of governor, 120, 121–22, 125–26; vs. power of local governments, 136–37; women in, 49, 51–52, *51, 53*

North Carolina House of Representatives. *See* North Carolina General Assembly

North Carolina Legislative Black Caucus (NCLBC), 42–43

North Carolina Senate. *See* North Carolina General Assembly

North Carolina Senate Judiciary Committee, 122

North Carolina State Board of Elections, 17, 41, 61, 62, 81

Randolph County, 28, 134
Rankin, Robert, 13, 29
Raymond, Ken, 61
Reagan, Ronald, 20–21
recreation, 133
recruitment, of candidates, 32–33, 56–57, 77
redistricting, 99, 107, 123–24, 141, 143–44; gerrymandering in, 3, 4, 27, 109–16, 129, 144, 176n4 (chap. 12)
REDMAP (Redistricting Majority Project), 115, 177n22
Red Shirts, 38
Reeves, Blair, 85, 91
referenda, 100
regional divide, *32*, 36
registered voters: data availability on, 159; demographics of, 73–75, *74*; party affiliation of, 71, *72*
representation, in politics: of Asian Americans, 46–47; of Black people, 39–45, *43*, 113; of Latinx people, 45–46; of Native Americans, 47–48; of women, 32, 50, 51–53, *51*, 54–56
Republican Party: and conservative Republican orthodoxy, 106, 107; and Tricia Cotham, 104–5; inclusion of unaffiliated voters in primaries of, 70–71; increase in conservative ideology of, 105; and race, 41, 44, 46, 47; realignment of white people to, 33, 40; and unaffiliated voters, 76; voter demographics in, 73–74, *74*; and voter turnout, 65; vote share for president, 26–27, *27*; vote share for president by region, 31–32, *32*; vote share for president by urbanity, 33–35, *34*
requests for proposals (RFPs), 87
Research Triangle, 46–47
Rhode Island, 12
Richmond County, 33
Robbinsville, NC, 32
Roberts, John, 113
Roberts, Susan, 76

Robeson County, 42, 47
Robinson, Mark, 168n28
roll-call votes, 169n25
Romney, Mitt, 26–27, 75
Roney, Kim, 52–53
Rose, Jeff, 77
Ross, Deborah, 128
Rotterman, Marc, 90
Rucho v. Common Cause (2019), 113
runoff elections, 136
Rushing, Stony, 113
Russell, Carolyn, 79
Rutherford County, 30, 176n4 (chap. 12)

salaries, of state legislators, 95, 96–97, 98–102, 141–42
Sampson County, 73
Sanders, Bernie, 21
Sanford, NC, 143
Sanford, Terry, 15, 18
Sarbaugh-Thompson, Marjorie, 146–47
Schiff, Kaylyn Jackson, 101
school boards, 133, 135–36
school choice, 103, 104, 146
Schwarzenegger, Arnold, 120
Scotland County, 30, 33, 35, 47
Scott, Robert W., 18, 121, 126
secretary of state, 12, 15, 50, 62, 126
semi-closed primaries, 71, *72*
senate bills: Senate Bill 3, 122; Senate Bill 4, 129; Senate Bill 20, 103, 176n4 (chap. 11); Senate Bill 568, 66–67; Senate Bill 749, 62
senate districts. *See* state house and senate districts
separation of powers, 12, 16
sewers, 133, 135
Sharp, Susie, 50
Shelby County v. Holder (2013), 41
sheriffs, 12, 18, 79, 133; unaffiliated candidates as, *81*
Shuler, Heath, 23, 109, 167n16, 176n1 (chap. 12), 176n4 (chap. 12)
sidewalks, 134